PRAISE FOR *PROGNOSIS*

"The morning after a fall from a horse, Sarah Vallance entered her kitchen to find she'd stored her reading lamp in the refrigerator, her groceries in the sink, and her toaster in the freezer. Diagnosed with a traumatic brain injury, Vallance went from holding down a senior government position to unemployed, with an IQ of around 80. *Prognosis: A Memoir of My Brain* tells the story of her journey back, aided by her loving rescue dogs, George, Bess, Sofia, and Scout, who 'robbed her of her reason for dying.' Vallance works to revitalize her brain, finally earning a PhD, reconciling with her impossible mother, and finding a loving marriage. *Prognosis,* **beautifully wrought and essential, stands as testament to the power of human reclamation and recovery.**"

—Susanne Antonetta, author of *A Mind Apart*

"A lot of memoirs are about redemption and survival, but Sarah Vallance has outdone most by writing a **rather brilliant and compulsively compelling** book about her harrowing traumatic brain injury without an ounce of self-pity, but with irony, wit, and a lack of the kind of self-absorption that critics sometimes see as the hallmark of the contemporary memoir. If you want to find redemption and a story of overcoming the odds, yes, you can certainly find it here, but I'd rather commend it for its crystalline prose, and Vallance's skills as a consummate stylist and storyteller."

—Robin Hemley, author of *Nola: A Memoir of Faith, Art, and Madness*

T0051103

"Sarah Vallance's *Prognosis* isn't just a **riveting** account of life before and after a traumatic brain injury or a meditation on what happens to the mind when the brain (almost) stops working. It's a book about what it means to care for others—parents, dogs, friends, patients—and how we can learn to care for ourselves."

—Jess Row, author of *Your Face in Mine* and *White Flights: Race, Fiction, and the American Imagination*

"In direct and unflinching language, Sarah Vallance faces the existential question of whether our cognitive perception constitutes the totality of who we are. Fortunately for her, and for her readers, it does not. The head injury Vallance suffers begins a journey on which she discovers that her openness to the world, to friends, lovers, and family, is crucial to her recovery. While *Prognosis* is about physical, mental, and emotional wellness, it has even more to say about the larger question of how to live a full and authentic life. **This is a brave and necessary book.**"

—Sue William Silverman, author of *The Pat Boone Fan Club: My Life as a White Anglo-Saxon Jew*

"In *Prognosis*, Sarah Vallance has produced **a harrowing but absorbingly immersive account of survival, rendering a life's worth of pain and trauma with clear-eyed and measured precision.** Also, I loved the dogs."

—Matthew Vollmer, author of *Permanent Exhibit*

"Spanning continents, lovers, dogs, and decades, *Prognosis* is a memoir of Sarah Vallance's amazing perseverance in the face of a traumatic brain injury, asking the crucial question of what our brain's relationship is to our sense of self. As she unravels the effects of her neurological symptoms in **prose as distinctive and meticulously crafted as William Styron or Joan Didion**, we learn about our own mortal bodies, our relationship to grief and time, the legacy of the families into which we were born, and ultimately our irrefutable ability for self-determination. In the end, this is a timeless love story told by a skeptical and wildly funny narrator who leads us into the landscape of her own gray matter—both biological and social—with such care and insight that we can't help but rethink our own relationships to illness, sex, aging, and one another. *Prognosis* **is an astonishing debut by a writer from whom we are sure to hear much more.**"

—Ravi Shankar, Pushcart Prize–winning author and editor of
W. W. Norton's *Language for a New Century*

"Sarah Vallance's *Prognosis* is **a triumphant blend of candid personal writing and meticulous research into the modern epidemic of traumatic brain injuries.** With artistry and sensitivity, Vallance weaves together her own often-hazy memories into a vivid narrative in which her personal relationships—both human and canine—proved instrumental to her recovery. **A must-read for anyone whose life has been touched by a TBI or memory loss.**"

—Justin Hocking, author of *The Great Floodgates of the Wonderworld:*
A Memoir

"Combining love, loss, and the restorative power of animals, *Prognosis* is a powerful testament from a writer who has experienced life-altering brain injury. Vallance writes in exquisite detail and with fierce honesty about what appears to be a minor bump, but her brain injury will continue to reverberate through her life as she, society, and the field of neuroscience learn and grow to better understand this all-too-common condition."

—Justin Hill, author of *The Drink and Dream Teahouse*, *Washington Post* Book of the Year, and *Shieldwall*, *Sunday Times* Book of the Year

Prognosis

Prognosis

A Memoir of My Brain

Sarah Vallance

This is a work of creative nonfiction. The events, scenes, and dialogue are written and portrayed to the best of the author's memory. Some names and identifying details have been changed.

Published by Little A, New York

www.apub.com

Amazon, the Amazon logo, and Little A are trademarks of Amazon.com, Inc., or its affiliates.

ISBN-13: 9781542043021 (hardcover)
ISBN-10: 1542043026 (hardcover)
ISBN-13: 9781542004206 (paperback)
ISBN-10: 1542004209 (paperback)

Cover design by Zoe Norvell

Printed in the United States of America

First edition

In loving memory of George and Bess

Contents

AUTHOR'S NOTE

I started work on this memoir during my MFA at City University in Hong Kong. I hadn't planned to write a memoir, and it took some time for me to get my head around the idea of exposing a large chunk of my life that I had kept private for so long to a group of eight strangers in a workshop, much less a broader audience. My memory had been deteriorating for some time, and I was terrified about the longer-term consequences of my head injury. To begin with, my motivation was to write about my life so I could remember and record it, but I had also hoped that the act of writing might help keep my brain active. It had worked for me once before; perhaps it would work again.

The more I wrote, the more convinced I became that mine was a story that needed to be told. Not for me, but for the hundreds of thousands of people that suffer traumatic brain injuries (TBIs) every year who are *not* able to tell their stories. TBI is often an invisible problem and one that is poorly understood, not just by the medical community but also by the friends and family and acquaintances of the individual who has suffered the injury. If this book broadens the understanding of what it is like to experience a traumatic brain injury, then it has served its purpose.

Like many people, including those who have not suffered a head injury, I have forgotten a lot, but my chief problem in writing this book has been determining correct chronology and timing. I have spent months researching parts of my own life, trying to determine accurate timings and sequences of events, relying wherever possible upon documents, passports, and the corroboration of others.

I have not written anything in this book I do not believe to be true.

1

ACCIDENTS WILL HAPPEN

Death is stalking me.

She finds me on a sheep farm in Crookwell, a three-hour drive inland from Sydney. I have come to visit my friend Tim and his wife, Belinda, and to see Tim's new quad bike. I'm traveling with my closest companions, George and Bess—city-slicker dogs who love nothing more than to pretend they belong in the country, riding around in flatbed trucks, tearing after stray sheep, hanging with the farm dogs who see right through them and sniff them with scorn. It is a sweltering day in early January 1995, during the peak of the Australian summer. The sun has leeched the color from the grass and torn open the earth below. This weather is ripe for bushfires.

Tim and I met when we worked in Corrections. I was Tim's boss. We spent our days visiting every prison in New South Wales. Tim was my bodyguard, the one shoving aside inmates who rubbed themselves against me as we walked through the prison kitchens and dining areas. After we'd been friends for a couple of years, Tim told me that his mother was doing time in Mulawa prison for fraud. She had done something dodgy with the accounts at one of his father's car dealerships. Tim felt funny visiting her, he said: the staff knew him as the policy adviser to the Minister for Corrections. Yet his mother was locked up inside.

Tim's bike is red and black with monstrous tires, and looks either like a lot of fun or like a death trap. "Be careful, you two!" Belinda shouts from the porch as Tim revs up the engine. She knows trouble follows Tim and me wherever we go. We unleash each other's inner lunatic.

"Don't worry!" Tim yells back and blows Belinda a kiss.

I hop on the back and let Tim drive me around the fields before demanding that it's my turn to drive. He lifts himself off, stands to one side, and tells me to drive up the side of the mountain. I do as I am told, Tim running behind me, trying to keep pace with his new toy. Near the top I grow bored and decide to change course, turning a sharp left.

"No!" Tim shouts, appearing out of nowhere, hurling himself at the side of the bike to keep it upright and stop it from rolling down the side of the mountain, with me on top.

"You can only go up or down on a mountain. Go sideways and you'll roll!"

"Calm down. I'm fine."

He holds the bike in place while I dismount, and as soon as I am standing, he folds himself onto a rock, his head between his hands. "It nearly killed you!" he says.

Waiting for Tim to get up, I ponder what it would be like to be crushed by a rolling quad bike. It scares me less than it should.

~

Nearly two years have passed since my father died from bowel cancer. He was sixty-four, and I was twenty-nine. I drank my way through the first weeks after his death, doing my best to forget I was alive. One particularly grim night, I lay on the road in the middle of Oxford Street, the drinking mecca of gay Sydney, arranging myself neatly inside the painted outline of a body, where a pedestrian had been killed. Friends had to scoop me off the road just as the traffic lights changed. These days I try to distract myself with work, but grief still has me in a head-lock. I seem to have lost the ability to make sense of the world. My grip on life feels fragile.

I knew that a rolling quad bike would never kill me, even if I wanted it to. It couldn't. No matter what I did, no harm could visit me. I was protected by an invisible lifesaving ring that I'd first become aware of as a child. It had allowed me to do things other kids couldn't, like lying facedown on my skateboard and riding from the top of our steep hill, around a blind corner, and down another hill before rolling to a stop on a street in the next suburb. When the other kids tried it, they all wound up headfirst in the gutter, their arms and legs embedded with gravel.

I was also a fast runner and a long jumper, which only fed my delu-sions of power. I had a remarkable ability to jump between branches of trees, to leap walls, to scale the mesh fences that surrounded tennis courts.

Most children outgrow such delusions. Not me. I harbored them right through adolescence into adulthood. If anything, age seemed to embolden me. The older I got, the more I enjoyed walking down dark alleys at night alone, venturing into places I knew to be dangerous and pitching myself against whatever fate might hold.

My father and I fought during my adolescence, but by my early twenties, I realized that—apart from his intelligence, which eclipsed mine, and my love of animals, which confounded him—I was his carbon copy. Combative, contemptuous of authority in almost all its guises, and driven by a compulsion to be right, I seemed to be the only person who understood him, and him me. He was the only person with whom I could be myself. I sought his counsel on everything, although I didn't always follow it. My mother and I had never been close and, as our relationship disintegrated, the bond I shared with my father became unbreakable. At twenty-nine, I had lost the only person I trusted, the only person I respected, the only person who loved me without conditions. My father's love had made me strong. Without that love I was rudderless. Part of me had died too.

"We're different, you and I," my father said to me on his deathbed. "We're not like Mum, not like your brother. You're the pea and I'm the pod."

~

Tim rocks back and forth on the ground, apoplectic, as I ponder my own invincibility. Finally, he pulls himself up. A bull ant marches across my shoe, and I flick it off with a stick. Moments later, Tim throws his leg over the side of the bike, pats the seat behind—officially now "my seat"—and drives us, in a straight line, down the mountain and back to the house where we sit down to the meal Belinda has prepared.

Ripe for a new thrill after lunch, I ask to ride Tim's horse. I have no clue that horses are more dangerous than quad bikes,[1] or that they are considered to be twenty times more dangerous than motorbikes,[2] due in part to their unpredictability and in part to the fact that the distance to the ground from a horse's saddle is much greater than the distance to the ground from the seat of a motorcycle. None of that even occurs to me. Mac is a big horse—sixteen hands at least—and Tim says he's docile. "You'll be lucky to get him to do much more than eat," he says.

"That's okay," I answer.

Tim goes off to the barn to get a saddle and bridle, and I introduce myself to Mac. I have an apple in my pocket that he swipes before I know what's happening. "Help yourself," I say, and rub his muzzle. He likes me. Why would he not? I have a way with animals, although my experience with horses is patchy.

~

My mother won hundreds of ribbons at pony shows when she was a girl. Most of the ribbons were blue or red. She sewed each ribbon together with the next and made bedspreads with them, so her equestrian triumphs could be displayed in the bedrooms of her family home. It was the same home I grew up in. Nigel, the piebald pony she had been given when she was twelve, lived on a paddock two blocks from that home in Roseville, a leafy suburb on Sydney's north shore. By the time I was born, single-story redbrick houses had sprouted up where the paddocks once were, and no one in our neighborhood owned ponies anymore.

My mother had hung an oil painting of Nigel on my bedroom wall, as if to preserve his memory in my young mind as well as hers.

For my seventh birthday, she baked me a horse-in-a-field cake. She used desiccated coconut soaked in green vegetable dye for the grass and chocolate fingers for the fence. From a toy store, she bought a plastic horse that bore a reasonable likeness to Nigel, and stood him in the middle of the cake. It was my favorite birthday cake, and the fondest memory I have of my mother.

By the time I was nine, I was obsessed with horses. An aunt had given me a book called *The Love of Horses* for Christmas, which I kept hidden under my bed, and at night I'd gaze at the photos with wonderment. I loved horses, although I don't remember ever meeting any. Nor do I recall having any desire to ride them. My ambitions went only so far as patting them, grooming them, and feeding them carrots.

For my tenth birthday, my mother surprised me with four riding lessons at the Terrey Hills riding academy in Sydney. She had given me the riding hat she used as a child, which I wore proudly as I sat astride the fence in our backyard. I had never needed a horse to indulge my riding fantasies. My parents didn't have much money, and my mother had scrimped for those lessons. She had every reason to believe it would be a good investment. She was a good rider; I was her child.

After the first lesson, it was apparent that I hadn't inherited any of her horsewomanship, and on the drive home she chanted, "Sit up straight, heels back in the stirrups, hands down." "Alright," I said. I would try to remember that next time.

By the end of my fourth riding lesson, my mother wore a look of defeat I would come to dread. I had failed her. She never said it, but her silence in the car and then the words, "Perhaps you would be better at the piano; let's try that next," after we pulled into our driveway left me in no doubt how she felt. In four hours over four consecutive weeks, I had convinced her I would never be a rider. Riding was the first of many things for which I exhibited no talent. Next came the piano, then the violin, and then anything that involved numbers or foreign languages.

~

Mac waits placidly while Tim saddles him up. I haven't ridden a horse in more than a decade. I try to count the times I have even been on a horse in my thirty-one years. Six? Seven? At lunch, I had a couple of glasses of chardonnay, which may be hampering my memory.

After a few ungainly attempts, I manage to mount him. He takes a moment to study the scenery, ambling toward a thick clump of dried grass next to a fence post. I pat his neck as if to say, *Take your time, Mac.*

"Kick his sides," Tim says.

I don't have time to.

Mac is galloping toward a fence. He leaps the fence. I have never jumped anything while riding a horse, and I have no clue what to do other than lean forward and hold on. He jumps another fence, and I feel alive for the first time in ages.

Mac and I are flying. I have cantered on a horse once but never galloped. Mac is like a racehorse. *He will have to stop sometime,* I tell myself. We head down a hill; this is not good. Leaning forward, I clutch at the long hairs on Mac's neck. *Should I lean forward or backward?* Gravity

8

says backward. Shocked by the pace we are moving and the steep drop below me, I feel fear for the first time since Mac took flight. My fear is for Mac. The hill is rocky, and Mac is not watching his footing. He may slip and break a leg. A horse with a broken leg needs to be destroyed and it will be my fault. I should have left him alone in his paddock. I let go of his mane, grip the reins tightly, and tell him to stop. Or at least to slow down. He takes my words and actions as a sign to speed up. Then he stops. Suddenly. Digging his feet into the ground and bracing himself.

I am flying. Alone, this time. I soar over Mac's head and somersault through the air. The sensation is remarkable. Time is suspended. I savor the moment—I am a diver, with no water below me. In childhood dreams I flew, but this is different: I cannot control the speed, the direction, the altitude. I have no control at all. It's almost more fun—except that I know I will land, and that is bound to hurt. I have no time to plan. I cannot extend my arms to protect my body. Gravity has taken over.

I will almost certainly break an arm. That's okay, although I won't be able to drive home. Never mind; Tim will drive me. And I'll get scratched. No way to avoid that. The earth is hard and covered with rocks, and between the rocks are thickets.

Those are my last thoughts as a person with a healthy, normal, functioning brain.

The sound my skull makes as it hits the rock is like no sound I have heard before. It's an assault. One part crack, one part slosh, one part thump. My brain shudders inside my skull. I feel it move.[3]

When I come to, Tim is leaning over me, speaking. I have no idea how long I have been unconscious. *Who is he talking to?* I wonder, before realizing he is talking to me. He is making sure I'm alive. Mac nuzzles my feet apologetically. *I got a bit carried away,* he seems to say, although it could just as easily be his way of saying, *Fool!* I know absolutely nothing about horses, I realize. They are not like dogs. I lie on my back and look at the sky. The clouds pass overhead like I'm watching a time-lapse film. It never occurs to me to test my legs to make sure they still move. I am in shock, but I seem to be okay.

"You've got a scratch down your arm," Tim says.

I look at my arm, at the cut that runs from my elbow down to my wrist.

"Take it easy. No rush to get up. Where did you land?" he asks.

I point to the back-left side of my head. "Here," I say.

"Let me have a look," he says. He peers at my scalp. "Not even a mark."

I stand up and walk slowly back to the house. As soon as I am upright, I develop a headache, the kind that feels like someone has split open my head from behind with an ax, and a lump begins to form there. I can feel it. It never occurs to me, not even for a moment, that life will be different from this moment on. I drive back to Sydney that afternoon. Three hours on the road in Sunday traffic. *I'm fine,* I tell myself as I tear along the freeway, darting in between semitrailers and cars driven by old people. And I believe it to be true.

As soon as I am home, I ring my mother. I am not sure why. I have no one else to call.

"I got thrown off a horse," I tell her.

"No, darling, you fell."

"I did not fall."

"Horses don't throw people off, darling. People fall."

"No," I insist. "This one threw me." Catapulted me, in fact, although I can't seem to find that word. *Was she there? Does she know? How do mothers acquire these frightening powers of omniscience?*

"Look, it doesn't matter. Pour yourself a strong gin and tonic. You'll be fine. I fell off countless horses, countless times, and look at me![4] Anyway, Marjorie is here, so I can't talk now."

I hang up, do as I'm told, and pour myself a strong drink.

The next morning, I wake as usual to find George's muzzle in my side, reminding me it is time for a walk. Home, after our walk, I feed the dogs. I open the fridge and am surprised to find the reading lamp from my study lying on its side beside a jar of goat cheese. I remove the reading lamp from the fridge and place it on the kitchen bench. Inside the sink I notice the remnants of a square of butter, a block of Parmesan cheese, a jar of jam, a tub of olives, and a pint of milk. *Why are these things in the sink?* I wonder. It dawns on me that they have been moved from the fridge to make way for the desk lamp. Confused, I notice the toaster is missing. Someone has broken into my home and stolen my toaster. I race upstairs and look in the top drawer of my dresser for my grandmother's sapphire bracelet. It is sitting in its blue velvet box. I race downstairs and check the living room. The TV and video player are still there; all that appears to be missing is the toaster. I check the doors and the windows, but there is no sign that anyone has entered my house.

I pack the things that were left out overnight back inside the fridge. I open the freezer and find the toaster, covered in frost and icicles. I look at George and Bess. "Did you do this?" I ask. They look at me guiltily. I'm not convinced. Bess is the kind of dog who would confess to anything for the sake of peace. I remove the toaster from the freezer and set it in the dish rack to thaw. I decide to buy myself breakfast at the ferry stop on the way to work rather than use the toaster, for fear of electrocuting myself.

At work, I enter my office and set down my bag. It is 7:45 a.m., which means I am fifteen minutes late. I have a job with a fancy title: the Director of the Executive Office of State Administration in the Premier's Department, the central agency in the government of New South Wales (NSW). I am the youngest person ever to have been appointed to the NSW senior executive service. I am a third of the way through my doctorate in public administration, and I believe that public administration is the most fascinating thing in the world. I take myself seriously and hope I am destined for big things.

As I bend down beneath my desk and flick the switch that turns on my hard drive, my boss enters my office and plonks himself down in my visitor's chair.

"How was your weekend?" he asks.

I sit up and start to answer, but I don't get far before he interrupts.

"What happened to your eye?"

"What's wrong with it?" I ask.

He peers in and looks at me closely. "Your left eye has turned inward slightly. And it doesn't seem to move."

"I got thrown off a horse," I say. "Yesterday."

"You need to see an eye doctor. Now. I'll find someone."

He gets up, and I go to the bathroom to inspect my eye. It looks fine to me. I cover my right eye to check that the left eye still works. It seems to. Back at my desk my boss has scribbled down the name and number of an ophthalmologist.

"He's just down the hill on George Street. Call at nine when they open and make an appointment right away."

The eye doctor tells me the problem lies with my brain rather than my eye. There is nothing he can do. He suggests I get myself to a hospital as soon as I can for a brain scan. As I leave his office and walk outside into the bright light of George Street, I have a brief realization: brain injuries can be serious.

I ring my ex-boyfriend Edward and ask if he will take me to the hospital. He lives nearby and is happy to help in an emergency. I call my mother. Again, I am not sure why. She says she will meet us there.

Little good comes from a head injury, but it does cut down the wait when you show up unannounced at the emergency room. Mentioning the words "horse," "thrown," and "head" pushes you right up to the front of the line, ahead of everyone apart from people who have stopped breathing, people whose hearts have given out, and people with severed limbs.

My mother arrives, and we sit down on three scratched green plastic chairs at the back of the room.

"What's the matter with your eye?" she asks.

I don't have time to tell her before my name is called. I look at her, shrug, and follow the nurse into the emergency room. Neither she nor Edward get up to follow me. I go in alone. I am not fearful. In my mind, I am here to make sure that my brain is not bleeding. A hemorrhaging brain sounds serious. And painful. Frankly I have no clue why I'm here. I feel perfectly normal. I seem to have no problem at all with speech or movement. And I certainly don't look as though I have anything wrong with my brain. Apart from my left eye, which, people are telling me, struggles to keep pace with my right.

The nurse leads me to a small office where a tall man wearing beige trousers and a light-brown jumper tells me he is a neurologist.

"What happened?" he asks.

"I was thrown from a bolting horse yesterday." I point to the back-left side of my skull, where I can still feel a lump the size of a small kumquat.

"I landed there," I say.

"Were you wearing a helmet?" he asks, his head tilted upward like he's trying to show me the insides of his nostrils. He does not have even a veneer of kindness about him, and I feel like I've intruded upon his day.

"No."

"Why not?"

"There wasn't one," I say. It is the first time the idea of a helmet has even occurred to me.

"Well that was very, very silly," he says. "You could have been killed, do you realize that?"

I kind of wish I had died, I think, although I don't tell him this, for fear of spending the next fortnight strapped to a bed in a psych ward.

"The first thing we need to do is get you a CT scan to make sure there's no bleeding in your brain and you haven't fractured anything. We'll send you off to imaging and then you'll come back here."

I do as he says and trundle off behind a nurse who leads me halfway to imaging and then directs me to take a left, then a right, then the second door to my left. "Just follow the signs. It's all clearly marked," she says, smiling. I nod. I have an excellent sense of direction, but I somehow end up in a room marked "Orthopedic Day Patients." A nurse leads me out and walks me to imaging. I am the only person waiting for a brain scan. I lie down inside a long plastic shell and close my eyes. My mind is blank.

Once the scan is over and after a few wrong turns, I find my way back to the waiting room, where my mother keeps clearing her throat and pushing her glasses up onto the bridge of her nose—the things she does when she is nervous. Edward is telling her about a new business idea he has, but I can tell she's not listening. It has dawned on her, I think, that being here—in the hospital, me talking to a neurologist and having a brain scan—might be an indication of something serious. The waiting room seethes with sick, hurt people, and I have been seen straightaway. I sit down beside them and wait only moments before my name is called. I get up, alone again, and follow the nurse back to see the neurologist. He sits at his desk in his tiny room, looking at pictures of my brain on a light box. It looks, to me, like a series of black-and-white photos of an old moldy orange.

"Another couple of centimeters to the right and you could have died. Can you see this?" he says without glancing at me, using a ball-point pen to point at the screen. I lean closer.

"Bruising. Can you see it?"

"I have no idea what a normal brain looks like, so no, I can't see it," I answer.

"A normal brain looks like this," he says, and points at a different part of my brain. "That's healthy brain tissue. See the difference?"

I shrug. "No."

"*Contusion*, we call it. Often follows a concussion. It could have been avoided had you worn a helmet."

"I think you've made your point about the helmet," I say. "What does it mean?"

"We don't know yet. We'll get you an appointment at the Brain Injury Unit in Ryde. They'll do some psychometric tests and show us what we can't see from the scans. You were really silly not to wear a helmet," he says.

"Shut up about the fucking helmet!"

My venom disarms me. It is the first time in my life I have sworn at a stranger. It is also the first time in my life I have exploded without warning. I sit back in my chair and watch a sneer spread across the doctor's face. I have lost whatever scant respect he may have had for me.

"The nurse will get you a slot at the Brain Injury Unit. Wait outside for a few minutes."

I find my way back to the waiting room.

"What's going on?" my mother asks.

"I don't know," I tell her. "I have to go to the brain place in Ryde for tests."

"Why? What did the scans show?" she asks.

"Bruising."

A nurse comes out moments later with a slip of paper. "We've booked you in at the end of this week. Friday, at two o'clock. Is that okay? They have your details, so all you need to do is show up."

"What else do they need?" my mother asks.

"I have no idea," I say.

"But there's nothing wrong with you apart from your eye!" she says.

"The doctor seems to think differently," I say.

"I'll take you," my mother says.

"No. Edward can take me." I don't even ask him.

"That's fine," he says. "I'll take her."

I start to argue with my mother. She has done nothing at all to provoke me, but a sudden fear about my brain, indignation about the helmet, and a lifetime of resentment toward her conspire inside me like a bomb that has just been detonated. "Fuck off!" I shout at her in the middle of the parking lot. The words leave my mouth, and I turn my head slightly, wondering where they came from. *Who said that?* My mother and I have always fought, but I cannot recall an occasion when I have talked to her like this. *What has happened to me?*

My mother takes me at my word. She gets into her car and drives away.

I spend the rest of the week at home. I don't hear from my mother. I don't hear from anyone. I must have rung my boss to let him know I would take the rest of the week off, but I have no memory of doing so. Edward picks me up on Friday.

"Your eye is back to normal," he says, looking at me closely as soon as I open the door.

"Oh, okay. I'm glad to hear it." I had forgotten all about it.

"I'm starving," he says. "Do you mind if we take a detour past McDonald's?"

"That's fine. Thanks for the lift."

"Don't be silly," he says, leaning in and slapping me on the knee.

We arrive at McDonald's and find an empty table next to a life-size cardboard cutout of Ronald McDonald, and I watch Edward eat two Happy Meals. He pretends he has no interest in the two plastic figurines that hide inside his Happy Meal boxes, but I see him slip them inside his trouser pocket. McDonald's makes him happy.

Edward is a nice man, but we ran out of things to say to one another long ago. I'm glad we broke up. He finishes his food, wipes his hands on a fresh pile of napkins, deposits his rubbish in the bin like a good McDonald's citizen, and we walk back to the car. Inside, he reaches across me and slips the two plastic figurines inside the glove box. He looks at me and smiles.

"Does Kate like McDonald's?" Kate is his new, improved girlfriend, with whom he got together in the final months of his relationship with me.

"Hates it," he laughs, "even more than you."

We don't speak at all in the twenty minutes it takes to drive to Ryde. I stare out the window and wish my father were here. He would know what to do. My father was an associate professor of geology, but he sprang to life in a crisis—an electrical failure, or a leaking roof, or a broken-down car. In matters that concerned me, he almost always took my side, providing a counterweight to my mother, who liked to blame me for anything she could. I watch the trees and telegraph poles rush by and realize I have lost the only person on earth who ever had my best interests at heart. I am completely on my own.

A psychologist named Toby leads me into his office and sits me down. He has curly brown hair, thinning slightly on the top of his head, and gentle green eyes. He wears jeans, a corduroy jacket with suede patches on the elbows, and oval glasses with gold rims. Toby asks what I do and where I work. I tell him, and he nods encouragingly.

"We're going to do some simple tests," he says.

"Okay. No problem." I do well on tests as a rule, apart from tests that involve numbers. I failed high school math. Not only did I fail, but I achieved a result of 8 percent when I was fifteen, before giving it up altogether. It wasn't that I hadn't tried but that I seemed incapable of grasping anything that involved numbers.

I tell Toby about my struggle with numbers so as not to alarm him. "That's okay," he says. "Let's try some basic numeracy tests anyway." I don't get the answers wrong. I can't answer his questions at all.

"Let's try something else," Toby suggests. "Basic verbal reasoning." I do my best to answer, but I feel a sharp pain inside my head each time I try to think. I can't process his questions, and as soon as they leave his mouth, the words begin to scramble; I can't grasp them long enough to make sense of anything. Summoning up the energy it takes to ponder ten simple questions exhausts me. They are not so simple after all. I slump back in my chair and wonder what is happening to me. Looking out the window, I notice the venetian blind is broken. Is there anything more forlorn than a broken plastic venetian blind? I stare at the blind and a tidal wave of hopelessness overwhelms me.

"Let's try this," Toby says, reaching under his desk and pulling out a large plastic cylinder full of wooden shapes in primary colors. He empties the cylinder on his desk. "Find the blue shapes," he says.

I stare at the shapes, conscious that Toby is watching me intently.

"Take your time," he says, which I interpret as, *What on earth is wrong with you?*

"Good," he says, when I've finally sorted them out. "Now let's try something else. I want you to find the red triangle on the desk and put it inside the cutout triangle here, and then do the same with the yellow circle." He points to an empty red space in the shape of a triangle. "Do you understand?"

Yes, I nod, registering that no one has asked me if I understood something since I was in kindergarten. It's a game meant for kids aged between two and four. I struggle. I manage to place the triangle in the triangle space—I remember what he pointed at—but when it comes to the circle, I can't for the life of me find it. It's a trick. "There's no yellow circle," I say.

Toby points at the circle.

Something inside me bursts. I bury my head in my hands and sob. Toby passes me a box of tissues, but I am beyond tissues. I sob while he tells me it will take him a day to write up his report and send it to the hospital. I sob as I leave his office and make my way to the car park, Edward trailing behind me silently. I sob all the way home and long after Edward has dropped me off and returned to his life with Kate. I sob as I take the dogs to the park. I sob until I fall asleep that night and moments later when I wake.

I don't go back to the hospital. I don't need to. The neurologist rings me at home to tell me he has received the results of my psychometric tests.

"Look, you probably guessed the results are not good," he begins. I don't speak.

"You scored very poorly on the psychometric tests. If we were talking in terms of IQ, yours would be around eighty."

He does not tell me what an IQ of eighty means, but I know enough to realize that an IQ of eighty is very low. Perhaps he thinks I will not understand.

"These kinds of results are consistent with a mild traumatic brain injury," he says. "Unfortunately, the longer-term prognosis isn't terribly good. I don't see that you're going to be able to return to work." He pauses. "Not to white-collar work, anyway."

I struggle to follow. What does he see me doing in the future? Going down a coal mine? Working on the railways?

"Outdoor work might suit you. Do you like the outdoors?" he asks. I don't answer.

"Working in a park, that kind of thing."

I cannot speak. The number eighty sloshes around inside my head, like dirty water inside a bucket. *What was my IQ at age eleven?* I knew it once; how can I have forgotten it? *Eighty. Eighty. Eighty.* A frighteningly low number for someone holding down an executive job, someone who is partway through her PhD.

"We'll organize some rehab for you. You'll have your own social worker, and she'll be able to help you. She'll let work know too. That you won't be going back. The main thing to avoid is another blow to the head. That could be very dangerous."

I listen, and as the words register, I feel as though something inside me might implode. "What about my PhD?" I ask.

He clears his throat, and I hear what sounds like a scoff. "There is no way you'll be able to finish a PhD."

And there it ends. My prognosis. Our conversation. Life as I knew it.

2

THE POCKMARK ON THE WALL

On the wall of my living room, directly opposite the fireplace and approximately one foot above the back of the sofa, was a slight recess about an inch in diameter, where part of the plaster was gouged from the wall.

I bought this house for my dog, Bess, after Edward and I were threatened with eviction from our old apartment block. Bess, a mixed-breed dog about the size of a spaniel, had barely been living with us for a fortnight when an elderly woman with gray hair set atop her head like fairy floss stopped me in the lobby of our block and hissed, "We have had multiple complaints about your dog. Get rid of it or find somewhere else to live."

I put the apartment up for sale and found a buyer almost instantly who paid double what I had just two years earlier. A week later I purchased an unrenovated terrace house barely a block away, on Darling Street in Balmain, and hitched myself to a large mortgage. Bess got a home, and, for the first time in my life but not the last, I had bought a house almost entirely based around the needs of a dog.

I painted the inside of the house after Edward and I broke up. An old brick house built in 1870, it was prone to the ills of old Sydney terrace houses—dampness, darkness, mustiness. I chose a hue of burnt yellow for its walls, which the paint chart called "corn bread," and I diluted it by half. I hoped yellow might improve my mood and help me forget that I had once shared the house with Edward.

It took me a week to prepare the walls for painting, plugging the holes with putty, waiting the requisite two hours for drying time, sanding them, applying a second layer of putty, and finally sanding again, first with coarse paper and then with extrafine. I used wood putty to mend the scars and scabs on the doors, molding, and baseboards before giving everything three coats of high-gloss white paint. I used turpentine and a clean sponge to remove the paint from George and Bess, who had leaned against the freshly painted doors, eager for me to finish. I was certain I had plugged every fissure, every blemish, every hole made by picture hooks over the past 120 years. My dedication to this task was astonishing. I am sloppy by nature, but the results I achieved were nothing short of remarkable. Had I been so inclined, I could almost certainly have tossed my job with the government and set up shop as a painter.

Days after I learned of my prognosis, I lay on the sofa, entranced by this gouge in the plaster. I didn't wonder how it slipped my notice when I was preparing the walls for painting. I wasn't struck by my pockmarked wall in need of putty to seal its holes as a metaphor for my life. I didn't imagine the pockmark was a hole that would suck me in and transport me to a different world.

I didn't think anything at all.

I just stared at it and lost all concept of time. Spittle ran down the side of my chin, reminding me that my mouth kept falling open. Time passed without me realizing it, and my memories of that period are murky and disordered. My life was crammed inside this spot on my wall.

I had just been told I had suffered a mild traumatic brain injury, but even in my brain-damaged state, the words "mild" and "traumatic" seemed contradictory. If my injury was mild, why couldn't I return to my job and resume my former life?

I was not the only one who was confused about the meaning of a "mild" traumatic brain injury (TBI). I have since learned that there is no consensus among health-care professionals as to what the term actually means, making diagnosis rather difficult. To complicate things further, the term "mild TBI" is often used interchangeably with "concussion."[5] Mild traumatic brain injury is commonly thought to refer to any loss of consciousness that lasts less than thirty minutes, any loss of memory of events immediately before or after an accident, any change of mental state (such as feeling dazed or confused), and any problems with focus. Patients are generally assessed according to the Glasgow Coma Scale, which is used, among other purposes, to measure the level of consciousness after a TBI by testing basic eye, verbal, and motor responses.

Not that I knew any of this at the time.

I spent most of each day stretched out across my sofa. George preferred the coolness of the floorboards, while Bess sacrificed her own comfort, and mine, to nestle against me and let me know she was there. The summer heat seeped through the walls of our house. I wore shorts and a T-shirt, and the skin of my arms and legs prickled with heat and dog hair. My head felt as though a train rattled through it as I gazed into the pockmark on the wall.

George and Bess stepped willingly into their respective roles as protector and caregiver. In the unlikely event someone knocked at our door, George barked savagely and bared his teeth. If anyone wanted to mess with his brain-damaged owner, they would have to deal with him first. Bess, a gentler dog than George, licked my hands and face and wagged her tail to let me know that everything that existed outside my brain-damaged world was fine.

George, our pack leader, assumed control over my days. He seemed to enjoy the redistribution of power in our household—he was the man and he liked to be in charge. Unless there was a thunderstorm, in which case all bets were off while he convulsed with fear under the kitchen table, or sat on my head when a storm struck during the night.

Each morning he woke me at seven to take me to the park. I dressed myself in whatever clothes I could find that were nearest to the bed and attached leashes to the dogs' collars. We walked in any one of three directions, depending on George's mood. Bess and I followed him, grateful that someone in the family was capable of taking charge.

Three parks were nearby, and George liked variety. At the park, he led Bess and me to an empty bench, where I sat, removed the leashes from their collars, and stared out at the harbor. George and Bess spent an hour or so gamboling with other dogs, sniffing trees and busying themselves. From time to time, if a man approached or came too close to my bench, George would bound up to him out of nowhere, snarling and flashing his teeth. I belonged to him. A former stray, George wasn't fond of men. His fondness was for pretty blonde women. If he spotted an attractive woman on the other side of the road, he would happily put our lives in danger, dragging us in front of cars and buses, in the hope of a pat or a kiss.

Once he decided our park visit was over, George mustered up Bess and they trotted back to my bench and sat obediently at my feet, waiting for me to attach their leashes. They walked me home and waited in the kitchen while I prepared their breakfast of cooked mince and dry kibble. We repeated the ritual at lunchtime and late afternoon. Before bedtime, they settled for a quick walk around the corner to a small patch of grass.

~

When we rescued Bess, I was twenty-six. I had been desperate for a dog ever since moving out of my parents' house, but the apartment Edward and I lived in didn't allow pets.

Looking out our kitchen window one Sunday morning, Edward spotted a dog not far from the seawall in Sydney Harbor, struggling to stay afloat. He shouted at me to follow him, and we raced downstairs.

Edward leapt the stone wall and waded into the water. Moments later he reappeared carrying a waterlogged dog. She was medium sized, white with black markings and a black patch the size of a baseball over one eye. We sat with her on the grass and waited for her to get her breath back. Moments later she lifted her head slightly, looked at us, and wagged her tail.

"We are keeping her," I said to Edward. "If she doesn't have a microchip."

"Dogs aren't allowed in our building!"

"We'll buy a house then."

Edward looked at me as if I was crazy.

"She doesn't have a collar," I said. "Let's see if she has a microchip."

Bess, as I decided to name her, didn't have a microchip. Our local vet had never seen her before.

We wrapped her in a large beach towel and carried her up in the elevator to our apartment. The first time we did it when the elevator was full, she let out a single yelp, signaling to our fellow passengers that she wasn't a pile of laundry, but a dog, and not just a dog, but a dog we were disguising as something else in order to smuggle her inside our building.

About six months after we settled into our new house, Bess and I were out for an afternoon walk beneath the enormous Moreton Bay fig trees at Birchgrove Park, when we spotted a terrified dog without a collar. A few blocks from our house, Birchgrove is one of the most exclusive suburbs in Sydney, comprising a ring of luxurious waterfront homes, a tiny harbor beach with an old wooden jetty, and a perfectly manicured sports field—not the kind of place you expect to happen upon a stray, hungry dog.

The dog was darting back and forth across the road, his tail between his legs. I tried to approach him, and kneeled down on the ground with my hand extended in his direction, but he refused to come anywhere near me. I ran home, left Bess there, grabbed some fresh meat from the fridge, and hopped in my car to find him. Three days later I finally caught him after I followed him onto the jetty and managed to slip a collar around his neck. More fearful of water than he was of me, he relented. We sat together on the steps of the jetty, and I stroked his ears. Despite being thin, he was handsome, about the size of a German shepherd, with the red-brown coat of a dingo.

Worried that he might slip his collar and leash, I picked him up and carried him to my car. Bones were visible on his sides, and his slack body felt like jelly. I took him home and introduced him to Bess. She was happy to see another dog and looked on amiably as he gobbled down a bowl of dog food. I decided to name him George, my father's middle name. It was a name I liked, and it seemed to suit him.

That afternoon, I took George to the vet for a checkup and a microchip. The vet estimated he was around twelve months old.

The rivalry between Edward and George was instant. A neighbor told me Edward locked George out in the garden when I was at work. George disliked Edward and spent most of his time pretending Edward wasn't there. The two vied for the position of top dog, and George won.

~

One day, the social worker came to visit. The unusual sound of a knock at my door sent both dogs into a frenzy. Breathless after climbing the three steps it took to reach my hallway, Rosie introduced herself and told me she was frightened of dogs. I neither liked nor trusted people who were fearful of dogs. Dogs were all I trusted. George looked Rosie up and down, snorted his disapproval, and retreated inside the house.

"Do you mind locking the dogs in another room while we talk?" Rosie asked.

George shot me a look that said, *How about we lock her in another room?*

"The dogs stay," I said. "They've never bitten anyone and are unlikely to start now. We have no secrets here."

Rosie raised an eyebrow. She then told me she had contacted my boss and "explained the situation," lingering over each word.

"You suffered a serious brain injury. You're not going to be able to return to work." She said it as if she were telling me what she cooked last night for dinner.

I sat for a moment, letting her words sink in. Weeks ago, I had a senior job in the government. Now I was being told I would not be able to work again. It was an outcome I could never even have imagined. "Please go," I said. I could not believe that a decision like that had been made without my permission, without consultation. It infuriated me to think that the state had stepped in and decided my future. My life was in the hands of Rosie, a well-meaning woman with spiky red hair and arms like loaves of bread, a woman I had never even met before.

"Go," I said, and she did.

∼

Rosie called me about a fortnight later to tell me she had managed to get me a spot in a rehab group in North Sydney, cutting up fabric for stuffed toys. "It would help you, I think," she said. I hung up. It was the last conversation we had—her final attempt at my rehabilitation.

Rosie's call made me decide to wrench the phone from the wall. I plugged it back in only when I needed to make a call.

George, Bess, and I settled back into our routine. Each night around nine o'clock George nudged me from my torpor and made his way over to the foot of the staircase, where he waited for Bess and me to follow him up to the bedroom. He was the first to hop onto the bed and insisted on lying crossways over its middle. Bess and I squeezed in around him, legs dangling over the side of the bed. The dogs fell into a deep slumber almost as soon as they were horizontal.

Sleep as I once knew it was impossible. When I closed my eyes, I was bombarded by flashing lights—my own private laser show. Sleep came in snatches of five or ten minutes and only when I sunk into slumber at the very instant my eyes were no longer able to hold themselves open. When I did fall asleep, I had horrifyingly vivid dreams of being locked inside a coffin and buried alive, with a torch flashing in my face. So disturbing were these dreams that I would wake to find myself standing somewhere in my bedroom, soaked in sweat, arms flailing, thrashing my way out of a locked wooden box. Back in bed, I stared at the ceiling, at the shadows cast by the fan that whizzed above us and threatened to break loose and chop us all into tiny pieces.

No one had told me that sleep disturbances affect most head-injured folk, sometimes permanently, or that a lack of sleep would significantly hamper rehabilitation. I would never have another normal night's sleep without medication. I squirmed around the bed, trying to claim enough space to stretch out like a beanpole between the dogs.

Grief consumed me, fanning the flames of my insomnia. I struggled to remember anything except my father's death. That episode had been carved inside my brain like a knife cuts into the trunk of a eucalypt. I remembered little other than the most rudimentary requirements of daily living—to wake, walk the dogs, feed them, feed myself, swallow painkillers for my aching head, wash, dress, and retire to the sofa until the dogs reminded me it was time for me to move. My father's death, though, I recalled as if it had just happened. I saw the outline of his body under the white hospital-issue blanket, like a matchstick bent in half. I heard him shriek with pain before we called the doctor and increased his morphine dose. I kissed his face, the face of a dead man. Every memory I ever had was wiped clean to make room for each minute detail of my father's death. It played out in my head, over and over again, like a tape on repeat.

Cancer had shrunk my father to half his former size. A tumor had burst the banks of his bowel and spread into his spine. Bowel cancer had become bone cancer, and the pain had been excruciating. He had still been handsome only a year before his diagnosis, but afterward he looked at least thirty years older than sixty-four. Gray flesh with eyes that retreated inside his face. A skeleton draped with skin.

One morning he got up after tea and took his mug back to the kitchen. My mother and I watched him use all his strength to lever himself out of his chair. He didn't stay upright long. Bess leapt up excitedly, thinking it was time for a walk, and knocked him back down. My mother and I picked him up and carried him to the bedroom. He never got up again.

A palliative care nurse visited and gave my mother and me a lesson in morphine injection. I took three months' unpaid leave from work, packed a suitcase, and moved into the family home with George and Bess.

I set up the sofa bed in my brother's room, but the springs poked through the mattress and I wasn't able to sleep. In the room next door, my father soaked his sheets with sweat and convulsed from the pain. He needed to be moved every couple of hours to control his pain and prevent bedsores, and my mother couldn't manage alone. She lay next to him and held his hand, helpless, while he writhed in pain.

It was my father's idea to move into my old bedroom. My mother needed snatches of sleep to prepare for what lay ahead. We promised him we would not have him hospitalized. He hated hospitals, loathed doctors. I assumed the full-time duties of nursing assistant.

The palliative care unit delivered our own hospital bed. It was brand-new, the nurse enthused, which I took to mean that no one had died in it yet. My father would be the first. She showed us its features, as if it were a car: a hydraulic pump to control height and bed position, adjustable side rails, lockable wheels, plastic bed sheets. The grim prospect of watching my father die in my childhood bedroom sank in as we set him up in this bed.

My room hadn't changed much in the eight years I'd been gone. Only the bed and its position in the room was different. My single bed had sat with one long side against the wall underneath a window. This new, shiny hospital bed stuck out from the wall at right angles, allowing us easy access to my dying father from both sides. My father would die in the same room where he had read to me before bed each night. "Here's Bod in bed," began my favorite book, *Bod's Dream*, and I never tired of hearing it. Years later it dawned on me that my father liked it because it was short. If it was particularly late, he would sit on the edge of the bed and recite "There Was a Little Girl" by Henry Wadsworth Longfellow, pointing at the curl on my forehead, hoping that would be enough. It never was. "No!" I would shout, worried he would leave. "Please! *Bod's Dream!*" and he would groan, reach across my bedside table, open the book, and begin to read. I was about five at the time. Now, some twenty-four years later, we experienced the devastating reversal of roles that occurs at some point in many parent-child relationships. His deathbed book would be *Flaubert's Parrot* by Julian Barnes, a book I could never bring myself to finish on my own after his death.

The curtains I'd chosen as a teenager still covered the windows of my bedroom. Red, orange, and yellow poppies had become bleached over the years. My parents had indulged my request for a bright-green ceiling when I was thirteen. It looked terrible, but once done it was hard to disguise, so we left it there for posterity. Shrouded between white hospital sheets, under the green reflection of the ceiling, my father looked like a plastic Casper the ghost, the kind left to glow all night in a child's bedroom.

He chose to take up residence in my room because it looked out onto our backyard. From one window he could see the large liquidambar tree in the corner of the garden. From the other he looked out onto the jacaranda tree in the neighbor's yard. In front of the liquidambar was an open stone fireplace—the kind of fireplace that could start a serious fire. Backyard fires were banned, and my mother had turned the fireplace into a flower bed, full of nasturtiums and lavender. George liked to sleep in it and catch the afternoon sun.

We dragged an armchair from the sitting room to my bedroom so one of us could sit next to him when he was awake. I lowered the bed using the hydraulic pump and shifted the chair alongside so I could hold his hand.

"How's the PhD coming along?" he asked.

"Um."

"What progress have you made, Pod?"

"Um, well, none."

"Really? Why?"

"I've been a bit distracted."

"Oh, I see. I'm sorry about that."

"It's not your fault."

I sat with him, holding his hand until he settled. I passed him a glass of lemonade, an invalid straw poking out its top. "Drink," I commanded. He took a small sip and handed me back the glass.

"Enough."

He had stopped eating a week earlier. Now a drip was keeping him alive.

"How's the pain?" I asked.

"The same."

"It's nearly time for your morphine."

I went to retrieve his stash of drugs from the kitchen and loaded up a syringe. *What would an air bubble do?* I wondered, as I flicked away at the plastic cylinder. *Kill him quickly? Make things worse?* I called my mother. She had a knack for injecting him so he didn't even feel the prick of the needle.

Fuzzied by morphine, my father looked blearily out the window. "Pod, would you mind moving that plant a little? I can't quite see out."

I got up and pretended to shift the imaginary plant a few inches to the left and looked back at him for his approval.

"Much better," my father said. "Thank you. It's quite a nice view, isn't it?"

"It is."

On another occasion after my mother had increased his dose, he grabbed my hand and whispered, "You're so much prettier than the other nurse. And nicer too."

"True," I said. "Would you like me to ask her to leave things to me from now on?"

"Would you mind?" he said, squeezing my hand. "Thank you."

The pain worsened. My father, not one to complain about pain, began to shriek. We called the doctor. *Double the dose,* he said. I jumped in the car, drove to the doctor's office, picked up the prescription, raced across the road to the pharmacy, pushed to the front of the line, grabbed the paper bag full of ampules, raced back to the car and home, ran up the front steps three at a time, and loaded up a clean syringe for my mother. It was a routine we repeated every couple of days.

The pain got so bad my father agreed to go to the hospital. He would stay only one night, we promised him, and we would sleep in chairs beside his bed. The next morning when the pain was under control, we would bring him home. We carried him downstairs and stretched him out carefully on the back seat of my parents' Toyota Corolla. I drove, my mother's arm twisted around from the front to stop him sliding off the seat. We kept our promises.

Home, with yet more medication, the pain became crippling.

"Pod, you have to help me. I can't go on like this. I want to die. Now. Today. Please help me. I can't ask your mother."

Stupidly, I told my mother. "He wants to die and he wants me to help him."

"You want to *kill* him?" she shrieked, as veins began to throb in her forehead. "To *murder* him?"

"Yes," I said. "And since he's dying I'm not sure how it counts as murder."

"Of course it's murder, you idiot! We could go to jail for that!"

"And who do you think is going to find out? He's dying! *We* are criminal if we sit by like this and watch him die."

Relations between my mother and me sank to a new low. "Sarah wants to kill him!" I overheard her say on the phone to the doctor, and again to my great aunt. She followed me when I went into the room to sit with him. I sensed if anyone was going to turn me in for helping my father die, it would be her. In the end, I gave her my word. I would not help him die.

I told my father.

"Why on earth did you tell her?" he asked.

"I don't know," I said. But I did know. I was scared because I didn't know how to do it. *How much morphine would it take? What if it wasn't enough? Or too much, and it made him sick?* I hated myself for my gutlessness. My father, the person I loved most in the world, had asked me for help only once in twenty-nine years, and I had failed him.

It was the one thing for which I would never forgive myself.

In the last ten days of his life I took to sleeping beside his bed. When my brother arrived from England in time to say goodbye, I gave up my claim to his old room because he was jet-lagged. Taking some cushions from the sofa, I made myself a bed on the floor next to my father. He drifted in and out of consciousness. I didn't want him to be alone. To die alone. I held his hand, told him I loved him, and asked him to squeeze if he knew I was there. Each time I asked, his hand pressed against mine.

On the tenth night, I waited until eleven o'clock and went back to the sofa. I hadn't slept in more than a week. Moments after I fell asleep, I felt my mother's hand on my leg. "He's gone." He had clung to life knowing I was there beside him. He needed me to leave, to allow him to die.

I sobbed—that mad, uncontrollable sobbing that only grief can cause—until eight the next morning when we rang the doctor. He came and pronounced my father dead. We called a funeral director. Three scruffy blond men showed up, looking like they had been dragged away from their morning surf. They banged their stretcher against the sides of the hallway as they made their way to my old bedroom. Minutes later they returned, my father hidden under their white sheet. They carried him down the front steps and loaded him into the open back of a station wagon. My mother, brother, and I watched in silence as the car disappeared down the driveway, my father finally gone.

I locked myself inside my father's study and wept. That same day I moved back home with George and Bess. I wanted my own bed and the familiarity of my own home. There was no point staying with my mother and brother. The glue that had held our family together was gone.

~

The longer I spent alone after my injury, the more I realized I vastly preferred the company of dogs to people. Dogs never give up on us, even after we have given up on ourselves. They accept us as we are, love us without conditions, and do not cast judgments. There is no greater gift for the brain-injured person than a dog.

I didn't return to work. I received no compensation, although I must have had some form of death and disability insurance coverage—a legal requirement for all government employees. No one told me about it, and it didn't even occur to me until years later, by which time it was too late to pursue. Months after my accident a solicitor friend suggested I sue Tim and Belinda. They should have insurance that would cover everything, he said. I called Tim and told him that the doctor had said I would never return to work.

Tim was appalled. Horrified. Apologetic. He had no idea. He took a day to find his insurance papers and discovered his coverage had expired a month before the accident.

"Go ahead and sue me anyway. We'll find a way to come up with the money," he said.

"Don't be ridiculous," I responded. "I would never do that."

My solicitor friend pressed me to go ahead and sue. I refused. *Who sues their friends?* It wasn't Tim's fault I had brain damage. I had insisted on riding his horse.

A couple of weeks after the social worker visited, a letter arrived in the mail from the federal government telling me that my injury meant I satisfied their requirements for a disability pension, a form of social security offered by the Australian government to people with disabilities that prevent them from working. Once a fortnight I drove to the Commonwealth Employment Service office in Leichhardt to collect my check. It barely covered groceries, bills, and dog food.

Ever since I had started work as a teenager—babysitting and stuffing the bodies of dogs and cats that had been euthanized into huge garbage bins at a nearby vet surgery—I had tried to save as much money as I could. I had just started high school when I overheard my mother talking to a friend on the phone. Her friend had asked my mother to go to a movie, and my mother declined. She didn't explain why, but I knew it was because she couldn't afford the ticket. My father, who was in charge of the finances, had grown up poor and was parsimonious with the money he earned. His priority, after supporting his elderly father, was to pay off the mortgage. Any money left over was used to indulge his passion for collecting rare books. The teacher's salary my mother earned went toward bills and groceries. At the end of each month, we never had much money left.

Overhearing my mother decline that trip to the movies made me decide that whatever job I ended up taking, I would need to earn enough money to be financially independent. I worked after school and during university, saving whatever money I could. With a small sum given to me by my mother's father, I stretched myself to buy a small apartment when I was twenty-two, and stretched myself yet further to buy my house. I would never rely on anyone for money, and I would never be poor.

Over the years, I had saved enough money to keep paying my loan for the next nine months. I had planned for a worst-case scenario, knowing somewhere in the back of my mind it was never far away. There is something to be said for pessimism.

The pain inside my head intensified. It felt as though someone had dropped a concrete slab upon my head. I made regular visits to the local hospital, to collect a supply of painkillers. Drugs muted the pain, but they didn't kill it.

My ability to think had been stolen from me. A walk down a supermarket aisle bewildered me; I may just as well have been pondering whether black holes produce thermal radiation. I didn't have the ability to remember what to buy, and I didn't have the clarity of mind to determine what I needed in the way of food, so I often just bought pasta, tomato sauce, and dog food. The routine with the dogs reminded me that I needed to eat also, but for the first time in my life, I had no interest in food. I ate the same thing every day without even noticing the taste. George turned his back on my leftovers, leaving me in no doubt that he thought my cooking was worse than his dog food.

One day I stood in the middle of a supermarket aisle and stared at the wall of pasta. Yellow-and-red packets, blue-and-yellow boxes, blue packets, red packets, yellow packets. I peered at the price tags lining the bottom of each shelf and couldn't tell which packet was cheaper, which more expensive. The numbers all looked the same. I took a step closer to the shelf to study the different types of pasta, and my head started to pound. Corkscrew pasta, tube pasta, long stringy pasta in different widths, pasta shaped like shells, pasta shaped like ears. What was the point? Choice confused me. Overwhelmed, I reached for three packets of tube-shaped pasta in red-and-yellow plastic and dumped them in my shopping cart.

Clueless as to how much things cost and unable to add things up, I handed the cashier nothing smaller than a fifty-dollar note. That way she couldn't look at me like I was crazy. I panicked at the prospect of being humiliated by the person at the checkout counter. My greatest fear was appearing stupid; a fear I will carry with me for the rest of my life—a tattoo across my forehead only I can see. All I wanted was to be invisible. As I paid the girl, I reminded myself to close my mouth. I had realized that clamping my mouth shut hid the worst of my damaged brain from the world—effectively solving both my unsightly slack gape and the nonsense that came out of it. My words were jumbled. I knew that from talking to the dogs. When I had to interact with humans, I said as little as possible: *yes, no, thanks, bye.*

After driving home and unpacking my shopping—two large bags of dog food, three packets of pasta, six jars of tomato sauce, I noticed the list resting on the counter next to the sink. I had forgotten bread, milk, fruit, vegetables, garbage bags, laundry detergent, soap, Vegemite, and a bulb for the bedroom light. It took me a week to make that list. I placed the dog food on the floor of the pantry while George nuzzled my leg approvingly.

My emotional range had shrunk drastically and now comprised stupor, anger, and depression. Anger was the worst.

I knew a lot about terrible tempers. My father was prone to sudden bouts of rage that sent him rampaging through the house, smashing things and beating my brother and me. As a child, I had no way of grasping what drove my father's rage. When I had time to hide, I watched him transform from a distance and saw the ugliness and the damage that rage wrought. He never hit my mother, but he once Frisbeed a plate in her direction, which crashed into the kitchen wall a foot or so away from where she had been standing.

Before my accident, I had a mild temper. I could turn it on and off and use it to good effect, or so I believed. I never lost control, and I was never violent. But the brain-damaged me was consumed by a simmering rage. Nothing quelled my fury. It assaulted me without warning. One moment I could be resting on the sofa and the next held hostage by an uncontrollable rage.

When Edward moved out, he left behind a set of old kitchen chairs that I stacked up inside the garden shed. Those chairs often took the brunt of my anger. At the first signs of rage, I would go into the back garden and shut the door to the house with the dogs inside. George, Bess, and all the dogs and cats I would ever own in the future were the only things I spared my fury.

Outside, I would remove a chair, lift it over my shoulders, and belt it into the ground with all my might. It took five hits each time before I would start to tire. Then I would curl up on the ground, rock back and forth, and sob. Rage robbed me of what little self-respect I had left. It signaled defeat, failure, and a complete loss of dignity. Exhausted, I would pick up what was left of the chair and stack it back inside the shed, ready for the next time I'd lose it. George and Bess would be waiting behind the kitchen door and would follow me back to the sofa.

Bess would hop up next to me and I would hug her until my heart stopped thrashing. Not one to miss out on a cuddle, George would always intrude on our embrace.

My rage was born of frustration, at no longer being able to do the things I once did without thinking. After the accident, the smallest things required an effort of gargantuan proportions, and even then often confounded me. Paying an electricity bill, deciphering a bank statement, or trying to find the key to the back gate. Those kinds of tasks caused me to erupt into an apoplectic rage.

Brain damage had left me with ultrasensitive hearing. Certain sharp or sudden noises made me snap and turn into a madwoman. A poorly tuned radio or TV signal, a screeching tire on the street outside, or a car backfiring threatened my mental stability. The sounds of daily life had become an intolerable cacophony.

Anger was something I would learn to live with, something I would hate myself for, something that would drive away those closest to me, that would strangle nearly every intimate relationship I ever had. Anger was the acid that would eat away at the people I loved. It was the reason I would spend many years alone, although that was the least of my worries then.

I was depressed. My life was stuck inside a chink in a wall that stretched out before me. The only way forward was through a long black tunnel burrowed into infinity. I couldn't escape, so I settled in and made it my home. I lay on my sofa inside my tunnel. If it were not for the dogs, I would never have dragged myself up. I would have stayed on that sofa, closed my eyes, and waited until time stopped.

Depression is the soulmate of brain damage, although no one told me so. Frankly, I had no good reason to live. The life ahead of me was terrifying. A life of disability checks, years spent trapped inside my house until it was taken from me because I couldn't afford the mortgage payments, lying on that sofa, unable to think, unable to remember, unable to work. I should have seen a psychiatrist. I should have sought help. But I lacked the insight to realize that. I didn't see another specialist about my head injury or any of its manifold consequences for nine more years. The hospital neurologist had left me with an intense dislike for members of the medical profession; I was completely without hope.

I had lost my father, lost my mind, lost my self. What else was left for me to lose but George and Bess? I trifled with the idea of suicide but stopped when I thought of the dogs. I had a responsibility to them. No matter how miserable I was, I pledged to keep myself alive for the rest of their lives. Then, I decided, I would permit myself to die. And even that idea was daunting. I was no longer competent enough to know how to kill myself. Something would go terribly wrong. I would nearly die but not quite. I would lose the use of my legs or some such thing. It did not even occur to me that it was the same fear I had about helping my father die.

My own death was beyond me. In the absence of antidepressants and psychiatrists, I drank. Every day. Around half a bottle of wine, sometimes more. They say that alcohol causes depression, but they ought not generalize. It may not have been the wisest coping mechanism, but alcohol made life tolerable.

～

In the months after my accident, I heard nothing at all from my mother. What did she think had happened to me? Did she care? I could not believe she'd abandoned me. And then, after a while, I could. I had disconnected my phone, but she knew where I lived, and her apartment was only a fifteen-minute drive away.

My relationship with my mother had always been brittle.

When I was twelve, I showed her a short story I had written. I did quite well at English in school and loved to write. She was an English teacher, and I trusted her opinion. She handed my story back to me and said, "Well, I don't think you're going to make much of a writer."

I was fourteen when my mother admitted she had never wanted a daughter. She had just attended a parent-teacher night at my high school, where most of the teachers had described me as "naughty" or "disruptive."

"All I wanted was two boys," she said, when she finally calmed down.

"Why?" I asked.

"Boys are easier and I like them more."

"Well, I'm sorry I'm not a boy," I said.

"I lost a baby," she said. "I never told you that before."

"Where?" I had visions of her leaving it somewhere and forgetting about it.

"Before you were born. I'm certain it was a boy. We were going to call him Matthew."

I looked at her but didn't speak.

"But you made your father happy! He wanted a girl."

That same year, a couple of months later, my mother told me she thought it would be best if I never had children of my own. "I just don't think you'd make much of a mother," she said, exhaling slowly.

At the time, I said nothing. But I filed those remarks away in a drawer of my brain marked "Things I Learned from My Mother." The accident seemed to leave that part intact.

I grew to suspect that my mother wanted to be the only female in my father's life. Perhaps she considered me competition. I wondered whether she had overheard him, weeks before he died, telling me that I had always been the most precious thing in his life, that he loved no one more than me. It was a time when my mother liked to listen in on our conversations. A time when she worried I might help my father die.

I certainly wasn't blameless in our relationship dynamic. From the time I was thirteen, I realized I had a unique ability to needle my mother. Sometimes all it took to get her to snap was a look from me. I had a combustible power over my mother, and I used it whenever I wanted a reaction.

Once, Edward punched me in the face. It was after we had been together a couple of years and a male colleague had turned up at our place drunk, shouting into the intercom that he was in love with me. Edward assumed I had led him on. His fist smashed my face, and I fell onto the corner of our glass coffee table. I ended up with a black eye and a bruised chest. The next time Edward saw my mother, he apologized to her and told her he had no idea what had come over him.

"Don't worry, Edward," she said. "I've been wanting to do that for years."

My mother's hostility frightened me. Weeks before my father died, I held his hand and sobbed.

"What will happen to me?" I asked him.

"Don't worry, Pod, you'll be fine. You're the strongest one in this family. Easily! And Mum will take care of you. Of course she will."

"But she is only ever nice to me when you're around!"

"I know," he said. "I do. I know exactly what she's like. But this will be different."

My mother never came to visit after my accident. I continued to stare into the pockmark on the wall, reliving my father's last months, tears racing down my cheeks. I had lost my mind. There was nothing left but the halfway state between sleep and waking. George and Bess huddled alongside me until my crying finally stopped.

3

BUILDING A NEW BRAIN (PART ONE)

One morning I entered my study. It was likely about two months after my accident, but I cannot be sure. Like many head-injured people, my serial memory is terrible, and I struggle with timings and chronology. I had decided to finish my PhD. I refused to believe I was incapable of doing so. A voice inside my head had spoken: *I can't continue to live like this. I can't waste my life. I must do whatever it takes to get my old life back.*

My study had been sealed up since my accident, and the carpet reeked. The room had served as George's toilet when I spent too long at the office—his way of letting me know about work-life balance. I yanked open the window to air the room.

Towers of photocopied books and articles smothered my desk. Glancing at the books, I didn't recognize any of them. How did they get here? Were they library books? Was I amassing a giant fine for not returning them? I removed books from the pile, studied their spines, and was relieved to discover they weren't library books. They belonged to me. I picked one from the top of the pile and held it in both hands. It didn't look even vaguely familiar. On the spine of the book was the word "Japan." My PhD topic focused on Singapore, Thailand, and the Philippines. What was a book about Japan doing there?

In the middle of my desk, surrounded by papers and notebooks and pencils and highlighter pens, sat my computer and keyboard. I stared at the computer, trying to remember how to turn it on. I ran my fingers around it, exploring the contours of the monitor before realizing the hard drive was housed in another large box at my feet. The on switch was down there. I knelt down, switched on my hard drive, and waited for my computer to boot up. Sweeping the books and papers to one side, I opened a file named *PhD v1*. Bess burrowed into the space beneath the desk and settled at my feet. George curled up on the landing, aloof. My study was his toilet, not his bedroom.

Inside the file there was a folder titled *Methodology*, which seemed like a good place to start, although I had no idea what the word meant. Was it the opening chapter? I wasn't sure. I had no recollection of writing it. Forcing myself to concentrate produced a sensation inside my skull like someone using an angle grinder on the back of my head.

I opened the document and studied the words. *What was a "hypothesis"?* I wondered. I turned to the *Oxford English Dictionary* my father gave me for my thirteenth birthday. He had also given me the two-volume *Shorter Oxford English Dictionary* for my birthday the year before he died, but the print was tiny and there were way too many words for me to be able to find anything. After a struggle, I found the *H*'s but couldn't find "hypothesis." Goose bumps spread down both my arms. I had written something that didn't make sense. *What was I thinking? What did it mean? Did I write this?*

I closed the document and burst into tears. Things were worse than I thought. Much worse. I tried to calm myself and opened another file titled *Introduction*. My eyes drifted along each line of text, hopping from word to word, but my brain registered nothing. My thesis was concerned with "The Influence of Culture Upon Administrative Practice in Singapore, Thailand, and the Philippines." I remembered the three countries but had forgotten the rest of the title until I saw the words written in black marker across the top of a manila folder.

I cradled my head in my hands and strained to remember any details about the time I'd spent in Southeast Asia three and a half years earlier. I pinched the skin on my leg, hard, thinking that what I needed was to wake up, to concentrate. I slapped my leg. No matter what I did I couldn't seem to turn on my brain. Its power had been drained. I gripped my desk with my fingers and forced myself to concentrate. A memory of getting food poisoning from a raw piece of chicken in the Philippines came to me. And I knew I'd befriended a Sri Lankan engineering student whose grandmother kept an elephant. I recalled writing a letter to my father each week, telling him what I had been doing, describing everything that I thought might interest him. He had still seemed healthy then, oblivious to the tumor taking root inside him.

My body trembled. The prognosis had been right. I could see my future, spread out in front of me like a frayed, dusty carpet. I would fester at home on the sofa until the dogs grew old and died. Then a friend, who happened to be a vet, would euthanize me. I would lie down on a Formica table in her surgery, and she would stroke my cheek, say goodbye, and this hell would be over. I comforted myself with my plan. It would take around a decade to execute, but it was a plan all the same. I turned off my computer and retreated to the sofa and the sanctuary of my pockmark.

On his deathbed, after I had broken down and told him I would not survive without him, my father squeezed my hand and said, "You're clever, Pod. No one can ever take that away from you. You will be fine, whatever happens." But something had happened, something my father could never have foreseen, and I was no longer fine. I turned this thought over and over in my head like a hard clump of soil.

The next day, fueled by thoughts of my father, I resolved to try again. Confined to his sickbed, he had made a valiant attempt to finish the book he was writing. Some years earlier on a visit to the British Museum, he had discovered the handwritten journals of Robert Brown, the young botanist who had been part of the voyage on the first circumnavigation of Australia. HMS *Investigator* set sail in 1801, and Robert Brown's brief over the journey was to collect scientific specimens, including plants, insects, birds, and rocks. My father had decided to annotate Brown's diaries, adding notes and interpretations, breathing new life into material that might otherwise have been lost. He had spent two years on the book before he became ill. In the end it was a useful distraction, something to keep him from thinking about dying.

I brought a laptop home from work and tried propping him up with pillows from the bedrooms and the sitting room. No matter how many pillows we used, how many positions we tried, he could never get comfortable enough to use the keyboard. It was easier for him to work with a pad and pencil. Pain hijacked his every movement. Bone cancer, the doctor warned us but not him, is one of the most painful ways to die. He eventually left his notepad on his bedside table, knowing he would never be able to finish.[6]

I thought of my father as I stood outside the study. He would expect me to sit down at my desk and work for as long as it took to resume a normal life. That's what he would do if he were in my position. I summoned all my strength and reentered my study.

The room was tidy and smelled as fresh as it ever would. I had a vague recollection of cleaning the room and airing it the day before. I took an article from the top of the pile of photocopies, placed it in front of me, and attempted to read: "The Dynamic Interplay between Employees' Feedback-Seeking Strategies and Supervisors' Delivery of Performance Feedback." *Was that even English? What on earth did it mean?* I refused to believe that title made sense to a person with a healthy brain, let alone someone like me. I spent a good twenty minutes trying to unscramble the meaning of the title before burying the article at the bottom of the pile and choosing another. The next one was "Intraorganizational Structural Variation: Application of the

Bureaucratic Model." I shuddered. *Who wrote this crap?* Worse, who read it? People like the person I used to be? That was a scary thought. *Who was I?*

I searched the pile for another. And another. Finally, I found one with a title I could understand: "The Filipino Family." It took me an hour to grasp the first sentence.

I devoted the entire day to interpreting a single paragraph. I read it, and I read it again, again, and again. Then I read it aloud. Again and again and again. Bess wagged her tail, and I felt it thump against my foot. She thought I was talking to her. I had not talked to anyone other than George and Bess for a very long time, and my voice sounded strange. It echoed inside my skull and made my head ache. From time to time as I read, I uttered words that did not appear on the printed page. Rogue words that came out of nowhere and made no sense.

Eventually, I seemed to grasp the meaning of the first eight lines. Like most introductory paragraphs in journal articles, all it stated was the purpose of the research and its scope. It would be a good day, a wonderful day, if I managed to read the first photocopied page of that article. Before the accident I read a book a day, two on a good day. Now I would settle for a page. I concentrated so hard my hands began to shake. Bess licked my toes as a gesture of encouragement. It was too hard. I threw the article on the floor, buried my head in my hands, and sobbed, again.

In my study the next day, my brain felt like it had been scooped out with an ice-cream spoon and replaced with porridge. Nothing worked, and my vocabulary had been scrubbed clean. Each sentence contained words I didn't recognize, words I couldn't understand. English was like a foreign language. I kept the dictionary close by, but looking up a word took an eternity, and even then there was no guarantee I would find it. I saw it on the page of the article, but I couldn't find it inside the dictionary. On occasions, I couldn't even find the right letter in the dictionary to correspond with the first letter of the word I didn't understand. Tiny particles of sweat formed along my hairline. I flicked through the dictionary, and the sweat began to trickle down the sides of my face. Thinking provoked pain. I slammed the dictionary shut and attempted to calm myself by stroking the top of Bess's head.

Rebuilding my vocabulary turned out to be harder than I'd hoped it would be. I decided I would attempt to work five hours each day, seven days a week, for as long as was necessary. It wasn't as if I had anything better to do. I recorded the meaning of every word I didn't recognize in an empty notebook. It didn't take long before I ran out of pages. At the end of each day I studied those words and attempted to remember their meanings. By the next morning, I would, without fail, recognize the words but not remember what they meant. The cells in two parts of my brain had died, and the pathways connecting the neurons had become obsolete. It would take a considerable amount of time and effort before new pathways began to form.

MRI technology has shown that the brains of head-injured people work significantly harder than those of non-head-injured folk to solve even the most basic problems, or to retrieve memories. My brain felt like an old, rickety bicycle I was trying to ride up a steep hill. Every yard or two, I was forced to stop, catch my breath, and gather my strength so I could creep forward another yard.

After a couple of months, I decided to attempt to make notes about each article on a writing pad. I had forgotten how to type, and writing anything on the computer took forever—studying the keyboard in search of the correct keys. But I could still write by hand. That much I hadn't forgotten, although I had a tendency to write sentences that included words I didn't plan on, words that belonged in different sentences than the ones I was writing, or words that belonged in sentences on completely different topics.

I hoped to find and record the salient points of a journal article. But as I read I was unable to siphon off the key points from the padding. Everything seemed vital. I could barely read, much less skim, and

I was distracted by everything. I copied the words verbatim from the page to my notebook. At first, I noticed mistakes. I stared intently at each word I had written. It took all my effort to subdue the thrashing sensation inside my head. I sobbed and tried again. I wrote the first sentence a second time and compared my writing with the author's words. There *appeared* to be no mistakes, and they seemed to match. My head throbbed. Yet it was the first time that I had been able to concentrate since my accident some four months earlier. It was a tiny step, but it felt like progress.

I didn't know this at the time, but the part of my brain that took the brunt of the impact during my accident was my left parietal lobe, in the area of the junction with the temporal lobe, which is known as the "language zone." Damage to that region can cause a range of different problems related to language, to expressing oneself through words and word finding. It may also disrupt the ability to understand spoken and written language. I experienced challenges comprehending written English for a couple of years after my accident, and to this day I struggle to understand spoken English in university lectures or when talking to an expert about something with which I'm unfamiliar. My best chance of absorbing new information is through reading. Sometimes that works, sometimes it doesn't, and I will read and reread whatever it is until the penny finally drops. Word finding, spelling, syntax, grammar, and vocabulary confound me. The condition is known as "dysphasia." The sheer force of impact of my head on that rock had produced a reverberation known as a "contrecoup," which had damaged my right parietal lobe. Networks within the right parietal lobe determine the ability to draw, to create things, and our visuospatial orientation.

After taking the dogs out for an unscheduled park break, I returned to my desk that afternoon. My task was to copy the whole page of an article into my notebook. I had started work on a piece about Singaporean society. I promised myself I would not leave my study until I had completed it and checked it for errors. It took me a week to transcribe that brief journal article; I got through a page per day. Without these self-imposed tasks, I would probably have festered at home on my sofa, spending most of my disability pension on dog food.

Each day I copied excerpts of books and articles into a notepad. In my mind, I was conducting important research, wading through a sea of papers that needed to be waded through. Why, I wasn't quite sure. I absorbed almost nothing of what I wrote, but that didn't matter. Each day transcribing became easier, and I accomplished it more accurately and more quickly. I continued reading everything aloud, to improve my speech, to check what I had written, and to limit the jumble of words that came out each time I opened my mouth. If someone were to stop me in the street and ask me how I was spending my days, I had an answer: "I am conducting research for my PhD!" I would need to make sure I closed my mouth when I finished saying it, but I believed I could make it sound convincing—as long as there were no follow-up questions.

As a demonstration of his support for my hard work, George took up residency inside my study. He found an unspoiled patch of carpet underneath the window that caught the afternoon sun and curled himself up like a pretzel.

~

One day I decided that I needed a particular book and that the only way of finding that book was by visiting the library at the University of Sydney. I told the dogs that I needed to leave them briefly to undertake an important mission. Even when I had a normal, healthy brain, I struggled to find anything in the labyrinth of Fisher Library, so I prepared myself for the worst. Research in the years before the internet involved searching through wooden catalog drawers for a card with the author's name, book title, and its location within the library. I hunted through the drawer for authors whose names began with *RA* and found nothing by the author whose book I needed. I looked again. And again. A line of students snaked behind me, clicking tongues, shuffling feet. The familiar beads of sweat congregated along my hairline, and my hands started to tremble. I gave up and headed upstairs to the fifth floor, where I had spent much of my time as an undergraduate. I walked through the shelves to the three hundreds as if on autopilot. Surely if I looked long enough I would find the book. I spent an hour looking. Exhausted, I left the library, angry with myself for giving up. I should have asked someone for help, but I was terrified they would think I was stupid.

Shame stuck to my sides, wherever I went, whatever I did. Shame was the reason I had locked myself away from the world and had severed contact with the people who had once been my friends. I couldn't bear the thought of anyone I knew seeing the person I had become. A person who was angry, depressed, stupid, and lost.

I was raised in a family of clever people, brought up by a mother who respected people, judged them, and made her own assessments of them based on their intelligence. Not their kindness, their compassion, their generosity, their humor, or their courage. I had done this too. Locked away from the world, I feared being judged by the same standards I had imposed on others. It took brain damage to make me realize how arrogant I'd been.

Years later I asked my mother what my IQ had been at age eleven, when Australian children were required to sit for a standardized IQ test. She seemed to remember it without any trouble.

"It was 127," she said, removing her eyeglasses and cleaning them with her shirt. "Lower than your brother's," she added.

Frankly, I was surprised my IQ was as high as it was, given my tendency to baulk at anything that required even a speck of mathematical reasoning. I'd thought of part of my brain as dead long before my accident. I was terrible with deciphering patterns. Before I started high school, I would stare at a row of numbers in those *What comes next?* questions and feel completely and utterly bamboozled. Not once in my life had I passed any kind of math test. And not only had I never managed to pass such a test, I had never managed to score more than 25 percent, and if I'm not mistaken, that was when I was eleven and tried to copy the answers of the girl sitting next to me.

My trip to the library was my first visit to the University of Sydney since my father had died. I had parked outside the geology department where he once worked, and as I walked back to my car, I looked up at the office on the fourth floor that used to be his and started to cry. I remembered lunchtimes as an undergraduate when I would pop in and find him sitting behind his desk in a room that stank of sulfur, poring through papers held in place by various bits of rock he had accumulated over the years. As a child when we visited the university on weekends, he would give me sticks of chalk from one of the lecture theaters, and I would use them when we got home to draw hopscotch or handball courts on our driveway. From time to time he'd let me draw on the blackboard inside a lecture theater while he rummaged through the papers in his office in search of something he needed. On the way out, after he had wiped the board clean, we would stop beside the large glass cabinet in the foyer of the geology department that housed hundreds of different rocks, and he would explain the difference between igneous and aqueous rocks, or some other such thing that left me cold.

"I really don't understand how you cannot be fascinated by rocks, Pod," he said, with eyebrows raised, as we made our way to the car.

"I'm sorry," I said, and we left it at that.

A year before he died, my father finished building a library next to our family home. It was a giant stand-alone structure built to house his collection of rare books. It loomed over the front steps of the house, next to an oak tree I had planted with an acorn when I was three. It was an addition that would make the house nearly impossible to sell after his death.

"No one wants a library," the first agent told my mother. "People around here want swimming pools and tennis courts."

Instead we had an enormous building gobbling up a tiny patch of land, with floor-to-ceiling bookshelves covering all four walls.

"Knock one hundred thousand dollars off the asking price or knock down the library," another agent said.

My father's dream became a bargaining tool for prospective buyers. He had built the library thinking he would use it for the rest of his life. Twenty, maybe thirty years.

My father loved books. Most of his books were shipped to him from booksellers in London and Dublin. Each book cost anywhere between fifty and one hundred pounds. He had bought rare books all his life. The result was a huge collection that took up all the wall space in my parents' sitting room, dining room, their bedroom, his study, and the library. Most of his books were about natural history, but his tastes were eclectic and he had a handful of novels, first editions of *The Life and Opinions of Tristram Shandy, Gentleman*, and *Sea and Sardinia*, and books about churches and architecture. His favorite was the first edition of Cook's voyages to Australia, which he had given to my mother in place of an engagement ring. His oldest book was an early edition of Boccaccio's *Decameron*, published in 1527.

With each new book, my father typed its title, the author's name, and the year and place of publication on a three-by-four-inch index card. In pencil on the back of each card he wrote the name of the bookseller and the price he had paid. As the faculty libraries at the University of Sydney updated their filing systems and got rid of their old wooden catalog boxes, my father bought them and began to create his own. He told my brother and me that he planned to divide the collection between us when he died. My mother made the decision to give the collection to the University of Melbourne library, where it sat in boxes for years, waiting to be unpacked. Having the books in the house was a constant reminder of her dead husband, she said.

∼

When I returned home from my visit to the university, the dogs treated me as though I had been gone for months. I told them I had not managed to find the book I wanted, and they appeared less concerned about that than I was. They seemed to think it was enough that I had made it home safely. It was the first time I had left the house to do anything other than shop, get more painkillers from the hospital, or collect my disability check. *She is slowly getting better,* George seemed to say to Bess when he thought I wasn't looking. We cuddled on the sofa until he reminded me it was time for a walk.

I read more quickly and was able to interpret the content of much that I read when I harnessed all my powers of concentration. I labored over every word and read each sentence again and again, in order to make sure nothing slipped through the holes in my left parietal lobe. Slowly, painfully, through a ponderous process of repetition, I was starting to improve. The feeling was at once horrifying and gratifying. I was reminded of everything I had lost, but I had flashes of optimism. The more I focused, the more progress I made.

My memory of life before the accident remained poor, but slowly my cognitive functioning showed glimmers of improvement. Of course, I was the only judge of this, and there were high chances I was wrong. But I had copied and summarized a great many articles and had started to create sentences of my own. Soon, I hoped, I would be able to begin writing. I had worked consistently most days for what I believe was around four months. I wondered if the results would have been the same if I were cutting up scraps of material for stuffed animals. The PhD, the albatross, the noose around my neck, my own Sistine Chapel, was saving my brain.

~

One day, around six months after my accident, George raced up to an attractive woman walking a dog in the park. She was blonde, under thirty, with a symmetrical face, which satisfied his criteria for beauty. I waited a moment before glancing around. She sat on the grass, and George rolled on his back beside her, his head reclined in her lap. He gazed up at her lovingly, and I walked toward them. The woman smiled at me, and George shot me a look that said, *This woman can't keep her hands off me and it would be very rude to leave.*

"Such a handsome dog!" she said, and I agreed.

George showed no sign of wanting to get up, so I sat down on the grass beside him. It was the first time I had talked to anyone for as long as I could remember.

"It's a lovely day, isn't it?"

"Very nice," I said, trying to remember how to make small talk.

"That's my boyfriend's dog," she said, pointing to a golden Labrador sniffing around after Bess. "I'm dog minding while he's down in Melbourne on business."

George nudged the woman with his snout, to remind her to keep petting him.

"He likes you," I said.

"I like him!" she said, bending her head down toward his and stroking the bridge of his nose.

"What do you do?" she asked.

"I'm working on my PhD."

She didn't look at me as though I was an imposter or, worse, a moron.

"What's it about? In thirteen words or less," she laughed.

I heard my voice tremble as I spoke and wondered if she noticed.

"That's great!" she said. "I just finished my master's degree in psychology. My thesis was on head injuries." I looked at her closely, thinking that perhaps I had imagined her.

"Head injuries?"

"Yes," she said, "and how the brain repairs itself after trauma."

I waited for a moment as her words sank in. "*Can* the brain repair itself after trauma?" I asked.

"It can," she said, "and often does. You'd be surprised."

"Wow," I said, and she nodded.

I did not tell her about my own injury. I walked away and never saw her again, but it didn't matter. Without knowing it, she had changed my life.

I was a person whose brain would repair itself, a person whose brain had already started to repair itself.

"How did you know?" I asked George as we started our walk home. I felt myself smile. I used muscles in my face that hadn't moved of their own accord for months. George looked at me, wagged his tail twice, and nudged the side of my leg with his head.

4

METAMORPHOSIS

If the brain *was* able to repair itself after trauma, why hadn't anyone told me? That thought jostled around inside my head after I embraced the prospect of getting some semblance of my old life back. The notion that the brain is "plastic" and able to change had been around for more than one hundred years, and the term "neuroplasticity"—the brain's ability to build new neural connections in response to internal and external stimuli—had been used since 1948. It was a complicated concept, and poorly understood, but it wasn't new. So why was I only hearing about it during a serendipitous meeting with a stranger in a park? Why had the neurologist been so adamant that my so-called "mild traumatic brain injury" meant I would never work again, never finish my PhD?

More than twenty years after my injury, how the brain repairs itself after trauma remains a mystery. We know that the extent to which the brain can heal depends upon a set of factors that include the patient's age and gender; the injury's severity, type, and force; the region of damage; and the patient's preinjury cognitive reserves and preexisting medical conditions.[7] But the research on neuroplasticity after traumatic brain injury is in its early stages and has been largely confined to lab rats. At the time of writing, little research into neuroplasticity after traumatic brain injury has been done on humans.

We know that in the days immediately following an injury, the cells in the region of the brain that were damaged die, reducing the pathways that transmit messages within the brain. Over time, healthy cells are "unmasked." Secondary pathways are recruited in place of the pathways that have died, allowing functions that were once performed by the damaged part of the brain to be performed by another healthy part of the brain. This adjustment process—the one I've provided a crude simplification of—is known as "compensation."[8]

I planted a lawn last year. I went to a garden shop and bought long rolls of grass that I laid out like a carpet over a bare patch of ground. Six months later, around two-thirds of my newly planted lawn had started to grow, but the remainder was parched and brown despite regular watering, fertilizer, and lawn pellets. Nearly twelve months later, the healthy parts of the lawn were thriving and slowly creeping across the areas where the new grass had previously refused to grow. I will never lay another lawn: gardening, it turns out, is not one of my talents. But the lawn is a good metaphor for the way in which the brain compensates for damaged cells. Eventually (perhaps in years to come), the healthy parts of the lawn will be so hardy that no one will notice the bald patches of dead grass. After my chance meeting in the park, that was my new hope for my brain.

As to why no one had told me that the brain can repair itself, the answer may lie in the attitude of health-care professionals toward victims of TBI. Researchers have found that qualified doctors in particular are known to blame TBI victims for their injuries. One study found that "among qualified health-care professionals . . . negative attitudes exist towards survivors of brain injury which can lead to adverse behaviors towards the individual."[9] It's a scary thought: you turn up in the emergency room after a bad knock to the head, and your treatment is compromised because the doctor who sees you assumes you were foolhardy and responsible for any injury you have sustained. I can't speak for everyone, but I am fairly certain no sensible person wants a traumatic brain injury, so any suggestion of blame seems misplaced.

According to the Center for Disease Control and Prevention, in 2013 around 2.8 million people in the United States suffered a traumatic brain injury that led to a hospital visit. Of that number, 50,000 died and 230,000 were hospitalized and survived. Those figures do not take into account the many individuals with undiagnosed TBIs who do not seek treatment for their head injuries. The estimated cost of traumatic brain injury in America during 2010, taking into account both direct (medical) and indirect costs (lost productivity), was thought to be around $76.5 billion.[10]

Despite the huge numbers of people suffering head injuries every year and the staggering costs associated, research into traumatic brain injury has been chronically underfunded. Alzheimer's, stroke, cancer, and Parkinson's disease are the sexy areas of brain research and, not coincidentally, the areas from which pharmaceutical firms are most likely to profit.

~

From the woman in the park, I had learned that my brain might be able to repair itself, and I intended to do everything within my powers to make sure that happened. My life had been suspended like the empty sleeve of a piñata dangling from a tree.

Emboldened by our meeting, I made the curious decision to return to Singapore, Thailand, and the Philippines to conclude my research. It was the first step I made to leave my cocoon with George and Bess and reenter the real world. Oddly, I have no recollection whatsoever about my decision to travel or of the trip itself. I would not have even known it happened had I not discovered my old passport with stamps showing I left Australia for the Philippines in the last week of July 1995, six and a half months after my accident, and returned home from Singapore a month later. I am told a friend moved in to my home and looked after George and Bess while I was gone, although I cannot recall this either. I have no idea where I stayed, what I did, or how I negotiated my way around Bangkok and Manila without getting myself killed. Singapore was clean and safe and easy to navigate, but given my brain injury, I was in no state to be wandering around Southeast Asia on my own. I very much doubt I was capable of conducting meaningful interviews. The lack of evidence of that trip makes me feel like I was trying to impersonate someone doing their PhD without actually doing anything. Whatever I did while overseas, it was not particularly productive. In the years that followed I remember writing numerous letters to the people I had met during my first trip into the field, before my father died, and asking them for help with questions I had been unable to answer.

Two types of amnesia affect people with traumatic brain injuries. Retrograde amnesia affects memories of events that occurred before the accident, while anterograde amnesia affects memories of events that happened after the injury. My head injury left me with difficulties remembering things that happened before and after the accident. But my greatest problem with memory has been locating an event at a particular point in time.

It isn't uncommon for people who have suffered traumatic brain injuries to experience clouded autobiographical memory, in which certain events can be recalled quite clearly while others are seemingly lost forever. The more poetic term "islands of memory"[11] has been used to describe detailed memories that can be located in time and space (when and where). These are memories that appear "in an ocean of forgetting." Autobiographical memory combines recollections of events, episodes, objects, and people at a particular time and place, along with a general knowledge of the world and its events. For much of the two years between my father's death and my accident, and for the year or so that followed, it seemed to me that random events had been documented on small strips of paper and thrown inside a hat for a lucky draw.

Emotion is one of the most important factors that allows autobiographical memories to be encoded and retrieved. Events that are emotionally charged, like getting married or losing a parent, are much easier to remember than the mundane comings and goings of daily life. That explains why my memory of the months leading up to and including my father's death is so clear to me, and also why I can remember my accident, my visit to the hospital the day after my accident, my session with the psychologist at the Brain Injury Unit, and the conversation with the neurologist when he told me I would not be returning to work. Those were the most powerful events I had ever experienced, and they changed my life irrevocably. My memory of the time I spent teaching myself to write and read and interpret information is also quite clear, perhaps because it caused me such distress.

While writing this book, I spent months with pen and paper trying to piece together events in the order in which they occurred, but it has been like trying to create a wall-sized fresco with a single box of tiles. Placing that trip to Southeast Asia within the broader story of my life became impossible, until I found the passport.

I do remember a birthday card my mother had sent me in the mail, which I must have received when I returned from that trip. "Happy birthday, Sarah, from Hilary," the card read. Enclosed was a check for $200. I went straight to the bank and cashed the check. The best wine shop in Sydney was only a few doors away from my house, and I planned to spoil myself. When I started my doctorate, I had received a generous scholarship for my research, which covered the costs of my travel, but my disability pension was swallowed up each month by groceries, bills, and the fresh mince George liked to eat.

I returned home with the wine, and called my mother to thank her for the money.

"How are you?" she asked.

"I'm fine," I said. "How are you?"

"Fine. Good, well bye," she said, and the line went dead.

I do not remember how much time passed after I returned home from that trip, before I decided to find a job. I needed to resume some approximation of a normal life, and I was running out of money. I do remember my job-hunting experience, even though I cannot place it in time.

One Saturday morning, I walked across the road from my house to the newsstand and bought the *Sydney Morning Herald*. I flicked past the news section and found my way to the jobs section. The first posting that looked even remotely suitable was for a policy director with a nonprofit organization in aged care. I tore out the ad and studied it closely. It seemed like a job I could handle, but I hadn't gone through an application process in years. I needed a CV and a cover letter, and it took me most of the day to prepare them. I found an unused envelope, wrote the address on it, and checked my application three times. The brain-damaged me spent a lot of time checking and rechecking things. A good thing too, as I often found I had forgotten something or made an error that had eluded detection not once but seven or eight times. Once I was satisfied, I walked to the post office and mailed my application.

~

On Tuesday morning I received a phone call inviting me to interview for the position that Thursday. The efficiency of the nonprofit sector surprised me. In government, seasons would pass before anyone got called for an interview. The quick response sent me into a panic. I studied the ad again, phrase by phrase, and started making notes. I imagined questions I might be asked based on each sentence in the job ad and scribbled them down inside a notebook. I wracked my brain for short, sharp answers to each of the questions. Hours after I had written down as much as I could, I went into the bathroom, taking the chair from my study, and sat down opposite the mirror. I practiced my answer to each question, looking intently at my reflection for any possible signs of brain damage. My habit of dribbling had stopped, and as long as I remembered to keep my mouth shut, I hoped I could pass as normal. I spent the evening in front of my bathroom mirror practicing, and eventually I seemed able to create a reasonable likeness of a person with a healthy brain. I tried to affect two expressions that might fool someone into thinking I was intelligent: The first involved a long (but not too long) serious look, a look of focus and concentration. The second was a look of mild curiosity, a look of interest but not eagerness.

~

The next day I sat on the sofa and pretended George and Bess were my interviewers. I spent the day going over every question and every answer. It had been so long since I had talked to anyone that I had lost the art of conversation. Now I needed to get it back. Fast. I repeated the answers again and again until the words came out in the right order. My plan was to go into the interview with my notes scribbled inside my diary in case I got stuck. I smiled at my dogs in turn and took my time to answer.

I decided the best approach was for me to say as little as possible. To think about my response and answer each question succinctly. A long, rambling response would almost certainly give things away. *Offer the least amount of words you can, without being too miserly,* a voice inside my head told me. No one is ever thought to be a fool by keeping quiet. *What am I doing?* I wondered. *Am I ready for this?*

Absolutely not.

Four people sat around a large conference table. The convener was an attractive woman who looked to be only a couple of years older than me; she wore frameless glasses and her hair in a bob. Her name was Rita, and she was the boss. An older man began asking questions, quizzing me about my career, my approach to developing policy, and the concepts behind aged care. I knew very little of aged care, I confessed, but it was an area I considered critically important. They seemed to swallow it. I went one step further—too far, perhaps—and told them that nursing homes have a lot in common with prisons.

Four confused faces peered back at me. I had blown it. I had likened old people to criminals.

"Not in terms of their patrons, of course, but in terms of their management," I added, after an awkward silence.

"Ah, yes, I suppose so," a man who represented the Alzheimer's Association said, and the others nodded along. "I'd never thought about it like that," he added.

So, I had almost blown it but not quite. I had managed to think on my feet. That in itself was an astonishing achievement.

The interview lasted a very long time. I remembered to clamp my mouth shut when I wasn't talking and to offer a half smile, to remind my interviewers I was human. I did my best to look intelligent, alert—but not too alert, for fear of looking crazed—and to ponder each question before I responded. It was a lot to remember, and I feared I might not be able to avoid looking like a moron. This was a serious job, and realistically I didn't stand a chance—my only offer of work since the accident had involved cutting up fabric for stuffed toys. Yet there I was being interviewed for a job in an office. I tried to banish that thought from my mind and focus on Rita, who was telling me about her goals for the year ahead.

The interview finally drew to a close, and Rita asked me about my salary expectations. I was dumbfounded. I had no expectations of anything much, including salary. I did not tell those kind, good-natured people that I was the recipient of a disability pension from the

Australian government thanks to my badly damaged brain, and that anything they offered was likely to be a significant improvement.

Instead, I told them what I'd earned in my last job, an amount that struck me as stratospheric. Rita looked at me apologetically and said that they could only go to $80,000. That was their limit. That was fine, I answered. I wasn't motivated by money. I was motivated by an intrinsic desire to improve the lives of the elderly.

I was also motivated by a mission to repair my brain and get my old life back, although I left that last part out.

Surprisingly, no one asked for references. That was a relief. After Rosie the social worker told my last boss I was brain damaged, I never heard from him again.

~

The following afternoon I received a phone call from Rita.

"Hi, Sarah, I wanted to tell you how impressed we all were by you yesterday, and to offer you the role." I covered the mouthpiece to hide my squeal.

"Oh, that's wonderful news. Thank you!" I said, trying to compose myself.

"Can you start work next week? We have so much work to do."

"Next week is fine!"

"I've got your address. Do you mind if I drop off your contract and some materials for you to read? I live nearby."

"Of course! Thank you."

I hung up the phone in shock. I had found a job. The only job I had applied for. It was unthinkable. I had survived a one-hour interview and no one had noticed my damaged brain. I was ecstatic. I was also terrified. The woman in the park had been right.

~

Before my accident my career had thrived. At university I had won prizes, and I had held a series of senior jobs; I looked good on paper.

By the time I was thirty, I was earning nearly the same money my father had earned when he retired from the University of Sydney. My father had argued vigorously against my decision to study government at university. He told me once, when I was a teenager, that he hoped I would become a scientist. He was passionate about science and nature. He was also slightly delusional. The fact that I played the violin and went to the Conservatorium High School—which didn't even teach science—and that I struggled with basic math meant science was not a viable option. When I pointed that out to him, he sighed, "You might be right." It saddened him to think that I was missing out on something extraordinary, something that had given his life meaning and a sense of purpose.

I had already learned the hard way that letting my parents make decisions about my future was a mistake. My mother, for some inexplicable reason, wanted me to be a violinist. Although I loved listening to the violin, I hated playing it, and, it turned out, the violin did not like me much either. That wasn't enough to deter me from applying for a place in the Conservatorium High School. Terror—coupled with my mother's prodding—had been my primary motivations for applying. There was a bully at my primary school who had threatened to kill me if we ended up at the same high school. We lived in the same catchment area, so there was no way to attend public school and avoid her. I had never even spoken to the girl when she chased me home for the first time. One day she waited for me outside the school gates wielding a bicycle chain. I lived in constant fear, and when my violin teacher told my mother that the Conservatorium was holding auditions, we all agreed I should apply.

The Conservatorium offered a limited academic curriculum, and for the last two years of high school we had to choose between studying French, German, and art. I had topped my class in art the year before and, after English, it was my favorite subject. My father thought art was a waste of time. He wanted me to study French. I was terrible at French, but my father was insistent. In the final exams I managed somehow to scrape through with a passing grade. If I had kept studying art, my results would have been much better. Not to mention I would have spent two years studying something that interested me. By the time I was seventeen, I decided that I would make all future decisions about my life. It turned out that I sought my father's advice on almost every one of those decisions. Occasionally, I chose to ignore it.

And while I felt confident eschewing his chosen path of natural sciences, he wasn't alone in thinking the study of government would guarantee any graduate's unemployment for many years to come. For a while I worried he might have been right. But I was lucky, and a good job came along before I had even graduated.

"You have made some truly baffling decisions," he said to me once, with both eyebrows raised, "but you have managed to land on your feet. You have forged your own way and done everything on your own terms. Few people can boast that. I am very proud of you, Pod."

My father grew up in a prefab house in a working-class suburb in the south of Sydney. His father was a milliner, a worker in someone else's hat shop. When my grandmother died at twenty-six, my grandfather was left alone to raise two young boys.

Every Saturday when I was a child, my father used to drive me across town to visit my grandfather. The house had not been refurbished in the sixty years since it was built. The floors were covered with the original brown linoleum that curled up at the walls in protest or rose to a peak, tsunami-like, in the middle of the floor. My grandfather seemed to know every crack and peak in his floor, and I never once saw him trip. He kept the house dark to save electricity. I remember when sewage pipes were finally laid in the street and a toilet replaced the large steel tin in the outhouse, which was emptied every morning by someone known as the nightsoilman.

My father had survived a nasty bout of polio and a year in leg irons when he was six. He did well at school and was the first member of the family to go to university. He won the university medal and then a Fulbright. After a year at Berkeley, he returned to a teaching job on the faculty at the University of Sydney and finished his PhD.

There was never any question in my mind that I would do a doctorate. My father had one, my brother had one, and not to be left out, I would get one too. Not doing a PhD would only confirm my mother's vocal doubts about my intelligence, or so I felt. My father and brother had enjoyed the luxury of full-time study when they did their doctorates, but I worried that a full-time PhD would stall my career. I also had a mortgage to pay down. Part-time study seemed the only practical option.

My thesis topic was "The Influence of Culture Upon Administrative Practice in Singapore, Thailand, and the Philippines." It was an odd choice given that Bangkok was the only city in Asia I had ever visited, and I had stayed there less than twenty-four hours. But during that brief visit, something inside me had been awakened. I had never experienced anything like the clamor and smell and chaos. Bangkok was home to some of the most delicious food I had ever tasted. I was eager to learn and experience more; I wanted to go back, and not just to Thailand.

When I read about a scholarship for doctoral students that covered the costs of field research in Southeast Asia, my ill-advised topic seemed more like a brilliant destiny. The timing was perfect. I submitted an application and months later received a letter in the mail and a generous check.

Not long after I returned from my first field trip to Southeast Asia, after hearing about my father's cancer, I made the mistake of asking him to read the first two chapters of my thesis. He delivered them back to me covered in red scribbles, his glasses resting on the tip of his nose.

"How on *earth* are you ever going to manage this?" he asked.

"What's wrong with it?" I asked indignantly.

"I don't know where to start," he said.

And that was well before my accident, when I was still in possession of a healthy brain.

Before he died, my father told me I was the only person who had ever stood up to him. The only person who had *dared*. He was proud of me for making my own decisions and sticking to them.

"You have guts," he said. "You really do."

"I am fearless," I said, and I meant it at the time.

"You are," he said, and smiled.

A better word might have been reckless.

~

I cannot determine exactly when I started my new job in aged care. I don't have any helpful records to assist me, nor was I in contact at the time with any friends or family who may have been able to recall on my behalf. My best estimation is that my first day occurred around ten to twelve months after my accident—making it either toward the end of 1995 or the beginning of 1996.

What I do recall is that my new workplace was nothing like my old one. I had traded prized office space in a building overlooking the Royal Botanic Gardens for what appeared—from the outside at least—like a dental surgery, the kind where a person might feel the need to remind the hygienist to use clean gloves. The office was situated above a sandwich shop, and the atmosphere was relaxed, the people friendly. There were no men in suits. No men at all, actually. I was shown to a room, which was more of a cubby than an office, with three plasterboard walls, a glassed wall at the front, and a glass door. Inside the room was a desk that faced the glass wall, a chair that swiveled, and a stack of metal filing cabinets. It was perfect. I had landed a job that didn't require me to cut up fabric for stuffed toys or sweep leaves in a park.

On my desk, amid a large pile of documents, was a note that said, *Welcome Sarah! Please read!* My boss, who was fond of exclamation points, was traveling. *Okay! Rita!* I thought to myself. *Will do!* I sat down with a yellow highlighter pen and waded through the stack of papers.

The job turned out to be dull. And depressing. In my first few weeks, I broke the monotony by visiting as many nursing homes as I could. I preferred being out of my tiny office, although seeing so many old and dying people took a toll on my already fragile mental health. Reading about old people in government reports was one thing, but seeing them clinging to life and staving away death with what little strength they could summon was another. I drove for hours with the car radio on and the sunroof open. "I hope I die before I get old," the Who sang as I drove over the Roseville Bridge on my way to the largest dementia facility on Sydney's north shore.

I was right: nursing homes *are* a lot like prisons. The big difference is that most people get released from prison. And the prisons I had visited, the low and medium security ones, anyway, were a lot more fun. The mood was lighter, with hope—the vague prospect of a fresh start—in the air. I traipsed through retirement homes, hostels, nursing homes, and dementia facilities. I smelled horrible things. Things that people who are frail or dying or disabled shouldn't have to smell. I saw disgusting meals served from old, scratched trolleys, and that same gray food nudged around plates. I felt an emptiness that ate away at my insides.

I greeted a lot of frail old people. I smiled at people who didn't know where they were or who they were, rattling locked doors to escape, to find their way to a home they couldn't remember. People who wept with frustration at being stuck inside a place where everyone around them was sick or dying. People who believed they were perfectly well, that their minds were alert. I saw people who couldn't get out of bed. People who lay on a narrow bed in a room, within the same four walls with a window that looked out onto a parking lot or a row of dumpsters, until they died.

And then I saw the saddest thing: In a bed next to a man in his nineties, there was a young man of around eighteen whose motorcycle had collided with a truck. He had suffered a severe brain injury and lost the use of his legs.

I looked at him, and my heart broke.

How could it be that a head-injured eighteen-year-old was stuffed away from the world inside a nursing home? That could have been me. The sad truth was that there was nowhere to put younger people with brain injuries, so they ended up in facilities completely ill-suited to their needs. It's still the case today.

~

Rita wrote nice exclamation-pointed comments on the papers I prepared for her and seemed to be quite happy with my work. One benefit of working alone was that I was able to labor over each of those papers without distraction, taking the time I needed, making sure they read well and made sense. I often took work home with me at the end of the day and spent hours writing and rewriting whatever it was I had written. Gradually it became easier. In any case, all seemed well with my job until the day Rita came into my office, dragged in a chair from the corridor, leaned across my desk, and said, "I need you to present a paper at a conference. It's in a fortnight, and there will be the usual crowd of nurses and care workers. Probably about 150 people. I want them to get to know you."

I suddenly felt ill.

Why didn't she mention this earlier, I wondered? Since my head injury, my confidence had been zapped. The look on my face must have given me away.

"You don't like public speaking?"

"I'm shy," I said, "and to be honest, I'm not great at it."

"But you had such a big job before!" she said.

"I never did much in the way of public speaking," I said. *And I wasn't brain damaged then,* I wanted to add.

"Look, I wouldn't ask you to do it if I thought you couldn't handle it," she said kindly. "You'll be fine. And I'll be there if you happen to get stuck!"

~

I drove an hour and a half to Gosford to the aged-care conference with 150 delegates. Looking at the program, I felt my breakfast lunge toward my throat. I had been listed as a keynote speaker. I sat down in a chair at the back of the room and considered stabbing my neck with a ballpoint pen—anything to get myself carted out of the room. I willed myself to faint. "Pass out, pass out," I chanted under my breath, but I had never fainted in my life, and I wasn't going to now. I tried to think about anything other than what the next two hours held in store. *Why do hotels and convention centers dress their chairs up in covers,* I wondered? *Is anyone fooled?* I lifted the peach-colored polyester dress and uncovered a metal framed chair with chipped chrome and a plastic foam seat. For all its ugliness, I preferred the bare chair—and the irony was not lost on me. I had lied about my head injury. Hidden it. But what choice did I have? If I had been honest, I would never have found work.

A gaggle of nurses approached me and took turns shaking my hand, introducing themselves. I tried to smile, but I heard nothing. All I could think was that soon I would be standing on a podium in front of all of them, humiliating myself.

When I stood up in front of the crowd, I froze. Everyone in the room was smarter than me, I realized, looking out at 150 faces, heads tilted expectantly like George and Bess, waiting for me to speak. Inside their skulls were 150 high-functioning brains. Some of them had likely experimented with drugs, so maybe their brains were not perfect. But no matter how much coke they had snorted, how much weed they had smoked, how many packs of temazepam they had snuck out of hospital medicine cabinets and swallowed in the bathrooms at work, they were still smarter than me. It was a terrifying thought, but it was true. It was over before I opened my mouth. Thoughts shattered inside my head as I tried to read my presentation. Because I was nervous, my voice quavered and I spoke too fast, in a steady monotone. I could not disguise my terror. All I could think was, *I knew this would happen. I warned Rita. I tried to tell her, but she wouldn't listen.*

I raced through to the end of my talk and stood back from the podium to catch my breath before the floor opened to questions.

Things only got worse. I fumbled around for answers to the questions they asked me and then gave up. "I'm sorry, I have no idea," I said. My mind could think only of Toby, the psychologist at the Brain Injury Unit, and my inability to find the yellow circle. I was kidding myself to think I could do an office job. The neurologist had told me I would never be able to return to this type of work, and he was right. I was a fraud—a fraud who was about to be fired.

I wanted to race out of the room and never go back. But in my high heels and skirt, I knew I'd trip and make an even greater spectacle of myself. Rita stood up at the back of the room and answered questions on my behalf. My life was over. I would return to copying slabs of text into a writing pad and staring at the pockmark on my wall. They would pay me out, I hoped, for a full month. I was still in my probationary period. That would help cover the bills. Then I would start all over again.

Except none of that happened. Rita was nice about my failure, although a tad surprised. "How could someone with such a successful career be so, um, *green* at public speaking?"

I had no answer.

"How about you go to Toastmasters to overcome your fear of public speaking? I found it really helpful."

I nodded.

I had no intention of going to Toastmasters and exposing another roomful of strangers to my damaged brain. I would be quite happy never to say anything to a group of more than three people for the rest of my life.

Back in the office, I approached Rita with a proposal. "I will write the presentations, and you can give them," I suggested. She thought about it for a moment and then nodded. "Okay." She happened to be an excellent public speaker and seemed to enjoy the limelight. "I'm happy with that."

I exhaled loudly as soon as I left her office. I'm not sure how, but I had made it through the first disaster of my working life and managed to keep my job.

5

IMPULSES THAT WON'T BE CONTROLLED

The accident had left me with a panoply of subtle and not-so-subtle changes to my personality. Beyond the extreme chair-destroying volatility I'd acquired, the new me found it hard to think, hard to concentrate, hard to remember. Everything I had taken for granted before the accident was an effort. The new me was bedeviled by the knowledge that I was stupid. My personality had been sabotaged by depression and anger. I had trouble adjusting to my new life. I was party to an arranged marriage with someone I didn't much like.

Following my accident, I had locked myself away from the world. My mother's lack of interest in my welfare had hurt me deeply. What kind of monster must I have become for my mother to have abandoned me?

I was sociable, if shy, before my head injury and enjoyed the company of others. It usually took a couple of glasses of wine for me to become talkative, but I was friendly, I laughed a lot, and I loved nothing more than making others laugh. Alcohol had always been an important part of my social life, and my closest friends reported that I was a lot more fun after a few drinks than I ever was sober. I was not lacking in sharp edges—those who knew me well would probably have described me at times as dogmatic, stubborn, or even acerbic—but I had a healthy reserve of charm at my disposal. Postinjury, my charm vanished. So did my sense of humor. It didn't seem like there was much to laugh about. I had no interest in seeing my former friends; doing so only reminded me of everything I had lost. I would rather be at home with George and Bess and a bottle of wine than out with friends or, worse, trying to make new friends.

I lost the art of socializing. I drifted away from people I had just met, unable to keep a conversation going. Soon after I got the job in aged care, a colleague who had done her best to befriend me told me I ran hot and cold. One moment I could be immersed in conversation, and the next I'd be in what she described as "shutdown mode." I apologized and told her I was distracted by something in my personal life. That I hadn't meant to be rude. In truth I had no idea how I came across to other people. That was why I tried to avoid them. When I relaxed, my mind wandered into cul-de-sacs, where the only word that accurately described my state was "stupefaction." It would take a very patient and persistent person to become my friend.

My impulse control vanished. I acquired the frightening ability to speak before thinking, blurting out comments that were insensitive or rude. I didn't mean to, but I couldn't seem to help myself. On one occasion I was running an errand in the center of Sydney when I saw an old friend from high school. She stopped me in the street and hugged me.

"Sarah! It's so nice to see you!" she said.

"Maria! You're supposed to be dead! I heard you had killed yourself!"

Which happened to be true. Another person I went to school with had told an old friend of mine that Maria had taken her life a couple of years before my accident. The words raced out of my mouth, and, as I heard them, I recoiled from myself in horror.

"That was my sister," she said, looking me over with an expression that suggested I was either evil or crazy or possibly both.

"I'm so sorry," I said, but the damage was done. I should have told her about my accident, about my problems with impulse control and my inability to hold my tongue. But I was hell-bent on hiding my injury from everyone around me. Maria walked away, and I never saw her again.

I wanted to find the nearest wall and bash my head against it. Perhaps that would help bring my old brain back. Instead I went home and shared my disgrace with George and Bess, and we cuddled on the sofa. I promised I would leave the house only to go to work.

Somehow, at work, the illusion of someone who was competent and professional held up. When I talked to people over the phone, I kept a notepad in front of me with a series of instructions I had prepared for myself that reminded me to *SPEAK SLOWLY!*, to *LISTEN!* and *BE POLITE!* As tedious as I often found my job, my sense of who I was and who I wanted to be was inextricably linked to work. Slowly I was climbing out from the bottom of a well, trying to rebuild my brain and my life. The job helped mend my battered psyche, and I couldn't afford to screw it up.

I bounced back and forth between my tiny office and my home, minimizing my exposure to the outside world and concentrating all my efforts on preserving the reputation I was trying to build at work. My only company was George and Bess. I had plugged my phone back in for practical purposes, but I didn't contact anyone. The only problem with my plan was an unexpected side effect from my injury: I craved sex, and lots of it.

Despite the paucity of interest in the subject, the research that exists suggests that most women with traumatic brain injuries lose interest in sex after their injury. One study that surveyed a sample of only twenty-nine Colombian women with traumatic brain injuries found that the majority had "reduced sexual desire, arousal, orgasm function, sexual satisfaction, and lubrication."[12] That wasn't my experience.

As my brain began to mend, there was a shocking shift in my sexual appetite. In the past my relationships with men had tended to last for at least a few months. I had never had a one-night stand with anyone. After my father died, I traveled to the Greek isle of Lesbos and met a woman from Amsterdam. We spent two weeks together, and I realized there was absolutely no doubt about it: I was gay. So my exclusive interest in women after my accident wasn't a huge revelation, but my attitude toward sex had changed dramatically. I no longer wanted to meet a woman and fall in love. Love and sex had become unlinked. I just wanted sex.

Before my accident, I had slept with three women. Maybe four. I had never met anyone in a bar. On the rare occasions I had attempted to enter a lesbian bar, I was turned away. The Sydney lesbian scene in the early 1990s was a tightly guarded community. Once, before my trip to Lesbos, I cajoled a friend from work to coming out to a lesbian club with me. The woman at the door ushered my friend inside but stopped me. "Straights are not allowed," she said. My friend had been happily living with her boyfriend for five years. "How is she ever supposed to know if she's gay or not if you don't let her in?" she protested. "Not my problem!" the woman said, holding her arm out to forbid me from entering. The problem seemed to stem from my face. I look frighteningly clean-cut, and I could be mistaken for a Sunday school teacher or the wife of an evangelical preacher—the kind of person who should be home sewing doll's clothes or baking gingerbread men for school fundraisers, not trolling lesbian bars for a date.

So I had a problem: I wanted to be alone, but I also wanted sex. In order to have sex, I needed to gain entry into a scene that had consistently rejected me in the past. To get past the gates into Sydney's lesbian bars, I needed a guide.

I gave in and called James, an old friend from my first job in Parliament House, and asked him to take me out. James was the first gay friend I ever had, and the only person I knew who was out at work. Everyone liked him because he had the courage to be himself. Impeccably dressed and fastidious about his appearance, he loved taking me aside and counseling me about my dress.

"Promise me you won't buy any more clothes unless I'm with you," he used to say, winking, as if to lessen the blow. It was true that I had no fashion sense whatsoever, and I stayed within the safety of navy, black, and gray skirts or trousers and striped or white business shirts, which I rarely bothered to iron. My appearance did not interest me in the slightest. If my colleagues hadn't realized it before, they did the day I turned up to work wearing one black shoe and one navy one.

"Why don't you ever wear makeup?" James asked me once. "Is it just laziness?"

"Partly," I answered. "And partly because I have no idea how to put it on. I would look like a clown."

"All you have to do is ask!" he said. "I could make you look gorgeous. If only you'd let me!"

"Thanks."

"You know what I mean. More gorgeous."

When I called James out of the blue asking him to take me out on the town, he couldn't have been happier.

"Where the hell have you been?" he asked as we flopped into two lounge chairs in a corner of the room in a bar on Oxford Street.

"I'm not sure," I said, and I meant it. James hadn't heard from me since my father died.

"Are things getting any easier?" he asked.

"No. I still miss him as much as I did when he died. I don't think it's ever going to get any easier."

"It will," he said, putting his arm around me. "It must."

For most of our friendship, James knew me as a poorly dressed heterosexual. My recently found gayness was a source of mirth. He insisted I give him an intimate account of my limited history with women.

"Well, who would have thought!" he chuckled, leaning back in his chair. "You're a lesbian!"

"I am," I said, slightly embarrassed. "And I don't want a relationship, just sex."

"You want a woman solely for the purposes of having sex?"

"More than one, if possible. A small number would be ideal, so I can rotate them."

"And they need to be pretty?"

I nodded.

He sucked air in between his teeth and looked around the room. "That might not be as easy as you think."

The bar was empty but for men.

"You'd better not leave me and run off with someone," I said. We sat and talked, and drank, and my induction into life as an out lesbian and a closeted brain-damage sufferer began. After about four hours and six Long Island iced teas, we were both drunk.

I stared into the dregs of an empty glass and came to believe that my real love, apart from George and Bess, was alcohol. The drunker I got, the less I thought about sex, and that could only be a good thing.

I was a late starter when it came to alcohol, but I made up for it fairly quickly. I did not drink anything until I was twenty because I didn't like the taste. I discovered my love for alcohol when I first started work at Parliament House, soon after I graduated. People who worked in politics drank wine with lunch, and then met after work for drinks in the parliamentary bar. Parliament House was home to a large assortment of alcoholics—mostly crusty old men with stained ties; jackets flecked with dandruff; and lank, greasy, combed-over hair.

My drinking went awry when I started working with Tim in Corrections. Fortunately for both of us, we worked together for only a year. Occasionally we would begin drinking as early as ten thirty in the morning when the bar opened at Parliament House. At lunch we would share a bottle of chardonnay—two if we were bored—and somehow, after a few hours' work, wind up back in the bar at five, and we would drink until it closed. How we ever managed to avoid getting fired remains a mystery. For one year of my life—my twenty-fifth year I believe—I behaved like a lunatic.

At a party once, a friend dared me to drink a large bottle of gin on my own; I did it and suffered only a dull headache the next morning. My ability to hold my alcohol was legendary, and friends watched me in astonishment. My parents enjoyed a glass of cask wine with dinner most nights, but they were not big drinkers and I had never seen them drunk. No one in my family had a history of alcoholism.

When I was twenty-six I saw an ad in the newspaper with the head-line "Worried About Your Drinking?" I visited a clinic at Royal Prince Alfred Hospital where a doctor took notes on my drinking history, drew some blood, and let me know I was well on my way to becoming a full-fledged alcoholic.

I told her I was the only person I knew who had never vomited from drinking. That was something I had always considered to be a badge of honor.

"That makes you higher risk for alcoholism than anyone else!" she said. "You miss all the warning signs."

She asked me how many drinks I had in a night, and I told her I tried to stop at six. Or eight. But that on Saturday nights that number could double with no ugly side effects. Well, none that I could detect, anyway.

"How many nights a week do you drink?"

"Four or five," I said.

I told her about the bottle of gin.

"You *are* an alcoholic," she said, insisting that a 750-milliliter bottle of gin would kill most people. "Do you really want to die from drinking? It's not a nice way to go."

The news that I was already an alcoholic rattled me. Sitting in the chair with the doctor opposite me, I was visited by an image of myself hunched over a shopping trolley stuffed with all my worldly possessions, dressed in filthy clothes, spending every last cent on gin. I pledged to eschew all alcohol for the next year. I lasted about half of that, but I did manage to moderate my alcohol intake somewhat when I started drinking again.

~

James cast his groggy eyes along the line of women who had entered the bar and were sitting opposite us. "None of those appeal?"

"Sorry." I shook my head.

"Let's go out on Sunday. Sunday is lesbian night in Sydney."

"Thanks," I said, and hugged him.

I met James on Sunday for dinner at a café on Victoria Street. The place to be, apparently, was a bar not far from Kings Cross railway station.

James looked at his watch. "We're going to be way too early."

"Why?" I asked. It astounded me that I had to stay up so late in the vain hope of having sex with someone. Heterosexuality was so much simpler. James and I took our time over dinner and headed to another bar he knew just around the corner before making our way over to the lesbian bar at eleven p.m. We sat on stools, getting drunker and drunker, and studied the patrons.

"None of them?" James asked.

"Nope."

Then a new woman appeared. She had shoulder-length blonde hair, brown eyes, and good teeth. She looked at me and smiled. I smiled back. She approached us.

"Hi," she said.

I returned her greeting. "Would you like to come home with me?" I asked. She turned around and walked away.

James looked at me as if I had lost my mind. "What the hell did you do that for?"

"What?"

"You scared her off!"

"Did I?"

"You don't get it," he said. "You need to do the legwork!"

"What legwork?"

"Buy her a drink, take her to dinner. That sort of thing."

"I don't want to have dinner with her! Is that what you do every time you see a man you like? Buy him dinner? If we did have dinner, I'd probably lose all interest in her!"

"Girls are different! You have to get to know her!" he said.

"I just want sex! Then, if it's good, I'm happy to get to know her. I'll buy her dinner then. What's the problem with that?"

James thumped his head on the table. "This could take years."

It took a month of going out twice a week before I met an attractive travel agent who actually offered to come home with me. In the taxi on the way back to my place, she stuck one hand inside my shirt and her other hand down the front of my jeans. I liked her immediately. So did the taxi driver, whose eyes were fixed on his rearview mirror. Once home, we headed straight to my bedroom.

"I get excited doing things to you," she whispered into my ear. I tried to reciprocate, but she pinned me down to the bed. She started to lick me and told me that she could do that all night.

"Go ahead," I said.

After we had sex—or rather, after I got sex—she told me she'd had a good night. I assumed, in jest, she meant meeting me. "That too," she said. She had also found a wallet in the street with $500 inside.

"Did you hand it in to the police?" I asked.

She looked at me like I was from another planet. "Why would I do that? If some idiot is stupid enough to lose his wallet, someone is going to take his money. That's what happens."

"Is it?"

"Yes, silly," she said, turning to kiss me. Before we fell asleep she told me she had a girlfriend but that they had been fighting.

"Oh," I said. "Does she know where you are?"

"She'd kill me."

I slept with one eye open, worried she was going to rob me. I woke before her and made sure my valuables were still where they should be. Nothing appeared to be missing. When she woke, she wanted sex again. Well, her idea of sex, to which I was not averse.

"Can I see you again?" she asked, before getting up and putting her clothes on.

"Um, sure."

"Good. I like you."

I smiled. I didn't like her particularly, but she knew how to find my clitoris, loved sex, was pretty, and had large, perfectly formed breasts that I liked very much. George, who wasn't an especially good judge of character, refused to leave her side. She tickled his ears and kissed his nose. Bess kept her distance. The travel agent called me later that day.

"Can I come over?" she asked.

But you only just left! I thought. "No. I'm sorry, but I'm really busy," I said. I needed some time to find and lock away my grandmother's sapphire bracelet. I toyed with the idea of hiding it in the chimney, but settled on a spot downstairs underneath the floorboards.

"Tomorrow?" she asked.

"Okay." She arrived at seven o'clock the next evening and led me straight to the bedroom. *Too bad she's a thief,* I told myself, but that seemed to be a small price to pay for my sexual satisfaction.

"Do you want to go out and eat?" I asked after we had finished. "There's a new Thai place up the road."

"No, I'm happy here," she said.

We continued to have sex for the next three weeks. I couldn't explain my sex drive. I was a brain-damaged, sex-crazed lesbian. Only one good thing came of this. The travel agent seemingly never picked up on any hint of my brain damage. It was a good sign. I had reached a point where I could disguise my shortcomings—until someone asked me what a hypothesis was, or to spell "rhythm."

Then one day we had sex, and when it was done, I decided I never wanted to see her again. It was over. I couldn't explain what had happened.

"I need to focus on my PhD. I'm feeling a bit overwhelmed by it all," I said.

"You used me."

"I'm sorry. I didn't mean to. And you do have a girlfriend." I showed her out. After a final scout through my house, I realized I was missing a jumper she once admired on me and a pair of knee-high boots.

~

My problem wasn't just my unfulfilled desire for casual sex but the puzzling internal conflict it created within me. Most of my friends were men. My troubled relationship with my mother had left me with an unconscious hostility toward women. I had a deep well of resentment toward my mother for walking away from me after my accident. And then, when I thought about it, I realized women had caused me grief for most of my life. The only exceptions were my grandmother, who died when I was eleven, and one of my high school English teachers.

In both primary and high school, a succession of female teachers seemed to dislike me on sight. I was rambunctious and didn't like being told what to do. Worse, I struggled to sit still and delighted in distracting everyone around me. Our family doctor had told my parents he thought I was hyperactive. They hoped it was something I would outgrow.

My aversion to authority came from my father.

"How can you be expected to listen to someone you don't respect?" he asked me after the only parent-teacher night he ever attended.

I looked at him solemnly and nodded. "Exactly," I said.

"Mind you, I think your English teacher is very good. And she likes you," he added. My English teacher was a Polish woman in her late twenties. And it was true that I liked her, even more so after she took me aside once and said, "I used to be just like you at school, really naughty. Don't change!"

Later that night I heard my parents arguing. "Tom, you really aren't helping matters when you tell her every teacher she has is an idiot."

"I liked her English teacher!" he said. "And she was the only one who had anything nice to say!"

~

One evening a couple of months after I stopped seeing the travel agent, I was invited to a birthday party where I met Laura. Laura had a pretty face with full lips, pale-blue eyes, and thick dark hair, and resembled a taller version of Kate Winslet. She was polite and well-mannered and had an excellent sense of humor. I looked at her closely and wondered, *What's the catch?*

As the night progressed, we found ourselves engrossed in conversation. When we weren't talking, we were doubled over in laughter or trying to compose ourselves. I hadn't enjoyed myself so much in a long time. At the end of the night, when I asked Laura for her phone number, she gave it to me and kissed me on the cheek. I called her the next day and asked her out for dinner.

We met in Bondi at a restaurant by the beach she had been eager to try. Laura was obsessed with good food and wine. I bought her dinner, and we talked until the restaurant closed. She told me about her favorite books, her favorite artists, her interest in design. I told her that I had always wanted to be a writer but that I took a few wrong turns and ended up in aged care. She dreamed of having a furniture shop—selling pieces she had handpicked from around the world and restored. For the first time since my accident, I forgot all about my damaged brain.

We left the restaurant and wandered around the rock pools at North Bondi Beach.

"I have a hypothetical question for you: What would you do if you found a wallet in the street with $500 inside?"

"Call the owner of the wallet if there was a contact number, or hand it in to the police," she said.

"Would you remove the money?"

She looked at me as though I was crazy. "Of course not!"

"Do you want to come back to my place?" I asked. "We don't have to do anything, but it would be nice to spend the night together. And you can meet George and Bess." It was a shocking and genuine request.

"Sure!" she said, and took my arm in hers as we walked back to the road to find a taxi.

She spent that night at my house. I wasn't seized by the need to lock away my personal belongings. I knew she wouldn't steal anything.

6

DOGS ARE THE BEST PEOPLE

It took a month of dinners, breakfasts, picnics, and trips to the beach before I mustered up the courage to tell Laura about my head injury. I was falling in love with her, and I didn't want to scare her off, but it was something she needed to know. The fact that she hadn't mentioned any concerns over my cognitive functioning or memory felt like a cause for celebration. But I could not keep my secret from her forever.

I told Laura about Tim and how we had always pushed each other to do silly things, indulged each other's dares. I told her about the time he lent me a blue flashing police light he had borrowed from a friend, and how I had attached it to the roof of my car and went on a joyride, menacing unsuspecting drivers. I told her how Tim had arranged for a police helicopter pilot—a friend—to take us on a tour over all the prisons in Sydney. I told her how Tim had arranged for me to drive a highway police car. Tim was a lot of fun, I told Laura, and I liked him a lot. I knew Laura would like him too. I told her about my life before the accident, my father, my job, and my PhD. Then I told her how it felt to somersault over the head of a horse and land on the back of my head.

"But you seem fine," she said.

"The neurologist told me I would never work or study again."

"Well, he got that wrong."

I told her about the disability pension. "I lost my job," I said, "and everything fell apart."

"Well, you're fine now!"

"You can see no evidence whatsoever of my damaged brain?" She was the first person I had asked.

"No sign whatsoever," she said. "I promise."

"You haven't noticed how many things I forget?"

"No! I forget things too. Everyone does. Your memory is fine."

Nothing made me happier than hearing those words.

Laura is an extrovert, and I was happy to let her lead our conversations. But I wondered if I talked more and she talked less whether the problems with my brain would become more obvious. It had been a long time since I had talked to anyone except James and my new work colleagues, and those conversations were usually brief and focused. Talking required a great deal of effort. It had been considerably easier for me to learn to read and write again than to form coherent thoughts in my head and utter them. I was out of practice.

Laura and I had been together only ten weeks when I asked her to move in with me. My brief time in the lesbian community had taught me that women like Laura came along with all the frequency of flying saucers. Now that I had found her, I wasn't letting her go. I knew ten weeks was a ludicrously short span of time in which to make such a decision, but gay women, even those who haven't suffered brain injuries, behave in odd, inexplicable ways. Particularly when it comes to life-changing decisions like living together, buying a house, getting a dog, or having babies. Mercifully, neither of us wanted babies. Only one of us wanted dogs.

The most immediate benefit of Laura moving in was a nutritional one. On the day she arrived, she opened the door to my pantry, peered inside, and shouted, "What on earth have you been eating!?"

"I don't know," I said. "Pasta?"

"Pasta with what? Barilla tomato sauce? How disgusting! You eat like a student!

"Where are the garbage bags?" she asked. She proceeded to throw out everything in my pantry except a large pack of caster sugar that she kept "in case we make meringue."

"I love meringue! Can we make some?"

"Sure!" she said. And she did, while I watched.

It was the best meringue I had ever tasted.

People with head injuries commonly lose their sense of taste or smell, or sometimes both, but thankfully my sense of taste had returned. Or perhaps it just took decent food to stimulate my appetite. In any case, Laura was an excellent cook. Slowly she began to educate me about food, and I rediscovered the pleasures of eating. She wanted to find the best chocolate there was; she'd come home beaming, armed with fifteen different types of chocolate, and we would sit down and feast. She did the same with coffee. With anchovies. With olive oil. Eating with Laura was a joy.

Six years my junior, Laura was still considerably more grown-up than me in every way I could imagine. She was maternal, though she didn't want children. She was serious and career-minded, like I used to be. She managed accounts for an advertising agency and loved her job. She had a clear career path mapped out with milestones to achieve every two years. She made lists and plans and crossed things off as she finished them. I had never known anyone as well organized as Laura.

I was the opposite. Living with Laura made me realize brain damage had stripped me of my ambition. I wanted nothing more than a normal life—a couple of dogs, a girlfriend, a home, and a job. That seemed to be a massive achievement, given the mess I had been barely a year earlier.

I tried to tell Laura about the difficulties I had faced returning to my PhD. "It's really hard for me to focus," I said. "My brain doesn't work the way it used to."

"Of course it's hard!" she said. "If it was easy, everyone would have a PhD."

"It's hard for me because of the accident."

"Don't be silly. You're just making excuses," she said.

And I started to think she might be right. In any case, I had decided to put my PhD aside for a few months and try to live a normal life.

Laura told me about her childhood. It was not without its own ugliness.

"My father died of esophageal cancer when I was twenty-one," she said. "I was away at college when my mum called to say that he had died."

"That's so sad," I said, and Laura shrugged.

"It was. Is."

"I'm so sorry," I said, leaning in to hug her.

"What about your family? It sounds like a bit of a disaster."

"When my father died, everything fell apart. My mother and brother are close, but I've never been close to either of them."

"What's wrong with your mother?"

"Nothing. She just doesn't like me much. After the accident, she made no contact with me other than a birthday card she sent in the mail."

"That is very strange. Most un-mother-like."

"You'll meet her at some point and you can make up your own mind."

I explained that my parents had met at the University of Sydney when my mother was doing her bachelor of arts. My father had lectured my mother in geology and, according to my mother, was highly desired by his female students. He was a handsome man: tall, with thick, dark, wavy hair and gray-blue eyes. When he kept his mouth closed he looked like a film star—but his stained teeth gave away his working-class roots. His many admirers, including my mother, had attended private girls' schools on Sydney's north shore. They'd enrolled in university, my mother told me once, for the sole purpose of finding a husband. My mother, a short brunette with excellent teeth, waited patiently until she graduated, when my father decided sufficient time had lapsed for him to ask her out.

My father's childhood had been unfathomably sad. His mother died from scarlet fever when he was three, and my grandfather made the curious decision to tell his boys their mother had abandoned them. Both boys had adored their mother and she them. My father and his brother learned the truth fifteen years later when my grandfather remarried. My grandfather seemed to blame my grandmother for dying, for leaving him to bring up two boys alone.

My grandfather's lie ignited a rage in my father that burned bright until his last few years of life. He never blamed his father, who had done the best he could under difficult circumstances. His rage landed on my brother and me. But my father had more integrity about him than anyone else I have known. I always knew where I stood with him, and I never doubted his love or support—even in his worst tempers.

My mother's father, Lionel, a journalist for a rural newspaper with a fondness for women other than his wife, divorced my grandmother when my mother entered high school. Once divorced, my grandparents never saw each other again.

Lorna, my grandmother, a beautiful woman with high cheekbones and long, shapely legs, lost her hearing after developing an infection in her twenties. My grandmother was gentle, loving, and kind—the polar opposite of my mother—and I adored her. She took me to the local cinema and bought me choc top ice creams. We did the kind of things normal people did, things I never did with my parents. Not once did our family go to a movie or a restaurant. We were short on money, but my father also had a strong desire to avoid unnecessary human contact.

My grandfather remarried a younger woman who had made a lot of money on the stock market and used to tell me, as an eight-year-old, to sit with my legs closed. They bought an apartment in an expensive suburb of Sydney with a view overlooking the harbor. They had their own drinks cabinet, complete with crystal decanters for gin, vodka, scotch, brandy, and port, each bottle labeled with a tortoiseshell tag slung around its neck. When we visited my grandfather, he always pretended I was more grown-up than I was and made me a nice drink: orange juice, bitters, and ice served to me in a proper glass with a plastic twirly stick. He was the only adult who ever trusted me with crystal. He was the only adult I knew who owned crystal. I held the glass tightly with both hands. In his spare room, my grandfather kept scrapbooks full of postcards of girls in bikinis. My stepgrandmother laughed about it. Each year they holidayed together in Hawaii, and he stocked up on more postcards that he filed away in his scrapbooks.

My mother sided with her father, and my grandmother grew old in a dark one-bedroom flat with carpet the color of the ocean. Each time we visited her we would find her hunched over a race guide, an old yellow Bic in her hand, wincing from the static between her tiny transistor radio and her hearing aid. She was a sensible gambler. A couple of times a week she walked up to the local betting shop on the Pacific Highway and placed her bets. She never betted much, and she did her research. Mostly she seemed to win. Her apartment was three blocks away from our house, which had once been her marital home. My grandfather sold it to my parents for a fraction of its worth after my brother was born. I was eleven when Lorna died from lung cancer, though she had never smoked. On the day she died, my mother came down to my bedroom where I lay spread across my bed sobbing and said, "You may not understand this, Sarah, but all I feel is relief. I am finally free."

My mother and her brother don't speak. Her father and her brother were estranged. A similar division formed in my family after my father's death, with my mother and brother on one side, me on the other. Conflict is in our genes.

My father maintained almost no contact at all with his brother and stepbrother. "We don't have much in common," he said, when asked why we never saw my uncles. "They're nice enough, but there's no need to *see* them, is there?" Had the decision been left to him we would have seen no one at all—no family, no friends, no neighbors. We were an odd family.

Some months after Laura moved in, we drove across town to my mother's apartment. Laura had been pressing me to meet my mother. To make up her own mind. My mother invited us in and made some tea. She sat on the sofa, looked earnestly at Laura, and said, "Well, you know Sarah is manic-depressive."

"What?" I asked. It was news to me.

"It's my opinion," she added.

"I'm not manic-depressive! Where did that come from? I had a head injury! I'm depressed!"

"I just thought Laura should know, that's all."

"She's not manic-depressive," Laura said.

"Alright," my mother said, shrugging. "It's just my opinion."

"You bitch!" I shouted, my rage flooding back in an instant. "You were saving that one up, weren't you?"

My mother looked at Laura as if to say, *See? You're dating a foul-mouthed psychopath. Enjoy!*

I grabbed Laura's hand and headed for the door.

"I'm not manic-depressive!" I said to Laura as soon as the door clicked shut behind us. "And if I were, why wouldn't she have tried to get help? We have barely spoken since the accident! She never talked to the doctor, never tried to find out what was wrong, never did anything to help!"

Laura pulled me toward her and kissed me on the ear. "You were right about your mother. I'm so sorry."

As we drove home, I realized that a seismic shift had happened in my relationship with my mother. She held an incendiary device and could toss it in my direction and wait for me to explode. From that moment on, my mother began telling her closest friends that she was scared of me. That I had a vile temper, that I lost it without warning, that she feared for her physical safety. She never told anyone about my father's frequent rampages through our house, smashing things and beating up my brother and me. I had never hit anyone, never smashed anything. But I did shout. Had she told them about my brain injury? I'll never know.

At home, Laura was disrupting the dynamics with my preferred family. George was surprised to learn that, while meeting his criteria of being under thirty with a symmetrical face, Laura didn't spend her time showering him with affection. She didn't get down on her knees, rub his tummy, and tell him he was a good boy. She didn't even tickle the tufts of baby hair behind his ears. She smiled at him, and sometimes nodded. That was the extent of it. Bess would approach Laura time and again wagging her tail, and seemed to bounce back when Laura nodded at her in response or ignored her altogether.

"I like dogs," Laura said a week after she moved in, "but they belong outside." I glanced at her and looked across the room at George, whose nostrils had flared in disbelief.

"I can't keep the dogs outside," I said. "They are inside dogs. Rescue dogs. I am compensating for someone else's neglect and cruelty. I am trying to make up for what went before."

"It's not cruel to keep a dog outside."

"You were brought up in the country with farm dogs. These are city dogs! And we live in a terrace house with a tiny backyard. And I won't," I said. This was something about which I wasn't prepared to compromise. I loved Laura, but the dogs had seen me through the most hellish time of my life, and they needed me more than she did.

The world, as I saw it at that time in my life, was divided into dog people and nondog people. Laura was a nondog person and a people person. I was a dog person and a nonpeople person. I had been a dog person all my life, but the nonpeople thing was new. After my accident, I decided that people (based exclusively upon my experience with my mother) were a colossal disappointment. George and Bess, on the other hand, had showed their devotion to me each and every day. It is true that they didn't have much choice, but I had experienced firsthand the ability of my dogs to calm me, to love me, and to motivate me to keep living. No one understood and supported the head-injured me better than George and Bess.

Laura was not as attuned to the positive effects of dog ownership. Stare into the eyes of a dog, and you may experience what researchers have called an "oxytocin-gaze positive loop," in which oxytocin levels are raised in both you and your dog.[13] You need to have known the love of a dog to understand the joys of dog ownership, and Laura, sadly, had not.

I did my best to explain that humans form opinions of each other based on their expectations and judgments. Dogs love us without conditions or judgments. Laura looked at me, cast her eyes upward, and exhaled, so I sang her a few bars from "Dogs Are the Best People" by the Fauves.

"Enough," she said, smacking my leg.

I sang the refrain again.

"Stop!" she said, placing her hand over my mouth.

My dogs and Laura were the two things that were helping my return to a normal life, and I needed them to learn to live with one another. I attempted to address Laura's concerns about the dogs' sleeping arrangements by buying two dog futons and placing them on the floor on either side of our bed. I explained to George that there was no longer room for him in the bed. He shot me a look of contempt, snorted, and wandered to the fireplace where he proceeded to lift his leg in protest.

"No," Laura shouted, as she saw the arc of yellow pee splashing against the fireplace, but once a dog starts to pee, it's hard to stop him.

"Don't worry," I said, racing out to the back shed to retrieve a mop and bucket.

"It's disgusting!" she said as I began to mop up the mess.

"There are a lot more disgusting things than a dog peeing inside the house."

"Like?"

"Come on! He's adjusting to having you here, that's all. We've been alone for years. Give him time."

Bess was even worse. Ever since Laura moved in, Bess had developed terrible separation anxiety. My days at work were shorter than Laura's, which gave me time to race home and clean up whatever surprise Bess had left us. Most days she would jump onto the kitchen counter and spray diarrhea over everything within reach: the toaster, the juicer, the blender, whatever we had left to dry in the dish rack. I started leaving the office earlier and earlier each day, allowing myself time to scrub the kitchen clean before Laura returned from work.

After a month of coming home each day to discover the same thing, I took Bess to the vet surgery two doors from our home.

"Separation anxiety," the vet said. "You could buy her a crate and lock her in it while you're out."

"I can't crate a twelve-year-old dog for nine hours each day," I said. "Do you have any other ideas?"

"You could try Bach Rescue Remedy."

I bought a box of the stuff—a tincture that claimed to calm a whole host of unpleasant emotions—and took it home. The next morning before I went to work, I placed two drops on Bess's tongue. That afternoon I discovered she had managed to spray diarrhea not just over the kitchen counter but also as far away as the fridge. I put on a pair of plastic gloves, reached under the sink for another bottle of Dettol, and began to clean. No worse than a sick kid, I told myself. A highly disturbed, sick kid.

~

My mother—as fearful of me as she claimed to be—kept up contact with me after she had met Laura. She was the type of woman who loved gay men but struggled to understand lesbians. I dated a plastic surgeon after my father died, and my mother adored him. Months after we broke up, I traveled to Lesbos. When I got home, I visited my mother and gave her a pottery dish I had bought for her in Athens.

There was a joke in our family when I was growing up that my mother liked to regift every present I ever gave her. Tea towels, scarves, and mugs I had carefully chosen were kept in their wrapping and given away at birthdays and Christmas. At Christmas, when I was seventeen, my mother gave an aunt a vase that was identical to the one I had given her months earlier. I waited until my aunt was out of earshot and told my mother. Ever the quick thinker, my mother insisted, "I liked the one you gave me so much that I bought another just like it for Mary!" In the car on the drive home, my mother said, "I'm sorry, Sarah, I had no idea that vase came from you." My father looked at me in the rearview mirror and raised his eyebrows.

After my trip to Lesbos, I felt compelled to tell my mother I was gay.

"I hope you like the dish. I got it in a shop in Athens, on my way to Lesbos. By the way, I'm gay." I have always favored the "ripping off the Band-Aid" approach when delivering bad news.

"You're what?"

"Gay," I said.

"What?"

"I'm gay."

"But what about Mike?"

"Mike and I broke up months ago."

"I thought you'd come to your senses and begged him to take you back!"

"No, I didn't do that."

She steadied herself on the side of the kitchen bench and looked at me. "It took you a long time to work it out, didn't it? You're thirty!"

"I like men!"

"Well, you're bisexual, then."

"No, Mum. I can love men without wanting to sleep with them. I'm just trying to tell you that I'm gay."

"Oh, well, alright. It's a bit of a shock, I must say."

With that backdrop, it surprised me somewhat that my mother embraced Laura. Months after Laura and I had stormed out of her living room, my mother asked me a question when we were alone.

"Just tell me, how is it possible to have sex without a penis?"

I felt my face flush.

She pounced on my silence. "You know your father would *not* have been happy to know you were gay."

"I believe you're wrong," I said. "And it's disgraceful to attribute sentiments to my dead father. I wonder what he would have thought about you abandoning me after my accident. Have you ever thought about that?"

She got up from the sofa, opened the refrigerator door, sighed loudly enough for me to hear from the living room, and tightened the lid on the Vegemite jar.

After our conversation, I became yet more wary of my mother. But she was family and I wanted our relationship to be civil.

Laura became our intermediary. People *liked* Laura. I, as my mother told me whenever she got the chance, polarized people. They either liked me or hated me. Certainly, after the accident, I felt that was true. My mother exhibited no signs whatsoever of liking me.

The only things my mother and I seemed capable of talking about without fighting were my dogs. I told her about Bess's separation anxiety. She had heard of a vet in Chatswood who specialized in animal psychology. I was desperate, so I booked a time for the vet to meet with Bess, and my mother came along. The vet suggested that I start leaving Bess alone in stretches of fifteen minutes and gradually build up to an hour to get her used to the idea that I would return.

I took a sick day the next Friday and left the house in blocks of fifteen minutes at a time. Each time I returned, I was pleased to find no mess at all. After two hours, I left for a full hour and went to a café opposite my house. Bess was not stupid, I realized, when, at three o'clock—after I'd spent the day leaving the house and returning to it, drunk eight cups of coffee, and eaten a cheese and tomato sandwich and three chocolate brownies—I looked across the road to my house and saw her standing on the back of an armchair with her head poking through the curtain watching me. I left the café and walked to the park overlooking the Harbor Bridge and sat there for an hour. Back home, Bess was fine. No harm done. I clipped on the dogs' leads and took them for a walk.

During the weekend, Laura and I left the house for breakfast, for a movie, then later for dinner. When we returned, Bess was fine. Come Monday when I needed to return to work, though, she was back to her old habits. Perhaps she had picked up on the fact that I hated my job. The Bach Rescue Remedy I had continued giving her for more than a week had no effect at all. I dreaded the day when Laura arrived home early and entered the kitchen.

That day came a few months later. I was late, running as many yellow lights as I could, desperate to get home first, when I got a call on my mobile.

Laura was hysterical. "The kitchen!"

"What's wrong with it?" I asked innocently.

"You'll see! You're cleaning it up!"

"Really? Okay. I'm on my way."

I got home to find the dogs locked out in the back garden and an ashen-faced Laura perched on the edge of the sofa. I walked past her into the kitchen. Bess had outdone herself. She had managed to cover the walls, the counter, the sink, the fridge, and the floor with diarrhea.

"Jesus! What happened?" I asked no one in particular. I opened the back door and Bess jumped up on me, frantically. "It's okay," I said, trying to calm her down. "I'll clean it up. You stay out here."

"You need to get a new toaster," is all Laura said. "And a dish rack and a kettle."

"Okay. I'll buy them tomorrow."

"Actually, you need a whole new kitchen. I've never seen anything more disgusting."

And you thought there was nothing more disgusting than a dog peeing inside the house, I wanted to say.

I realize that some people in this world find animals more disgusting than people. I'm just not one of them. If a human had diarrhea in my kitchen I'd be selling the house. I gag while cleaning a dog's mess, but I can manage.

"If that happens again, I'm moving out," Laura said.

"It won't happen again," I said, knowing full well it would. "Don't worry. She must have eaten something in the park that made her sick."

"Fine, but why did she do it on the sink?"

It was a reasonable question. "I really don't know."

I cleaned everything up, tossed out everything that wasn't fixed to the walls, and took the dogs to the park. I found a bench and talked to Bess.

"You can't keep doing this, Bess," I said. "It's serious now. You have to find another way to cope with your stress. Do you understand?" She nodded her head in agreement, licked my hand, wagged her tail, and hopped up onto the seat beside me. "I have to work, Bess. We need the money to pay off the house I bought you," I said.

I understand, she seemed to say. *I'll try to calm down.*

Six months passed and the problem only worsened. I hid it from Laura as best I could, but it placed a considerable strain on our otherwise surprisingly healthy relationship.

"Put her down," Laura told me one evening, after she overheard me on the telephone discussing Bess with my mother. "It's the kindest thing."

I refused to speak to her for twenty-four hours.

Then she said it: "She goes or I go."

"Go!" I shouted. As soon as I said it, I wanted to stuff the word back inside my mouth.

"Think carefully, Sarah. Do you want me to leave?"

"No," I said. The prospect of Laura leaving terrified me. She was my one chance at a normal life. But I loved Bess, and I couldn't bear to lose her either.

Each day when I got home, I dumped my bag on the dining room table, went straight to the kitchen, pulled on a clean pair of plastic gloves, and scrubbed every surface. It was starting to take a toll on me. *Why is Bess so stressed?* I wondered. I wish I could have filmed her somehow to see how it all started, but webcams hadn't been invented yet. I put it off as long as I could, and then one afternoon I found myself at the veterinary surgery again. It was a spontaneous thing. I'd had a bad day and returned home to a kitchen that looked and smelled like a dysentery ward in Calcutta.

I walked in and asked the vet for her opinion.

"We've seen an animal psychologist, tried the Rescue Remedy, tried leaving her alone in short snatches. Nothing has worked," I explained.

"Put her down," the vet said.

Bess was roughly twelve. She had lived a good life with me, I told myself. But I couldn't possibly kill this dog.

The separation anxiety she experienced was causing her such distress that from 8:00 a.m. until 5:30 p.m. each weekday, her world would close in and she was swamped by terror, which wasn't good for her. Laura had given me an ultimatum: Bess goes or she does. I was stressed. Bess was stressed. Laura was stressed.

It took all of an hour for me to arrive at my desperate decision. At the time, it seemed to be the right one to make. I walked the ten steps back home and collected Bess while tears rolled down my cheeks. At the vet I lifted her onto the table, held her head, kissed her nose, and told her I loved her. She lifted her head slightly and licked my face while the vet slipped a needle into her leg. She was gone.

I was gone too. The vet asked for money, but I was crying so hard I thought I was going to vomit. We made arrangements for Bess to be cremated and her ashes to be returned to me in a small silver urn. Back home, I lay down on the sofa and sobbed. George jumped up beside me. *What happened?* he seemed to ask. I buried my head in his fur and told him.

"I killed my dog," I told Laura when she got home. "Happy?" She had never seen me cry before and now I couldn't stop.

"I'm sorry," she said, "but you did the right thing."

"I did the right thing for you," I said.

I hated myself. It was the same self-loathing I experienced when my father asked me to help him die. I loved Bess as much as I loved Laura. And I chose Laura.

Watching Bess die reminded me how easy death could have been for my father. I cursed myself for my lack of courage. A single needle prick, an infusion of morphine, his pain gone. Bess neither wanted nor deserved to die, and I had killed her. My father wanted desperately to die, and I kept him alive, prolonging his suffering. Grief for Bess seeped into my grief for my father.

Laura and I had lived together only seven months, and I had killed my dog to keep her. I began to believe Laura would leave me and I would be even more broken than before. I tested her and prodded her to make sure of it. I deluded myself into thinking I no longer even cared.

With Bess dead, I insisted that George be allowed on the bed for cuddles on Saturday and Sunday mornings.

"No," Laura said.

"Yes!" I shouted. I thought my sacrifice had placed me in a position of strength. On Saturday mornings when I woke, I whispered to George, inviting him up to lie alongside me.

I am not sure how, given everything that had happened with Bess, but Laura and I managed to survive the first year of our relationship. We had fun together. Little things reduced us to tears of laughter. I realized how lucky I was to have her, and not just because she was a good cook who made me laugh. She was normal, by my standards anyway. I was a person with a damaged brain, and I suffered from the familiar symptoms of depression, bitterness, anger, and an inability to control my impulses. I was difficult. Why she stayed with me was a constant source of wonderment. I felt sure that she could do much better. She would leave me for someone else, at some point, I was convinced of it. And I couldn't blame her if she did. Until then, I embraced the fact that I was a much happier person with Laura than I was without her.

7

BUILDING A NEW BRAIN (PART TWO)

Work on my PhD slowed after Laura moved in. Stopped, in fact. Laura
had always been encouraging of my studies; it was me who had grown
lazy.

"You're going to finish that damned PhD, Sarah Vallance, if it's the
last thing you do!" she announced one Sunday morning after I emerged
from my study five minutes after I entered it to suggest that a nice lunch
out might increase my productivity.

It's a universal truth that the person who shares a home with a person who is completing her PhD part-time, even under normal circumstances, suffers. That diminished happiness shrinks even further when
the candidate also happens to be recovering from a traumatic brain
injury. Not only was Laura forced to suffer life with a depressed person
who was prone to inexplicable bouts of rage and craved sex constantly,
but she also had to endure living with a PhD hanging over our heads
like a rope. It was more than any person should bear.

My mother, back in the picture thanks to Laura, made her position
clear. "Drop it. You don't need a PhD!" she said, which made me realize I had no choice but to finish it. I *did* need a PhD. One life lesson I
had learned was that my mother's advice was rarely in my best interests.

Finishing the PhD was a critical step in reclaiming my life, and it had become vital for my self-esteem.

I got back in touch with my doctoral supervisor. He'd assumed grief over my father's death was responsible for my hibernation. I feared that if I was truthful about my accident, he might question my ability to graduate. I questioned that too. Luckily for me, doctoral students take time off from their research for all kinds of different reasons. Grief over a parent's death was as convincing as any of them.

Laura marched me into my study each Saturday and Sunday morning and commanded me to work. *If only it were so simple,* I thought. To prevent me from leaving my study, she tied me to my chair with a long cotton scarf so that I couldn't move anything but my arms. My challenge became more about breaking free rather than working. I turned out to be quite the escape artist. More than once Laura happened upon me lying on the floor spooning George, serenading him with the Carpenters' "Top of the World." Another time she found me tucked up in bed, pretending to sleep. When she discovered me straying from my research, she would drag me back inside the study and secure me in place with the scarf around my waist and a leather belt around my thighs strapping me to my seat for good measure. I couldn't move. She would lock the door from the outside and leave.

My mind wandered. When doing a PhD, almost anything seems more interesting than the research, but I even had difficulty focusing on my distractions. Each one was pasted upon the last to create an elaborate distraction collage—a bird calling out, upon a neighbor opening a window, upon a car door slamming—until I had lost all sense of whatever I sat down to do. I struggled to clear my mind of the chaos inside.

During my first field trip to Singapore, Thailand, and the Philippines, before my father died, I had filled a pile of notebooks with my own observations, interview notes, and scribbles from publications

I had discovered in government offices and university libraries. I had started to type up my notes not long after I returned from that trip, but my father's illness meant I had not finished. In a desperate attempt to focus, I decided to work my way through the remaining notes, writing at least one sentence from each bullet point scribbled inside a page of my notebook. Some of my notes made no sense at all. I couldn't read my own writing, or the words and symbols I had scrawled across the page while attempting to record the salient points of an interview turned out to be gibberish. I studied my scribbles and attempted to turn them into meaningful sentences. For example, *Phil Gov emp extra jobs < income* became *Many government employees in the Philippines are forced to supplement their income by taking second jobs or participating in the underground economies which exist within the civil service.* It was a slow and frustrating process.

One weekend, when I had sat at my desk for more than two hours and achieved nothing, Laura had a brain wave. "Break it down into small chunks," she suggested. "Make a list of exactly what you want to achieve with each chapter you are working on."

That struck me as pure genius.

"Then work your way slowly through each list. Cross things off as you finish them." She sat with me and showed me what she meant, taking a particular chapter and drawing different colored circles on a page, filling each circle with different ideas and connecting them to one another. It was a form of wizardry. Slowly, I was able to weave the various threads together in the semblance of an argument.

On the hour, Laura brought me a snack—a caffe latte from the coffee shop across the road, a piece of cake she had baked, a cappuccino, a panini, a bar of Toblerone, some pieces of licorice. At six p.m., whether I had spent the day productively or not, she would appear holding two glasses of champagne. It was selfless, an act of kindness for which I will be forever grateful. Yes, she had pushed me toward killing my dog—a dog I missed every day—but she had pushed me toward a great many good things too. It made no difference to Laura whether I graduated or not, but she understood that it would make an enormous difference to me.

After months of work, snacks, and champagne, I finally finished. I knew it was bad, but I was hopeful that my examiners would flick through it carelessly, as legend said some do, or, if I was truly lucky, skip the second shoddily constructed case study altogether. Somehow, I had always managed to scrape through by the seat of my pants, and I expected I would do it again. It was, after all, a miracle I'd made it this far—even if only Laura and I understood that. I had managed to write a doctoral thesis with a damaged brain! I submitted it and hoped for the best.

~

"Let's go overseas," Laura suggested over breakfast at a local café the Saturday after I submitted my thesis.

"We could use a holiday," I said.

"No, I mean go overseas *to live*."

"What about George?" I asked instantly, looking down at George asleep on the ground with his head on my foot.

"Bloody George! Does George mean we will never go anywhere?"

I stroked him behind the ears and hoped he wasn't listening. "Not unless Mum will take care of him while we are gone," I said.

"Wouldn't you like to experience a different culture? Live somewhere else?"

"I'm okay here," I said, and I meant it.

She rolled her eyes and groaned. "Jesus! What is wrong with you?"

"Where would you like me to start?"

"You're a pain in the ass," she said, and got up to leave.

"I know," I said, unraveling George's lead from the spine of the table. "But I don't mean to be."

I couldn't explain why I had become so reluctant to venture far from home. Before my accident, I was eager to leave Sydney. The reason I had chosen my PhD topic was so I could move overseas when it was done—after George had died—and live in Southeast Asia. Life, for the healthy-brained me, had been an exercise in accumulating experiences, savoring different things, meeting interesting people. Now I wanted none of that. I needed stability in order to rebuild my life from the ground up. I craved predictability, familiarity, and to be in a place I knew.

But my behavior was anything but consistent. At around the same time I was refusing to move abroad because of George, I decided it would be a good idea to get my motorcycle license. Laura insisted my brain was fine, so I forgot all about the neurologist's warning: *do not sustain a second blow to your head.* Motorbikes were a lot of fun, and I couldn't wait to get myself one.

For six weeks I went to motorcycle-riding classes each Saturday for an hour. I rode a bike around a vast empty parking lot, learning how to use the gears, how to stop, and how to corner. When I took the test for my motorcycle license, I met my examiner in an underground parking garage not far from the local Roads and Traffic Authority office. Unfortunately, the test finished not long after it started, when I drove the motorbike straight into a pylon. I was traveling very slowly, which made things all the more humiliating.

"What say you take a few more lessons and try again in a couple of months?" my examiner said to me as I tried to dismount the bike.

"Have you got that out of your system now?" Laura asked when I got home and told her I would not be getting a motorcycle anytime soon.

I looked at her sheepishly and nodded. I hadn't realized that my coordination, which had been excellent, was another casualty of my accident. Walking the dogs and going to work each day hadn't tested my physical abilities in any real way, but it was clear from the disastrous test that my visuospatial skills had taken a battering thanks to my damaged parietal lobes. It seemed like all the things I'd been most proud of, the things by which I'd identified myself, had been stripped away by my accident.

A week or so after my failure with the motorbike, Laura returned home with a bundle of papers about the Harkness Fellowship, a scholarship program run by the Commonwealth Fund in New York.

"Look at this," she said. "They are looking for people who work in health care. Aged care is a category."

I glanced at the form and passed it back to her, unable to mimic her excitement. "I know nothing about aged care. My PhD is in comparative public administration."

"You work in aged care! How hard can it be?"

"Hard!"

"It's all public policy, isn't it? You should apply. You can choose a topic, as long as it has something to do with aged care."

I stared at the wall.

"Come on! They pay for you to live and study in America for a year! It's one of the best scholarships around. I can study too. I can finish my master's degree! It would be fun!"

"Not long ago, I had an IQ of around eighty. I think that pretty much disqualifies me, don't you?"

"Your brain is fine!"

I reminded her about Toby, the psychologist at the Brain Injury Unit, and the yellow circle, and the fact that less than two years ago I was told I would never work again.

"Do me a favor," she said. "Apply. If you get a fellowship, you can always turn it down."

Her glibness about my accident was a double-edged sword. It made me believe I could pass for someone who was normal, but it was also frustrating. I let it go and did as she said. One of the things I liked most about Laura was that she took charge, allowing me to follow. I put together an application. I wanted to study aged care, my application began. But I really thought it was depressing as hell. The study of dying. I showed her my application.

"It looks dreadful!" she said, screwing up her face to make her point. "Let me type it up properly and make it look nice."

Despite the new application looking attractive, it happened to be frighteningly short on content.

"Let's wait a few days," I said. "I'll show it to Phil." Phil was a professor I had met through work who knew a lot about aged care.

Phil took one look at my application and shook his head. "No one is going to give you a scholarship based on this," he said.

He helped me prepare a different proposal. A decent one. Then he offered to write a reference and suggested two other colleagues whose references would be well regarded.

Laura got to work on my second application. We mailed it, with a two-by-four-inch color photograph of me taken by Laura's friend who was a professional photographer. In it, I was cocking my head slightly and smiling. I looked ridiculously wholesome. I didn't expect to hear back, and not just because of the photo. The fact was that I was a poor choice for a competitive fellowship. But one day about four weeks later, I received a phone call asking me to an interview in front of a panel of four: three professors of medicine and health policy and a senior employee of the federal health department.

I called Laura as soon as I hung up the phone.

"I have zero chance," I told her, trying to manage her expectations. These were clever people. I couldn't fool clever people. I toyed with the idea of pulling out.

"Pull out and I will never speak to you again," Laura said.

"Fine!" I exhaled.

I don't remember the interview, except the chubby, bearded face of the senior government person, who kept tilting his head and looking at me as though he was examining his first dead body. I had taken a beta-blocker an hour before the interview to ensure I didn't experience a repeat of the *Gosford Aged-Care Conference Frozen with Terror Incident*. I may well have looked like a moron, but no one was going to accuse me of looking like a *nervous* moron.

Two weeks later I was driving home from work when my phone rang. It was the chubby, bearded man calling to congratulate me. I had won a Harkness Fellowship. Their recommendation was that I go to Georgetown University for a year, but that was a matter for further discussion. They would send paperwork in due course and I'd apply for a visa. I was expected in New York for an orientation in early August.

At the time of the call, I was driving around a curvy stretch of road and nearly slammed my car into a sandstone wall. I pulled onto a quiet street and called Laura. I could barely speak. She screamed so loudly that I dropped the phone onto the floor of the car. By the time I picked it up and said goodbye, nausea had crept up through my insides. I nursed the phone in my lap and waited for it to ring, for the chubby, bearded man to let me know he'd made a mistake. It didn't ring.

At home I called my mother.

"Well, that's lovely, darling, but who do you suppose will look after George?"

"I was hoping you might."

"Were you," she said, as a statement not a question.

"Well, yes. It's only for a year."

"*Only* a *year*?" I had hoped my mother would be so astounded that I had gone from being on a disability pension to winning a scholarship to America for a year she would have happily taken George. I hung the phone up on her and burst into tears.

114

When I managed to compose myself, I thought of my father, who would have been thrilled with my news. Delighted. Proud. He would have insisted that they cared for George while I was gone.

In the absence of my father, my secret weapon with my mother was Laura. My mother adored her. Laura was thoughtful and well-behaved, and never said things like "fuck off," except to me, and my mother never saw that. My mother, highly critical of almost everyone, couldn't find fault with Laura.

My mother and Laura had lots in common, including wanting my dog dead. "Oh, putting down Bess was the smartest thing you ever did!" my mother said, causing me to explode, when she saw us a couple of weeks after Bess had died. "Nobody can be expected to live with a dog like that!" She rolled her eyes for emphasis.

They talked about the theater and books they were reading. I felt left out, but I was happy to have an ally, someone who could negotiate with my mother. I felt like I was Palestine, my mother was Israel, and Laura was President Clinton.

"You have to help get her to take George!" I told Laura. "Otherwise I'm not going."

"You're an idiot if you don't go!" she shouted.

"Please ask her to take George. She listens to you. She loves you!"

Laura called my mother and invited her along to an organic food market on Saturday morning. She looked at me and winked while she made arrangements to collect my mother.

At lunchtime, Laura returned home from the market with three bags of fresh produce and a big smile. "She's taking George!"

I threw myself at her and we nearly toppled over.

"You know the reason you and your mother don't get on?" Laura asked as she unpacked the groceries.

"She hates me."

"She's jealous of you. Not of your brother, just of you. Because you're the girl. You've had the good jobs, you're doing the PhD, and now you've won a Harkness Fellowship. She gave up everything to become a mother. You represent everything she sacrificed."

"If she was jealous of anything, it was the relationship I had with my father. Let's not forget I have a damaged brain. Not much to be jealous about there."

"But you've recovered from it."

I shook my head. "You're wrong."

"Trust me on this. I know what I'm talking about. Your mother is jealous. So now you know what the problem is, it's time to get over it."

8

AMERICA

In August 1997, approximately two and half years after my accident, Laura and I reluctantly checked out of our suite in the sumptuous Warwick Hotel in New York City, where we had stayed during the weeklong orientation. We weren't accustomed to such luxury but would very much have liked to be. During the orientation we had met the other fellows, their partners, and their offspring.

I had hoped there might be another moron among us, someone who had also managed to slip through the fissures of the selection process, but I was disappointed. The other fellows were very clever, and almost all of them were medical doctors. "We are the top one percent," I overheard one of the British doctors telling a small group of fellows, and I felt something inside my stomach lurch. Later, I smiled when I heard another British doctor refer to the first British doctor as an arrogant prick. I was in the top 1 percent of Harkness fellows who had suffered a mild traumatic brain injury. I decided to keep my mouth shut almost permanently, so people would mistake me for a deep thinker and selective mute. The truth was, the selection panel would have been hard-pressed to find someone less qualified and less capable than me. I was an entirely unsuitable candidate, so I channeled all my energy into hiding my limitations from the others.

The other fellows were nice, interesting people, but I felt like an alien. During the orientation week, small groups started to form, but I stayed on the fringes, hovering around on my own, wary of everyone and everything. They probably considered me to be prickly or rude, or perhaps just woefully socially inept. I didn't mean to be rude, but it was difficult to hide my awkwardness, and the massive chip on my shoulder seemed to double in size each day since we had arrived in America. At the various social gatherings during our orientation where our significant others were invited along, I stuck to Laura's side, allowing her to do the talking for both of us.

Luckily for me, the Harkness Fellowship program wasn't just one of the most generous fellowships around, it also happened to be one of the least onerous in terms of output. Fellows were given free rein to spend the year as they wished. The 1997–1998 cohort, of which I was one, was the first focused exclusively around health policy. Each of us had been matched with a mentor who would supervise our research. At the end of our year, we were expected to present a paper outlining our findings to members of the Commonwealth Fund, the other fellows, and their mentors. That was the only requirement of our year in America. One paper. Apart from that, the fellows would convene every quarter in New York to meet with one another, listen to guest speakers, and do fun things like attend baseball games. One of the purposes of the fellowship was to allow us to immerse ourselves in American society and culture.

The other fellows were about to be sent to various universities across the country: the University of Washington; Harvard; Johns Hopkins; Columbia; and the University of California, San Francisco. I was the only one due to travel to Georgetown.

Laura and I caught the train to Washington, DC, and began our search for an apartment. We settled on a one-bedroom place in an old converted hotel in Dupont Circle, which was within our budget and a short walk to most of what we wanted in DC. Dupont Circle was close to George Washington University, where Laura planned to take three marketing classes for her master's degree, and a thirty-minute walk from Georgetown. It was also the epicenter of DC's gay community.

Our building looked majestic from the outside and boasted a spectacular marble foyer and ballroom on the ground floor. Inside, our apartment had slits for windows and synthetic gray carpet and felt like a prison cell. The kitchen wasn't much bigger than an orange box. Ours was one of hundreds of apartments in the building, and most of our neighbors were gay men. They were friendly with the exception of the middle-aged bald man living opposite us, who wore tight leather pants and bright-pink tank tops and had thick black hair sprouting out from any exposed skin. Slung across his shoulder was a teddy bear backpack. When we smiled and said hi, he stared straight through us.

Our apartment was on Fifteenth Street. What could be more thrilling than a city so vast it had run out of proper street names! On the day we moved into our apartment, the building manager took us aside and warned us about the neighborhood. He was a weedy man not much older than twenty with acne and a giant Adam's apple. Judging by the *Playboy* magazine he buried under his desk when we entered the office, he wasn't a homosexual.

"Don't go past Fourteenth Street," he said. We looked at him blankly. Australians are not used to being in a city with streets that needed to be avoided. "Just make sure, okay?"

"Don't even think about it," Laura said to me as we rode the elevator to our tiny new apartment. "I know you. I know what you're thinking!" I smiled and nodded.

Neither of us slept during our first night in the new apartment. Helicopters circled above us, their searchlights shining into our bedroom. Sirens raged all night, up our street, down the next. Fire trucks, police cars, ambulances. War had broken out. We lay in each other's arms waiting for our building to be hit by a missile. *We will die here, on our first night in our tiny apartment in Dupont Circle,* I thought. The next morning we were relieved to find our street in exactly the same state it was the day before. Buildings hadn't burned to the ground; bombs hadn't wiped out entire apartment blocks. We visited a pharmacy and bought two sets of earplugs.

A week later, when Laura was at university, I locked the apartment door behind me, took the elevator downstairs, and walked outside into a bright sunlit day. I walked past apartment blocks just like ours, past stand-alone buildings too big to be private residences, past consular buildings representing countries I had never heard of. I turned a corner and walked past a small park with a single empty bench and neatly trimmed hedges. At the first set of traffic lights, I crossed Fourteenth Street. More apartment blocks, more buildings. Cars whizzed past and trucks stopped in the street, their hazard lights blinking as men traipsed inside lugging large pieces of furniture. I reached another set of traffic lights and waited for the pedestrian light. Thirteenth Street. At the next block, the gardens in front of the apartment blocks became overgrown and crowded with useless bits of electrical equipment and old, rusted chairs missing cushions. In the driveway of one block a car was supported on bricks with its hood open. Three men sat on crates beside the car sharing something from a thermos. I smiled at them and they smiled back. I crossed another set of lights and had started walking up another block when I saw a man walking toward me with a golden retriever.

I smiled at the man. "Do you mind if I say hello to your dog?"

"Please, be my guest."

I knelt on one knee and patted the dog, who wagged his tail and licked my face.

"Beautiful dog."

"Thanks," he said. "You're not from around here, are you?"

I laughed. "Is it that obvious?"

"You're the only white person here."

I told him I was from Sydney and that I had only just arrived in DC.

"Sydney, Australia? That's a long way from here."

I nodded.

"Can I give you some advice?" he said.

"Please."

"Turn around and walk back. It's not safe around here. You know, lots of guns and drugs and stuff."

"Even if you're just passing through? In the middle of the day?" My chest thumped with excitement.

"Especially if you're just passing through," he said. "I'll walk back with you. I'm headed that way too."

DC was an exciting city to explore. Even if Laura and I spent the year just poking around its streets instead of studying and going to class, we wouldn't have been able to see it all. Since hearing I had won a fellowship, Laura had devoted her time to writing details of every museum, gallery, park, restaurant, bar, and café she deemed worthy of a visit in a tiny green notebook. She devised a color-coded system using sticky notes to distinguish museums, monuments, food, drink, and so on. She was an excellent traveler, keen to maximize every spare moment we had and to make every meal, every coffee, every glass of champagne we swallowed memorable. I, of course, would forget pretty much all of it. But the distractions of a new city and the opportunities to do new things meant I also forgot about my depression. And without my depression, my rage subsided. Laura was right. Leaving home was the best thing we could have done.

We stood in awe of the Washington Monument, the Lincoln Memorial, the Jefferson Memorial. We spent our days wandering through seventeen Smithsonian museums without paying a cent. We visited every art museum, and I saw every Edward Hopper painting on display in the capital. I sat in front of his paintings for ages without even twitching. I reclined on a chair in front of *People in the Sun*, and Laura snapped my photo. It felt like a holiday, and when I could distract myself from the fellowship and detach myself somehow from my damaged brain, I realized I was happy.

Because I kept nagging about wanting to see the real DC, not the sanitized stretches of polished marble and rainbow flags dangling from café windows, a friend who worked for the State Department took us on a drive around the southeast quarter.

"This is the dangerous part of the city," she said. It was lunchtime and the streets were stark. There was no one around apart from a small group of kids huddled outside a corner shop. We passed what my friend told us were crack houses, dilapidated old buildings that jumped to life at night. I wanted to see things come alive, to be part of the action.

"Can we come back one evening?" I asked my friend.

"Are you crazy?" she asked, tilting her head to one side. "I would never come here at night. *You* should never come here at night either."

"Just ignore her," Laura said.

My friend laughed.

"Hard to believe she's thirty-four."

That afternoon, my friend took us to the State Department building. We walked for what felt like a mile along a linoleum corridor on the seventh floor. I hoped to catch a glimpse of Madeleine Albright, or at least her office. Outside the secretary's suite two Corinthian pillars led into the Treaty Room. We were disappointed to learn that Ms. Albright was out of town.

I spent my days wandering the streets of the nation's capital, stopping only to eat and to drink. New York is my favorite city in America, but DC comes a close second. I took the bus and got off at random stops to explore new neighborhoods. Laura, a far more conscientious student than I, spent her days in the library at George Washington.

I immersed myself in the novelty of American television and did everything I could to delay starting work on my research project, but eventually I called my mentor and introduced myself. It was a short conversation. She was curt and told me how busy she was, and I felt, even before I had met her, that I was wasting her time.

At her office in Georgetown, I knocked on her door, and she asked me to wait outside for a few minutes. When she invited me in she pointed to a chair. I liked her less in person than when we had spoken on the phone.

"You can get a PhD from the University of Sydney?" she asked.

"Yes, yes you can."

"And why would you want to do that?"

Her question disarmed me, and I had no answer. She was clever, and I was not. I dropped my head and prepared for the worst.

She didn't like my research topic and told me I should choose another. I didn't much like my topic either. I had cobbled it together quickly to win the scholarship. I never had even the vaguest notion of following through and conducting the research, because I didn't believe I had a snowflake's chance in hell of winning a Harkness Fellowship.

"I will try to think of one," I said, looking behind her at a credenza covered in photographs of her and Bill Clinton, her and Bill and Hillary, and a lot of other people I didn't recognize who were clearly very important or they wouldn't have been sitting in silver frames on her credenza.

"You do that," she said.

I felt like an impostor. A fraud. This woman had a mind like an MRI machine. She had peered inside at the wasteland of my brain and wanted nothing to do with me. I didn't blame her. I took the long way home, wondering how best to break the news to Laura.

Laura pondered my news and decided a drink might be in order, so we caught a cab to a bar in Adams Morgan and drank as much wine as we could. I woke the next day and realized I still needed a research topic. Two weeks later, I showed up at my mentor's office for an appointment I thought we had made. She scolded me and told me

I had made a mistake. She couldn't see me for another three weeks due to her travel commitments.

Laura kept in touch with a couple of the other fellows. They loved their mentors and were making excellent progress with their research. I had achieved nothing. Since meeting my mentor, I spent my days at home, slumped on the sofa in front of the TV, convinced that coming to America was a huge mistake. I was way out of my depth, and it was going to become frighteningly obvious to everyone around me. I hadn't been able to disguise my damaged brain from my mentor. I was certain she'd contact the Commonwealth Fund and let them know they needed to cancel my visa and send me home. I decided to lie low until that happened and watch as much TV as I could. On *Jerry Springer*, I saw a white man who liked to dress up in a Ku Klux Klan outfit, smear fried chicken all over his body, and screw black prostitutes. The world is full of crazy people, I decided, and a lot of them seemed to be in America.

Around one month after we had settled in DC, a dinner was organized for the Harkness fellows at a hotel on Pennsylvania Avenue, and I was seated next to a woman who headed up the Visiting Nurse Association in New York. Her name was Amy, and I liked her almost instantly.

"How are things coming along with your research?" she asked.

"Not great," I said. "I haven't come up with a topic yet."

"I'm sorry to hear that," she said, looking concerned.

"It's my own fault."

We talked a bit more, and she asked if everything was okay.

"This sounds ridiculous," I admitted, "but I'm scared of my mentor."

"That's not good," she said. "You have a whole year here."

"I know," I said, feeling pathetic.

"A good friend of mine is a professor in the Department of Social Medicine at Harvard," Amy said. "She's a lovely woman and very approachable. I'm sure she would be happy to take you on. I can get in touch with her and ask. You can't waste a year with someone you don't like."

Later that evening, I talked to Laura about the possibility of us moving to Boston. She was ecstatic.

"I can switch across to Harvard and finish my coursework. That would look better on my CV. Let's do it!" she said, hugging me. "It's going to be fun!"

I woke the next morning to find an email from Amy telling me that the Harvard professor had agreed to mentor me. My mood shifted almost instantly.

My new mentor was warm, sharp, funny, and kind, all of which I gathered from our first fifteen-minute phone call. She was polite enough to say she would be thrilled to mentor me. I explained that I really hadn't made any progress, that I needed to find a new research topic, and she assured me not to worry. She had a couple of ideas that might be of interest.

I called the program coordinator at the Commonwealth Fund to tell her the news. She wasn't happy. Switching mentors presented an awkward and unprecedented situation. "What about all the trouble your Georgetown mentor has gone to?" I explained that I had only met my mentor twice and that on the second meeting she couldn't see me because I had apparently made a mistake with the date. I tried to be as polite about her as I could, but I made it clear we had got off to a poor start. When I mentioned the name of the dinner guest who had set things in motion with the professor at Harvard, the tone of our conversation changed.

"Alright," the woman from the Commonwealth Fund finally conceded. "Let's see what can be done."

People needed to be talked to, and agreements made. Then I needed to ring my Georgetown mentor and explain why I didn't want to work with her. I had wasted the first six weeks of the fellowship, and I couldn't afford to waste any more time. I wrote down exactly what I needed to tell her, counted to ten, and picked up the phone. She was cold and aloof, and I was relieved that I would never have to see her again.

Laura and I bequeathed our front-row tickets for Gladys Knight and the Pips to my friend in the State Department and bought tickets instead for a train to Boston that weekend. Our departure from DC happened to coincide with the end of the Promise Keepers rally, in which one million Evangelical Christian men had gathered to keep their promise to the Lord, stay faithful to their wives, and tend to their children. The whole experience was creepy. Union Station heaved with men, heads bowed, holding hands, spreading the Lord's word. It was an odd spectacle for an Australian: a giant gathering of men where no one was drunk, vomiting, smashing beer bottles over people's heads, or urinating in the street. I wondered what was worse: a cheating husband or a man who enjoyed events like this.

Our train car was packed with Promise Keepers going home after the rally. One of them strummed a guitar while the others sang. It was a long nine-hour ride, but we were going to Harvard!

The first thing we did in Boston was visit Filene's Basement, where we purchased some of the ugliest, most affordable cold-weather clothing we had ever seen. We had lost a lot of money breaking our lease in DC, and rents in Boston were even higher. In her bright-green ski jacket, Laura looked like a cross between the Michelin woman and a giant toadstool. I resembled Joseph in his amazing technicolor dreamcoat in a fluorescent-green jacket with purple-and-red trim around the collar and sleeves. At least I would not have to worry about crossing the street at night in that coat. We looked absurd—two grown women wearing coats favored by small children—but we consoled ourselves with the fact that we were warm. The night before, a homeless man had frozen to death in Boston Common.

We spent a day walking around campus in our bright new coats. The Harvard students dressed in the uniform of the wealthy and privileged: black overcoats and occasionally muted tones of brown, any color reserved for scarves and mittens and their rosy upper-middle-class cheeks.

"Harvard attracts millions of badly dressed tourists each year," I told Laura, watching her cringe as we explored the campus. "On the balance of probability, some of them will look even worse than we do. So let's not worry about looking conspicuous. In any case, would you even *want* to be mistaken for one of these Harvard students?"

"Yes," she said.

There was a bit too much Ralph Lauren on campus for my liking. I was happy with my practical winter coat, and I enjoyed flaunting it around.

In Harvard Yard, Laura fumbled inside her pocket and produced an old camera loaded with black-and-white film.

"That's the answer!" I said. "Let's use that camera for all our winter photos! No one will ever see our coats!" We each took turns standing in front of the John Harvard statue and took photos. It was incredible to think that I was at Harvard. On a scholarship. I squeezed Laura's hand to make sure I wasn't dreaming.

She hugged me.

"How did we end up here?" I asked her.

"I have no idea, but we did!"

We walked across to the Coop later that day and bought a Harvard collar and leash to send home for George.

Laura's charm garnered us an invitation to stay at another fellow's apartment in Cambridge until we found a place of our own. We had arrived at a bad time of year for real estate, and the only available apartments in our price range looked like the crack dens we'd seen in DC. After a week of looking at all manner of hideous, windowless, roach-infested apartments, we realized we couldn't afford to live in Cambridge or Boston. We set our sights on Somerville, the slightly rough-around-the-edges town that borders Cambridge to the north, and we liked the first apartment we saw there. It was the only residence on the street that didn't have a PebbleCrete front garden filled with statues of angels and garden gnomes. Better still, we liked the landlord. I let Laura deal with him. He seemed to like her, and she liked him until he told her he had a passion for collecting guns. American men liked Laura. No one looked twice at me, apart from a chihuahua in a trinket shop on Commonwealth Avenue that stared me down from his velvet bed on the shop counter before lunging and clamping his jaws down over my hand.

~

My mother emailed us days after we moved into our apartment. She had experienced twenty-four hours of hell with George when a thunderstorm hit while she was at work. When she returned home, she found a broken window and no George. George, it turned out, had leapt straight through a glass window—but not just any glass window. He chose the lounge room window above the garage, where the drop to the ground was more than twenty feet and the ground below was concrete. George's hair and blood were stuck to what remained of the windowpane. My mother wrote that she left a frantic message on her answering machine: "If you're calling about a brown kelpie called George, please leave your name and number and I will call you as soon as I get back from looking for him. Thank you."

She drove around the neighborhood, past George's favorite haunts—the back of the Pizza Hut, the back of KFC down the road. George had mates there who snuck food out to him, or so my mother believed. She had found him there before, too tired to walk home, his belly the size of a soccer ball. It horrified me to think that my mother let George roam the streets; I never let him out of my sight. My mother said that as the rain got harder and there was no sign of George, she went home and found a message from a woman at a childcare center about a mile away who had found George.

My mother hopped back into her car and raced over a railway line, over the six-lane Pacific Highway. It was a miracle George crossed either without being killed. She pulled up outside the childcare center to find a pretty blonde woman sitting on the front step with her arm around George. Then my mother had to endure the indignity of tugging George by the leash to get him to leave his new girlfriend. Eventually the woman coaxed George into my mother's car. The email ended with: *The glazier just left. $300 for a new window.*

My instinct was to take the next flight home. Laura promised me that would not be necessary.

"We'll buy your mother a nice thank-you present and post it to her. Today," she said. And without further discussion, Laura went into Boston that afternoon and bought my mother a scarf. She mailed it with a thank-you note she signed from both of us.

~

I met my new mentor, Liz, in her office at the Department of Social Medicine. There are highly intelligent people, like my Georgetown mentor, who make no secret of their intellectual superiority. And there are highly intelligent people like my Harvard mentor—humble, generous, and kind—with no need whatsoever to assert their superiority over anyone. Five or so years older than me, slight, and dark haired, Liz had two young kids and a husband who worked as a management consultant.

In one of our earliest conversations Liz told me that she struggled with depression. I wanted to leap up from my chair and hug her for her candor. The fact that she also happened to be one of the smartest people I had ever met left me in awe of her. My new mentor spoke to me like a friend, a confidant. But she also illuminated all of my intellectual anxieties, and I worried that in befriending her, I would let her down. I wasn't ready to be honest about my own struggles with anyone other than Laura.

On the way out from her office, I spotted a flyer on a communal table that listed volunteering opportunities for Harvard students. A charity called Little Brothers–Friends of the Elderly needed volunteers to spend time with low-income elders. I scribbled down the name and contact number of the person who managed the volunteering program and called her later that day. I had always liked old people, and better still, most of the old people I had known throughout my life had seemed to like me too. My happiest childhood memories involved my grandmother. After she died I befriended an elderly neighbor who was bedridden with asthma. I used to drop by after school and sit with her and hold her hand while she wheezed. She loved to listen to my stories about school—stories I embellished because my school life was so dull. When she died I found another elderly neighbor to visit. I may have been a terrible candidate for a Harkness Fellowship, but I was the perfect volunteer for the elderly.

I contacted Little Brothers, and after attending an interview and submitting to a police check, I was matched with three very poor elderly women. I set up meetings with them almost immediately. Liz put me in touch with a couple of other research students who were working with her, and I slowly began to learn about the issues confronting the poor elderly population in Massachusetts.

All of Liz's students raved about how lovely and supportive she was, and all the glowing tributes turned out to be true. Thanks largely to Liz, I was enthusiastic about my time at Harvard and my research project, even though I had still not chosen a topic. It was liberating to be able to study something unrelated to my PhD. I knew that if I kept my research topic simple, I would be able to deliver something that would be acceptable both to Liz and to the Commonwealth Fund. My job in aged care turned out to have been a blessing. I had already spent around eighteen months writing research papers.

From one of Liz's students, I learned about a foster care program, through which the government of Massachusetts paid a weekly stipend to people who offered a room in their house to poor elders. The idea struck me as extraordinary. Few things seemed worse than being consigned to a nursing home, but the idea of moving into a house with strangers and being dependent upon them for care and food seemed fraught with danger. I decided that my research topic would be to determine the effectiveness of this rather odd program. Liz seemed to like the idea, so I set up a series of meetings with the people who established the program and the people who oversaw it, and they put me in touch with a number of families who "fostered" an old person through the program and agreed to let me visit them. Out of curiosity, I asked the three women I volunteered with how they would feel about moving into a stranger's home. They reacted with horror. "I'd rather die now," one of them said.

I formed a close friendship with one of the elderly women whom Little Brothers had matched me with. Constance Bailey was an eighty-eight-year-old African American woman with no friends or family. Once we got to know each other, I visited her almost daily and soon came to think of her as family, the family I wished I had had. Connie's life had been tragic, yet somehow she had emerged from all the trauma with the ability to laugh. She was funny and kind, and she loved animals more than people. She told me she had never had a friendship like ours before, and I felt the same. I loved Connie in a way I had never loved anyone but my father, and I saw myself in her. When it would finally come time to return home, she would be the person I missed most, the indisputable highlight of my time at Harvard, and my fondest memory of my year in America.

Worried I had wasted the first six weeks of the fellowship, I had started my research as soon as Liz agreed to my new topic. I worked hard, doing everything I could to finish the interviews and allow myself a lot of time to write up my findings. Flying by the seat of my pants might have worked for me when my brain was healthy, but I knew it wasn't going to work this time. The other fellows were not only considerably smarter than me but also a lot more ambitious. I told myself I would have to work around one hundred times harder than they did to pull off a reasonable piece of research.

The second half of my year at Harvard took an unfortunate turn when I was taken to the hospital in Cambridge early one morning with chest pains. After a night in intensive care and a day of tests, my results came back: borderline positive for tuberculosis. The doctor ordered a lung X-ray and noticed calcification on my left lung; I was sure it was a result of a bad case of pneumonia I had had in my late twenties, but he was having none of it. He thought I may have picked up TB during a visit to the Philippines.

"The law in Massachusetts requires every person who tests positive to undergo a course of medication that ensures the disease does not return," he said. "If it comes back, there's a ninety percent chance it will kill you."

"Can't we wait till then?" I asked.

I visited a TB clinic around the corner from our home in Somerville and left with an armful of pills. A lovely nurse from Haiti told me I had to take the medication each day for one year.

"You aren't infectious, so no need to worry about spreading it around, but during the year, you can't drink alcohol," she said.

"No alcohol for a year?"

"That's right."

I did not want to even contemplate the prospect of a year without alcohol.

Isoniazid is a highly powerful drug that can lead, in a tiny number of cases, to chemically induced hepatitis. Within weeks on the medication, I fell ill, and blood tests revealed I was one of the tiny number of cases. It seemed to me that I was one of the unluckiest people on earth. Not only was I still struggling with the aftereffects of a brain injury, I had been struck down by hepatitis. Physically, I felt terrible. Emotionally, I felt almost as bad.

By the time I got sick, I had managed to conduct most of my interviews and to consult all the relevant publications for my research paper. The interviews had gone well, and I had been able to concentrate for the allotted time and to ask most of the relevant follow-up questions. I had also managed to improve my note-taking and could, for the most part, decipher my own handwriting. None of the people I interviewed would have imagined that I had suffered a traumatic brain injury three or so years earlier. I hoped not, anyway.

As soon as I felt stronger, I started to write up my research. My conclusion was the concern I had had from the start: that paying people to open up their homes to elderly people was fraught with risk. Without thorough screening of families and frequent follow-up checks, the opportunity for abuse seemed to outweigh the benefits. I managed to cobble together a draft of my paper to send to Liz. She made some suggestions, and after a couple of follow-up calls, I was able to finalize my presentation.

Somehow, I managed to present my research paper to the panel of professors assembled by the Commonwealth Fund and the other research fellows. I can say with absolute certainty that mine was the lamest presentation by a country mile. But thanks to Liz, who stepped up to help answer questions from the audience, and a beta-blocker that helped control my anxiety, the presentation passed without humiliation.

Lying in bed one morning, I heard a letter drop through the slit in our front door. The envelope was from the University of Sydney, and I opened it eagerly. My eyes scanned the page and stopped at a sentence that said I needed to rewrite a chapter of my dissertation in order to graduate. The examiners actually *had* read my second case study, after all. I crawled back into bed and pulled the covers up over my head.

9

ANGER IS A (NOT SO) SHORT MADNESS
HORACE (EPISTLES BOOK 1)
(WITH A SLIGHT MODIFICATION)

After more than a year in America, Laura and I returned to Sydney in September 1998. We loved America, and Laura wanted to stay forever. But while the time away from home had given me fleeting moments of joy and freedom, I had spent the majority of my time in America peering over the giant chip on my shoulder, waiting for someone to expose me for the idiot I was. The facade of trying to appear something other than moronic had exhausted me.

We arrived at the airport, hired a rental car, and drove straight to my mother's house, where we planned to stay for a couple of days, until the furniture was moved back inside our house. I was so excited to see George I could barely contain myself. As soon as we arrived, I left the key in the ignition, slammed the car door shut, and leapt up the front steps. George was asleep on the sun-filled porch, wearing his crimson Harvard collar. "George!" I squealed. He glanced up, squinted at me for an instant, then got up and wandered inside the house.

"George! It's me!" I called after him, following him inside and ignoring my mother. He refused to even glance at me. My mother hugged Laura. "It's so good to see you!" she said. We shared a perfunctory hug before I set off in pursuit of George again. He loped toward the kitchen and drank water from his bowl, spilling most of it on the floor. I knelt on one knee in a puddle of water, threw my arms around him, and squeezed him. I kissed the top of his head. He fought his way free of me and wandered through the house to the front porch.

He had not forgotten me. He was giving me the cold shoulder. I spent an hour following him from room to room as he did his best to ignore me. I tickled him behind the ears; I tried to roll him on his back so I could rub his belly; I told him how much I loved him, how much I had missed him. He wasn't interested. I had abandoned him. Left him alone for eternity with my mother. Surely, I of all people should have known what that would be like! How was he to know I was ever coming back?

I'm only a dog! he seemed to say as he sat with his head pointed in every direction but mine.

Relations between my mother and George appeared frosty.

"He was not an easy houseguest," my mother said, looking at him as though she had just found a stash of crack in his bedroom.

He shot her a look that said, *You are a nightmare! I jumped out a glass window and crossed a highway and a railway line to get away from you! That's how bad it was!*

I tried tickling him under the chin, but he eyed me coolly and then stared at the floor.

"He likes his afternoon visits to KFC. Don't you, George?" my mother said, trying to be funny. "I lost count of the times he rolled himself back up the front steps looking pregnant."

George glanced up at her quickly and walked into another room. What I really wanted to ask was why she had left the front door open for George to go wandering the streets, but I thought better of it. My mother had always been one to leave her front door open. I could almost hear her shriek, *Why should I live like a prisoner in my own home! Just because I'm looking after your bloody dog?*

Two days later, on the morning we were due to move back home, George finally thawed. Laura and I were sitting on my mother's sofa drinking tea when he ambled across to me and rested his head in my lap. He prodded me with his muzzle, and I tickled the hair behind his ears. He closed his eyes, and I started to cry. We stayed like that for nearly half an hour. He had forgotten his anger. It had been a hell of a long year, but we were together again. That was all that mattered.

~

My body needed the better part of a year to recover from my bout of chemically induced hepatitis. Home in Sydney, I visited a respiratory physician who studied my test results and ordered a CT scan of my lungs before telling me he could almost guarantee I didn't have, nor had I ever had, TB. My mother remembered that I had been vaccinated against TB when we lived in England for the year of my father's sabbatical, when I was seven. That would account for my borderline positive test result. *Why hadn't she mentioned this when Laura had rung her from Cambridge to tell her I was starting treatment for TB?* I wondered.

Laura had finished her master's degree in America, and she found a job in a large advertising agency within weeks of us returning home. When Laura went to work, I spent most of each day in bed, stirring myself only to walk George or to do the grocery shopping. Home from work, Laura tended to me, cooking healthy meals and being kind enough to drink in private so I wasn't tempted to do more harm to my poor, poisoned liver. Slowly I started to feel better.

I had given up my job in aged care before we moved to America and found myself back home with no source of income. I contacted the bank and made arrangements to reduce my mortgage repayments until I was feeling well enough to work. Money we'd collected from letting our house while we were in America had paid down the mortgage, and I was still ahead with my repayments.

To save myself wasting yet more of my life on something I knew wouldn't be a long-term plan, I enrolled in a graduate diploma program in Human Resource Management at the University of New South Wales. My goal was to find work in the corporate sector. Switching from government or the not-for-profit sector to private enterprise is difficult at the best of times, and it didn't help that I was innumerate. A qualification in HR might make the move simpler. I had set up my career with the intention of working only in government, but there was no way I could go back; not after Rosie, the social worker, had told my boss in the Premier's Department I was brain damaged and incapable of returning to work.

If I had the talent and the means, I would have stopped work to write full time. I dreamed of writing a novel or some short stories. But I feared that my mother had been right when she dismissed my early attempts at writing, and I had convinced myself that while *not* writing would make me unhappy, trying to write and *failing* would be heartbreak. I might never recover. A delusion can be a handy thing to cling to, and by not writing—and therefore not failing at it—I could kid myself into thinking I still had the possibility of succeeding.

If there was an easier option, something I had less chance of screwing up, I would grab it. There was also the matter of money. I had a mortgage and a dog, and I needed an income. I dragged myself to lectures a couple of evenings each week, learned about recruitment and employment law and remuneration, and was delighted when I came first in three subjects. Nearly four years had passed since my accident, and I was starting to feel normal again. My brain was a lot better than it had been at any time since the accident. I thought more clearly, I could hold an argument, and I no longer had periods when my brain shut down midthought.

I used the period of my convalescence to rewrite the case study chapter for my doctoral thesis. By the time I had finished, I was confident that I had done the best that I could. My supervisor read the revised chapter and agreed; it was ready. I resubmitted my entire thesis and hoped like hell my three examiners would be satisfied with the result.

Within a week of finishing my HR exams, I found myself inside the offices of a newspaper company, interviewing for a job as HR manager. I sat in front of the publisher, the executive editor, and someone whose job title I didn't catch. It was the first HR job I had ever applied for. My CV boasted a stint at Harvard, a glowing academic record from my graduate diploma in HR, and the word "submitted" next to the words "PhD in Government and Public Administration." On paper, no one would ever suspect me of having a damaged brain.

As we approached the end of the interview, the publisher inched forward in his chair and asked me if I was a "people person."

"Um, no," I said, deciding there was no point in lying. "I'm afraid not."

"When can you start?" he asked.

I started work in December 1999 at one of the largest papers in the country, with an editorial, advertising, and circulation staff of around four hundred. A desk had been cleared for me in a small room in the Finance Department while a permanent office was prepared. I had a phone but no computer. A huge pile of old newspapers sat underneath my desk waiting to be transported to the library for safekeeping. In the meantime, the pile spawned colonies of paper lice that feasted on my legs. I spent my days scratching at my shins like a madwoman, waiting for something to happen that required the services of an HR manager.

One morning, after I was relocated to my permanent office and given a computer, everything changed. It started slowly, with a trickle of people wanting to talk to me. Within weeks a line of people snaked outside my door. The issues raised were mostly trivial, sometimes strange, and occasionally disturbing.

Someone had smeared feces over the walls of the men's toilets, and the cleaners had—justifiably—complained. I was expected to establish the identity of the perpetrator. Inexplicably, everyone I spoke to seemed to believe the culprit was one of the paper's section editors. Eventually I put this one in the "too hard" basket and gave up.

Another time, a senior sub editor had been caught watching granny porn on his office computer, in full view of his female colleagues. A photographer had "stolen" a company car for the weekend and driven his family to Brisbane. A sub editor picked his nose and arranged his snot in patterns on his computer screen, while participating in a virtual-reality game in which he referred to himself as the "Clit Commander." My graduate diploma in HR had not prepared me for any such incidents, so I made things up as I went along. That was the fun part of my new job.

Months after I started at the paper, I returned home from work to discover a letter from the University of Sydney. Less than six months after I sent it off for review, my examiners had reread my thesis. I tore open the envelope and was delighted to find that I had satisfied the requirements for a doctorate, and that I would graduate in October 2000. My legs started to give way, so I sat down on my old IKEA sofa, beneath that long-forgotten pockmark, and read the letter again.

So much had happened since I had returned home from Tim's farm on the night of my accident and placed my toaster inside the freezer. That night I had no clue I had sustained a traumatic brain injury, no clue I would lose my job and end up on a disability pension, no clue about what lay ahead. Five years later I had achieved what I once feared might have been impossible. In a matter of months, I would be standing on a stage in the Great Hall at the University of Sydney, wearing my father's square academic hat, and receiving a doctorate.

For four years I had clung to the idea of that PhD as the benchmark of my recovery. Only when I had been awarded the degree would I consider myself to be normal again. I had sat at a desk in a room that stank of dog urine and taught myself to read and write. I had spent days scouring a dictionary to comprehend words I no longer understood, and weeks writing each of those words and their meanings into a notebook. I had spent months copying slabs of text onto a writing pad, and reading and rereading things until I was certain my words matched the words on the page of a book or journal article. I had spent years trying to teach my brain to think on its own, to analyze and interpret ideas, and to make judgments of my own based on what I had learned. When I knew nothing but depression and anger, I'd poured myself into those self-assigned tasks. My PhD had given me a goal and kept me going, even at my darkest times, when I feared I had no chance at all of finishing.

My dissertation was not very good. I knew that. But my circumstances had been extraordinary. Years after I had started my PhD, I had received a letter, which started with the word "Congratulations," telling me I had *satisfied the requirements for a PhD*. I sank back into the sofa and read the letter a third time. I wished my father was alive so I could tell him.

I called Laura, and she guessed my news from the tone of my voice. "You did it!" she shouted into the phone.

"*We* did it!" I said. "You deserve it as much as I do! Where shall we go to celebrate?"

~

My new job as HR manager was the first position I had ever held where I was at everyone's disposal. A lot of unhappy people worked at the paper, and they were delighted to have a sounding board. I tried to point out that my job wasn't to buy people new laptops, or to restock the stationery cupboard, or to shift the panels of a workstation to improve someone's view. No one seemed to hear me.

My days were suddenly filled with listening to people who wanted a new chair or a promotion or a pay increase because they were worth a lot more than $200,000 a year. The fact they had penned only two stories that ran in the past twelve months, one with an error that had cost the paper hundreds of thousands of dollars in legal bills, had nothing to do with anything.

Then there were the ones who wanted a gratis parking spot because they worked such long hours, or a three-day-week arrangement on the same salary so they could write a book. Plenty of nice, diligent people worked at the paper too, people who never asked for anything. I just didn't get to see much of them.

Every now and then someone would come to see me who genuinely needed help. The paper was dealing with changing technology that had made twelve people redundant. One of them, a short, slender man, came to my office to talk to me. He was timid, with light-gray eyes that darted around like tiny reef fish.

He stood in my doorway and smiled at me nervously. "I'm sorry to waste your time," he said.

"Please come in and take a seat," I said, getting up to close the door behind him.

"I just received this." He reached into his back pocket and pulled out a letter of termination. He placed the letter on my desk, using his right hand to uncrease it, and pointed to the line that said his termination payout would be $50,000. "I've worked at the paper for ten years," he said. "And I don't want to make a fuss." He stopped.

I looked at him and nodded.

"The problem is," he started, before tears welled up in his eyes, "that my wife is dying."

"I'm so sorry to hear that," I said, passing him a box of tissues.

"She has a couple of months left, at best. We have five kids, all in school. They're helping to care for their mum so she can die at home. Our mortgage is four times the amount I've been offered. And there's no way I'm going to be able to get another job like this. No one needs us. Machines do everything now. I'll have to sell the house. Like I said, I don't want to make a fuss, but I'm not sure what to do." He paused for a moment, put his head in his hands, and sobbed.

I looked at him and tried to compose myself.

He stopped crying and glanced up to see a trail of tears running down my cheeks. He held out his hand to squeeze mine. "I'm sorry!" he said. "The last thing I wanted to do was to make you cry." His concern for me made me even sadder.

"Leave the letter with me," I said. "Let me talk to the publisher and see what we can do."

As soon as he left my office, I went upstairs to talk to the publisher. He agreed to increase the termination sum and to pay for a job placement service. All the people in his department who had lost their jobs would have that service available to them. But this would go down as the saddest story I encountered in all my time in HR. My patience for the people who wanted a leather chair instead of a vinyl one or free parking wore thin, and I discovered the line between sadness and anger was a flimsy one.

Some days I went home after work and was so frustrated that I thought I would burst. Laura needed only to utter an expression such as, "Whatever," for me to erupt. Sometimes all it took was for her to show me the facial expression that accompanied her "whatever" without her even saying it. Almost anything would ignite me. Laura was a calm, easygoing person, and I was a lunatic.

One night I started an argument with her over something small— maybe she forgot to tell me she was going out or had neglected to walk

George if she had arrived home first. Without warning, I started shouting. Veins protruded in my face and neck, and I frothed at the mouth. "Psycho!" Laura spat, and she was right. I ran at her, brandishing a wishbone from a chicken. I held it up to her face and shouted. She turned on me and kicked me in the shin, and I crumpled in a heap on our living room floor. The pain caused by the kick from the hard toe of her boot was excruciating. I helped myself up and limped to the bedroom to examine my wound. A huge black bruise that looked like someone had spilled a bottle of ink down my shin had appeared almost instantly.

Days later, the skin started to ulcerate and eventually I had a gouged, yellowing leg that looked like it belonged to an old person.

"You're lucky that's all I did to you," Laura said when I reappeared downstairs.

"I'm sorry," I said. "I can't help it!" I reached out to hug her, but she pushed me away.

"Sorry doesn't help. You're always sorry. Stop saying it and do something about it."

I had been *trying* to contain my temper ever since Laura moved in with me. Controlling it had been easier when I worked in aged care. My job wasn't stressful, and I could work on my own. Then we moved overseas, and there were so many distractions, I rarely became angry. America had lulled me into the false belief that I'd conquered my rage. But back home in Sydney, I had a job that involved constant contact with people. Pressure built up inside me until I burst. Laura had no experience with bad tempers. She thought angry people were unhinged. I tried to explain that my brain damage had made it almost impossible for me to regulate my emotions. I reminded her that I had never experienced rage before my accident.

"There's nothing wrong with your brain!" she shouted, and those words triggered another eruption.

"Of course there's something wrong! Do you think I made it all up? That I want to be like this? I can't control it! And you not acknowledging the root cause doesn't help! On the outside, I'm fine! Inside, there are times when my brain turns me into a monster!"

"Funny how you say you can't control it, yet you never lose your temper at work. Or with the dogs."

She was right. I did manage to control my temper with the dogs and at work, and I couldn't explain how I did that.

"If I lost my temper at work, they'd fire me! And what kind of person loses their temper with an animal? The dogs are the reason I'm still here. They stuck by me through the worst of this."

"I've stuck by you too."

"I know you have, and I am so thankful to you. Truly. If it helps at all, I hate myself as much as you do." And I did. Probably more.

My temper became a roadblock between us that wouldn't budge. Every noise was amplified. I couldn't focus on reading something in the living room while the TV was on, or while pots and pans were being loaded into the dishwasher. My ears hurt. My head was a dormant volcano.

"You need to see someone about your temper or I'm leaving," Laura said, days after I chased her with the wishbone. "I'm not your fucking punching bag." She slammed a door and poured herself a glass of wine.

My rage was slowly poisoning our relationship. The more I shouted, the less inclined Laura was to spend time with me, to have sex, or to hold my hand when we went out in public. I couldn't blame her. Every problem we had ever encountered in our relationship had been my fault. I was a nightmare. I waited until an empty, postapocalyptic calm set in before joining her in the kitchen. "I'm so sorry. I will talk to someone if you promise not to leave." I gave her a hug, apologized again, and poured us both a glass of sauvignon blanc.

I would have loved nothing more than to curb my anger. Not only for Laura, but also for myself. There was no dignity, no fun in being at the mercy of an uncontrollable rage, and no joy in the remorse that followed. I spent so many nights awake, hating myself for the things I had said to Laura. But rage crept up on me like a madman with a gun. I leapt the chasm from rationality to complete, unabated irrationality without warning. I read in an article once that women with traumatic brain injuries are more likely than men to experience aggression.[14] I was living proof.

I flicked through the Yellow Pages and found the name of a local woman who claimed to be able to help the angry. I chose her because she was a five-minute drive from home, and because there weren't a lot of options. It wasn't like I could ask friends for recommendations. I was the only person I knew who was afflicted by rage.

Walking up the gravel driveway to the counselor's office, I experienced a twinge of foreboding. Her room was perched on top of a garage, and as I started up the wooden steps, I wondered whether I should not just turn around and run. But I had promised Laura I would see someone, and I would keep my word.

The counselor wore a long flowing dress and a plastic beaded necklace. On her desk sat a bowl full of colored stones and a photograph of herself in India inside a picture frame made from shells. I don't know why, but I have always found the sight of white women in saris ridiculous. A lava lamp, emitting a soft purple glow, sat next to the photo. My counselor eased herself into a wooden chair and pointed for me to sit in an identical chair opposite. These chairs belonged around a dining table, not inside the room of a woman who purported to cure people of their rage. I looked at her again. She radiated a false serenity that made every hair stand up on the back of my neck.

"Sarah, is it? What can I do for you, Sarah?" she asked, her sentences ending with a jarring Australian inflection.

"Have you ever cured anyone of their anger?"

"Of course."

I very much doubted it. "Have you ever been angry?"

"No," she said. "Not really."

And in that instant, it struck me that I needed to speak to someone who knew what it felt like to be undone by rage, not a middle-aged woman who looked like she spent her days giving tarot card readings over the telephone.

The wooden chair was as uncomfortable as it looked. The middle spindle at the back had a decorative flourish in its center that poked into my spine. I turned around and glared at the chair to make my point. Surely the least this woman could do was provide a comfortable chair. It didn't take much to set us angry people off, after all.

I got up from the chair, lifted its soft blue foam cushion, rested it against the spindles, and then sat back down. "My partner says she will leave me if I don't control my temper."

"Oh, so that's serious. How does that make you feel?"

That question alone made me want to pick up her uncomfortable wooden chair and smash it over her head. I didn't answer, so she tried another tack.

"Why are you angry?"

"Head injury."

"You had a head injury?"

"Yes."

"And now you're angry?"

"Very."

"And you don't want to talk about it," she said, looking at me as if I was a small child.

"Correct." I looked over her head and spotted a magpie perched on the roof of the garage next door.

"So why are you here?"

"I told you."

"So your partner doesn't leave you. Anger is a very dangerous thing, Sarah. It can harm us and our loved ones. You'll drive your partner away and lose her forever. Anger will render you unlovable. Do you understand that?"

I sat silently and pondered the word "unlovable." It's the kind of word that catches in one's throat before metastasizing inside one's intestines.

"Have you ever hurt anyone?"

"Physically? No! Of course not. I abhor violence."

"Well, that's something. Have you ever been hit?"

I nodded.

"By?"

"A boyfriend."

I told her about Edward. That he punched me once and gave me a black eye, and that I landed on our glass coffee table.

She looked at me for a moment without speaking.

"He was jealous of a work friend."

"Did you report him to the police?"

I shook my head. "No."

I didn't like this woman enough to tell her about my father. I had told no one but Laura about my father's temper.

"What an asshole," Laura had said.

He wasn't an asshole, although I couldn't blame her for not understanding. Without knowing it, I had carefully curated my own memories of my father. He had only one failing, as far as I was concerned, and that was his temper. After his death I had chosen to focus on those things I loved about him, rather than the one thing I hated. My father loved me without conditions. How could I blame my father for a failing I now shared?

I was sixteen when a beating from my father left me with thick ridges down my buttocks and the back of my legs. It was so painful I couldn't sit for weeks. I didn't tell the counselor, but I couldn't help thinking about it.

I could never recall what I had done to provoke him, but he stormed down to my bedroom and, without uttering a word, reached under my bed where he knew I kept two ropes that I used for climbing trees. A neighbor who owned a hardware store had given them to me, and apart from my skateboard, they were my most treasured possessions. He chose the nylon rope, looped it around his hand, and began belting me with all his might. He said nothing.

I curled up into a ball, hoping to make myself small, to limit the area of flesh he could wallop. I kept my mouth shut for as long as I could, not wanting to give him the satisfaction of hearing me yelp. But he kept going. He seemed possessed. When I finally screamed it just made things worse. The pain was agonizing, and he kept thrashing away at my buttocks and legs.

When he had exhausted himself, he reached under my bed for the other rope, swung the two over his shoulder, and strode through the house to the garden where his chopping block stood. He placed the ropes carefully on the wooden block and cut them into tiny pieces. He knew how much I loved those ropes, and he chopped them up to spite me. Alone in my bedroom, I examined the back of my legs and bottom where my skin had split open. Hundreds of droplets of blood seeped out along the ridges where the rope had struck me. I did not dare go to the bathroom to clean myself up, for fear of encountering my father again. Instead, I pushed my wardrobe up against my bedroom door so he could not come back.

My mother had been in the kitchen and had heard my screams, and she did nothing to help me. I refused to speak to my father for the next six months. I hated him. I hated my mother even more. It wasn't weakness that stopped her intervening; it was her belief that I was getting what I deserved—her acute sense of schadenfreude.

At school the next day, my least favorite teacher thought I was being disruptive and sent me to see the headmistress. When I explained that I couldn't sit, the headmistress lifted up my school uniform, glanced at my legs, and demanded to know what had happened. When I told her, she flipped through her Rolodex and called my father at his office. He didn't answer, so she tried my mother at her school. Years later my mother joked with me about the indignity of being called out of a class she was teaching to explain what had happened to her daughter. I didn't see the funny side. The headmistress made her promise it would never happen again, and then warned my mother that she would report my parents to the Department of Family and Community Services if it did.

It never happened again.

My father never apologized, and my mother didn't mention it until I was in my twenties. "I knew he was hurting you and I should have stopped him," she said. "I'm sorry." It seemed odd that she was apologizing for something that had happened nearly a decade earlier.

Familial love is complex and inexplicable, and I forgave my father for that beating. In my mind, he had lost control, become possessed by something inside him. My mother, however, made a conscious decision to allow him to continue hurting me. That was harder to forgive.

"Do you work?" the anger counselor asked, stirring me from my childhood memory.

I nodded, still thinking about my mother.

"Doing?"

"Human resources."

"Oh," she said, shifting back in her seat, surprised. Perhaps she thought that angry people worked in abattoirs or demolition. I bet the angriest people of all work in jobs like mine that require regular, constant, unrelenting contact with other people. The calmest probably work in IT.

She took a moment before speaking. "Do you like working with people?"

"Not especially."

"Do you like people?"

"A handful," I said. "I love animals though."

"So why do you choose to work with them?"

"I lack the kind of skills that would allow me to have a job with no human interaction."

"But do you need to work in HR? Aren't there other things you could do?"

It was a good question. "Possibly."

This dialogue continued for a while before she suggested I count to ten each time I felt the seeds of rage grow within me. It couldn't hurt, although it wouldn't help me in those instances when I exploded without warning. I paid her $150 in cash, as she only took cash payment. I had paid $150 to learn the trick of counting to ten and was none the wiser about controlling my rage, but going to that counselor meant that Laura wouldn't leave me. At the time, it seemed like money well spent.

~

A couple of weeks later, Laura and I were driving out of Balmain, a suburb of Sydney famous for its narrow streets, when we came upon a car parked in the middle of the road, absent a driver. I counted to ten, looked at Laura, and took her hand.

"I'm counting to ten for the second time," I said.

She looked at me and smiled. "Good girl." The car didn't budge, so I counted to ten a third time.

"What's this idiot doing?" Laura asked. I felt a surge of rage.

"May I find out?"

"Sure," she said.

I got out of the car, stood with my hand on the hood, and counted to ten again, this time using my fingers for Laura's benefit. I waved to the cars backed up behind me blaring their horns, and as I walked to the gate where the car was parked, a man appeared. The poor man was attempting to unload things from his car and take them inside his house, but I couldn't stop myself.

"There's a line of cars trying to get past you!" I shouted.

He looked at me warily, as if I were crazed.

"Move your fucking car!"

He ran out, jumped inside his car, and drove it around the block.

"That was perfectly okay," Laura said when I got back inside the car, although she hadn't heard the exchange because it had taken place behind a large tree approximately twenty-five feet away from the vehicle in which she was sitting, with her window up. "Well done," she said, patting my leg. We drove off, and I smiled smugly, feeling like a child who had just done something naughty and gotten away with it.

The next morning at work, I was horrified to see the same man walking around the news floor. *How did he get in,* I wondered? *Had he followed me? Was he a man with a vendetta? Was I the straw that broke the camel's back?* Turned out, it was Tony Horwitz, the Pulitzer Prize–winning journalist and author, who was in Sydney for a year while his wife, Geraldine Brooks, finished a book she was writing. I felt appalled, ashamed, and horrified. I had berated an extraordinary writer whose books I loved. I would never be able to ask him to sign my well-worn copy of *Baghdad Without a Map* or tell him I had read everything he had written for the *New York Times*. He was slated to spend the year ahead as a contributor to the paper—the "star in our stable" as the editor kept telling me. He moved to a house just around the corner from me and Laura, next to George's favorite park, where I saw him pretty much daily on my walk with George. We would nod politely to each other and say hi, but he never recognized me, because for the year he stayed in Sydney, I never left home without a baseball cap and dark glasses.

~

Six months after my failed counseling experience, I decided to try a different approach to controlling my anger. I figured that trying to find another counselor was pointless, but a friend at the paper had taken up kickboxing to manage her stress. One evening I trailed along with her to a studio above a cake shop where a middle-aged woman taught other women how to kick. I signed up for ten sessions. It was fun, and it drained me of all my anger before I got home. Laura noticed a difference. I was less stressed and happier, and I hadn't lost my temper since I started classes. I decided I had found the answer to my problem, to our problem. Until one night, during the warm-up session of lesson eight, I kicked my foot in the air and my anklebone snapped. A bone-density scan revealed that I had osteopenia, the precursor to osteoporosis. My kickboxing days were over, and I spent the next six weeks hobbling around on crutches, frustration boiling inside me. I tried to remember to count to ten.

Years later, long after Laura had left me, I tried to understand the cause of my rage and learned that 70 percent of all head-injured people experience explosive anger or constant irritability following their accident. Not coincidentally, a significant proportion of that group end up in prison. There was a clear link between violent crime and brain damage. In a *New York Times* article, Daniel Goleman referenced two studies involving twenty-nine murderers on death row across four American states, which found that almost all had evidence of a serious brain injury that may have triggered their violence. The two biggest risk factors for violence among these inmates were brain damage and a history of domestic abuse during childhood.[15] I had been hit as a child and had also suffered a traumatic brain injury.

Perhaps the real miracle was that I hadn't killed anyone.

~

My inability to control my anger meant my relationship with Laura slowly began to deteriorate. She had started spending more time with work friends, coming home late and drunk. We hadn't had sex in months, and I had given up trying to initiate any kind of intimacy. She had told me that if I wanted to have sex with someone else, I should, because she was no longer interested. As long as I didn't tell her about it. Laura never said whether she planned to seek sex outside our relationship, and I never asked. But we seemed to be sliding further and further apart.

I had been at the paper for two years when George's health started to decline. He was only thirteen, but he looked much older and had trouble getting around. His eyes were cloudy and he often bumped into the furniture. I took him to the vet for a checkup.

"I don't want to alarm you, but this might be serious," the vet said. She took some X-rays, did an ultrasound, and then stood in the doorway to her office and beckoned me in from the waiting room. I could tell from the look on her face the news was bad. "Cancer," she said. "Take him home and watch him for a week. He's not at the end just yet." I did as she suggested, but he went downhill quickly.

A week later on a Friday morning I asked Laura to come with me to the vet.

"It's time," I said, trying not to cry. "Please come. I don't want to do it alone."

"I'm sorry, but I can't," she said.

Her callousness shocked me. "George is dying. It will only happen once."

"I need to go to work."

She left for work without saying goodbye to him.

I carried George out to the car and drove to the vet, tears streaming down my face. George had been the only constant thing in my life for the past twelve years. He had given me the longest and most satisfying relationship of my life. I was still crying when I reached the vet's parking lot, carried him inside the surgery, and followed the vet down a narrow corridor to a tiny consulting room. Three months earlier he had been too heavy for me to carry, but he had shrunk so severely that he didn't require much effort at all. He looked up at me, and I kissed him on the nose. The vet stretched him out on the table, and I put my arms around him and hugged him tightly.

"Ready?" the vet asked.

I nodded.

"You hold his head," she said.

I kissed his forehead, his muzzle, and the soft spots behind his ears while he slowly lost all life.

When the vet left us alone, I held his dead body and sobbed. I left the room with his Harvard collar and matching lead. I made arrangements for George to be cremated. Someone would call me when his ashes were ready for collection, the receptionist said, as I settled the bill. I got into my car, my whole body shaking.

Laura didn't pick up the phone when I called her.

That was a pivotal moment in my relationship with Laura. Laura had saved my life. I knew that. But for all the ways she had stood by me, pushed me to do more, loved me despite my many and serious flaws, she chose to be absent when I lost George. For a long while before I met Laura, George and Bess had been my closest friends. Bess had gone, at Laura's prodding, and now George was gone too. I knew her attitude was that he was just a dog, but to me he had been my family. I wanted to love Laura the same way I loved her before George died, but something inside me had changed.

I left the vet surgery and drove straight to work. Inside my office, I closed the door and hoped no one would disturb me. I was trying to distract myself with something or another when the door opened slightly and Grant, the most senior union rep at the paper, appeared in the doorway. Our relationship hitherto had been somewhat frosty, but I invited him in and he sat down in my visitor's chair.

"Are you okay?" he asked, looking at my bloodshot eyes.

"Yes, thanks. Fine," I said.

"You don't look fine," he said.

"I just had my dog put down," I said, and burst into tears.

"Oh, that's terrible. Is that him there?" he asked, pointing to a framed photo of George on my desk.

"Yes," I said between sobs. "George."

"I'm so sorry. We have a rescue dog at home. Pax. He looks very similar to your George. He's part of the family."

I looked at him and smiled.

"I can't imagine what will happen when we lose him," he said, spotting at his eye with his sleeve. "I really feel for you."

"Thanks," I said. "That's kind. So what can I do for you?"

"Oh, don't worry about it. Silly stuff. We can do it another time. When you're feeling better. Rescue dogs take priority over everything else."

And in that brief interaction, Grant—an unlikely ally—had done what Laura was unable to do: he understood how it felt to lose a much-loved dog. And a friendship was formed, the closest friendship I ended up making at the paper. A friendship that made both our lives a bit easier.

~

"He was a dog, Sarah. Dogs die," Laura said when we sat down for dinner that evening.

"I know," I said feebly before I started to sob again. I fell into a deep hole of depression, and the only way to climb out of it was to rescue another dog. Sick of my moping, Laura eventually gave in.

A fortnight after George died, we drove across town to the largest animal shelter in Sydney, and I asked to see the oldest, saddest dog they had—the dog nobody wanted. We waited our turn before a skinny middle-aged woman with blue streaks through her blonde hair led us to a cage. Standing in the corner and staring at the ground was a dog with vacant-looking eyes, a mix of kelpie and rottweiler. Her back was missing all its fur.

"Some kids poured petrol over her and set her alight," the woman said. "We wanted to put her down—thought it would be the kindest thing to do—but the lady who found her is paying to keep her here. Maybe someone will take her, but I doubt it."

"How old is she?" I asked.

"The vet thinks ten or eleven, but it's hard to say for sure."

We coaxed her out of her cage, and I held out my hand for her to sniff. She had no interest. She had given up.

"What do you think?" I asked Laura.

Laura looked down and nodded.

"We'll take her," I said.

We named her Jessica, after Jessica Lange—my favorite actress, the most beautiful woman in the world, and my first real crush. Jessica took nearly a week before she made eye contact with either of us. Then one evening while we were watching TV, she got out of her bed, wandered toward us, and sat at our feet. She looked at us for the first time, and I started to cry. We sat down beside her and hugged her. She responded by licking my face and Laura's hand. From that night on, she slept on our bed. Laura was fonder of Jessica than she had been of George or Bess. It may have been because Jessica was *our* dog, not *my* dog. Whatever the reason, we were both in agreement that we would do whatever we could to make her remaining years as happy as possible. Perhaps we both wanted something that could bind us back together.

~

I was standing in the elevator well at work one morning on my way out to buy coffee, when an attractive woman with red shoulder-length hair got out of the elevator and smiled at me.

A couple of days later, we ended up sitting opposite one another in a meeting about performance appraisal. Her name was Anna.

That afternoon she called me and asked whether I would like to meet her for lunch. She wanted to learn more about performance appraisal.

At lunch there was an unmistakable attraction between us. I told Anna about Laura, and Anna told me about her partner. The next day we met again, and ended up going back to my place. I had never cheated on anyone before, and I was so conflicted about whether or not I *was* cheating that I refused to allow Anna inside our house. So we had sex in the backyard, up against the back door, watched by an elderly neighbor wearing a fedora hat, from the bathroom window of the house next door—whom I spotted lingering around waiting for an encore.

A couple of days later, Anna and I had another encounter, this time in the changing room of the Versace section on the top floor of a luxury department store. I found the tackiest, shiniest gold-lamé thing I could and asked to try it on. The shopgirl ushered us into a small room. It was the perfect spot for sex, and frankly, I was surprised more people didn't make use of its facilities for precisely that purpose. There was a velour-covered sofa, plush shag pile carpet, and a door with a lock. The only problem was, having visited there once, I was not sure we would be able to go back. We stayed inside a bit too long, and I'm pretty sure the shopgirl realized that something was up.

~

One night the publisher decided to take a small group of his direct reports to dinner in Chinatown. I, for some reason I cannot fathom, asked if Anna could come along. It was a strange request, to say nothing of stupid on my part, but the publisher agreed. I was so desperate for sex at that point I seemed to have lost all my sense. We left the office, Anna and I trailing along behind the rest of the group, and as we passed a back alley off Sussex Street, Anna shoved me up against a wall and started kissing me. That was a bad idea. The brain-damaged me didn't enjoy kissing as an end in itself. Kissing was a precursor to sex. To distract myself I tried to think about Bess, George, my father, my grandmother—about any grief and loss I could conjure. When that didn't work, I tried to think of the most off-putting thing I could, which happened to be vomit. That did the trick. I peeled myself away from Anna, and we caught up with the rest of the group.

At the restaurant, an elderly Chinese woman seated us at a large round table with the publisher on one side of me and Anna on my other side. After drinks were served, Anna slid her hand across my lap. I reached for my napkin to cover her hand, but the napkin slipped off onto the floor, and I noticed the publisher glancing down to see Anna's hand stroking my thigh.

I tapped her foot with mine to stop her, but it made no difference, so I tried stamping on her foot. When that didn't work, I got up and went to the bathroom. She got up and followed me.

"What are you doing?" I asked in disbelief.

"I want sex," she said.

"We aren't having it here."

"Why not?"

"Are you insane?"

"Who cares!" she said.

"I could lose my job over this!"

Luckily for me, there was a rich tradition at the paper of people having sex with one another, and the publisher was polite enough never to mention the evening again.

Three weeks after we had met, Anna told me she was falling in love with me.

"I like you too!" I said. "But this can't go anywhere. You have a partner and I have Laura. I'm not going to leave her."

She was hurt. I vowed never again to have sex with anyone other than myself.

As the HR manager, sex with another employee turned out to be a grave mistake. The email system at the paper wasn't secure, and apparently anyone's email, including the CEO's, could be accessed by typing in the person's name and the word "password." That explained why the paper leaked like an origami boat. A journalist had been reading the emails between Anna and me. Although I had written very few emails to Anna, her emails to me told a fairly racy story. Racy, anyway, if you're a man in his forties who takes pleasure reading an exchange between two women who enjoy having sex. Eventually, the excitement grew too much, and he forwarded a couple of choice ones to his closest mates, and they forwarded them to a few of theirs. By three o'clock that afternoon, the whole paper knew.

Sex will be my undoing, I thought. *I will end up scorned and humiliated like a fat old politician with a face like a walnut and a fondness for hookers.*

Anna and I weren't the first people at the paper to have their sex lives brought to light by someone who had cracked the email system. But we were the first lesbians. And I was in a senior HR position and should have known better. I had acted irresponsibly. Unprofessionally. I admitted my foolishness. The union threatened to intervene. "What HR manager fucks the staff?" the head of the union asked me in a meeting. Luckily for me, my friend Grant, my rescue-dog-owning ally, helped hose things down. If not for his intervention on my behalf, I would probably have lost my job. I experienced a couple of weeks of hell until it all died down.

And then there was Laura. Laura may have given me her blessing to sleep with other people, but no one else knew that. Word traveled fast, and people who knew us as a couple looked at me with disgust. No one knew about my head injury, but it wasn't hard to tell that I was the difficult one in our relationship. Among friends, Laura had acquired the status of a saint for putting up with me. And now I had, in their eyes at least, cheated on her. The only person who didn't seem to know of the affair was Laura. Or if she did know, she had chosen to bury it forever. I had sunk as low as a person could sink. I felt I was loathsome and totally undeserving of Laura's love.

~

After three years, I left the paper. I had just turned forty and felt tired and old, and I needed a rest. I used the time between jobs to find a neurologist. My memory had been troubling me for the past six months. Little things had started to happen more frequently. I would reach the front of the line for the ATM and forget my PIN. I would make a reservation at a restaurant and forget my phone number. These things were happening at least a couple of times each week. Why would my memory get better after the injury and then worse? I worried I had a brain tumor. *What else could it be?*

A doctor friend of a friend recommended a neurologist. A family friend who was a specialist recommended the same person. He was said to be one of the best neurologists in the country.

I told my new doctor about my problems with my memory. He listened attentively and asked intelligent questions, and I did my best to answer them. After the consultation he sent me to a small, ancient radiology center above the supermarket at a shopping center. There was not much he could tell me without a brain MRI.

I went to the radiology center on my own. A weary-looking nurse in her fifties led me into a small room with a locker, handed me a gown, and instructed me to change. I did as I was told, then followed her out into a room where a huge coffin-like machine awaited me.

"Lie down," she said. "It's going to be noisy. And you need to keep still for twenty minutes."

I lay down and she clamped a brace around my skull to hold it in place.

"If you really can't stand it," the woman said, "just press the buzzer and I'll come in. That hardly ever happens. Close your eyes. That makes it easier."

The brace was tight and my head ached.

"Ready?" Her voice inquired over a loudspeaker. "We're going to start."

She pressed a button, and I slid up inside a large cone. The machine whirred, and a wheel around my head started to rotate, slowly at first until it built up momentum. The noise was deafening, and the inside of the cone was a fluorescent orange. My whole body felt like it was rotating. I closed my eyes, but that made it feel like I had the worst hangover imaginable, one of those hangovers where you spin around and around and can't stop. Actually, it felt like having that hangover, being tied to a rope behind a car, and taken into a field where the driver did donuts. My head throbbed. I lasted a couple of minutes before I pressed the buzzer.

The woman walked in the room and sighed. "Yes?" she asked, one hand resting on her hip.

"I can't do it. I'm claustrophobic."

"Get dressed then," she said, not doing much to hide her irritation. I did as she said and followed her to the reception desk. "You still have to pay." I nodded and handed over my Visa card.

I returned to the neurologist, who gave me a copy of the report, which didn't say much at all.

"Too noisy?" he asked.

I nodded.

"Yes, it's an old machine, I'm afraid."

I skipped straight to the conclusion: *Limited study only. Patient declined further series. No obvious hemosiderin deposit is seen. There could be some atrophy involving the parietal hemisphere on both sides.* I glanced at it while he looked at the slides of my brain.

"It's a real shame we don't have the initial scans taken after your injury. But from the look of these pictures I really wouldn't worry," he said. "You suffered a serious head trauma, so it's not surprising you might be experiencing some aftereffects. There's nothing here to show anything of real significance. In fact, there might be no change at all since the accident."

"Can we rule out a brain tumor?"

"You do not have a brain tumor."

Relieved that I wouldn't be requiring surgery, I thanked him and left. At the time, it didn't occur to me that I should have asked to be tested on a newer machine that was less noisy and uncomfortable. Nor did I think to ask about the longer-term prognosis for people who had suffered traumatic brain injuries.

Reassured that my memory problems weren't unusual given my accident, I started looking for a new job, and a headhunter approached me about a senior human resources job with a large Australian bank. During one of the interviews, my future boss asked me to explain what my PhD thesis was about. My mind went blank. I couldn't remember. I made up something about it being complicated (it wasn't) and dull (that was for sure) and managed to squirm out of an answer. The rest of the interview went well, and I ended up getting the job. The only problem was that the bank was in Melbourne, a city I had visited only twice in my life and didn't particularly like on either occasion.

Laura decided to move with me to Melbourne, even though the problems between us had started to snowball. She gave up her job as global account director for a large advertising agency in Sydney and took a part-time job with a smaller firm in Melbourne. My salary would support us both. Our year in America had fueled her desire to travel and to explore new places, and Laura had been desperate for a change of scenery. Melbourne was hardly top of her list, but at least it was new. We had been together for about seven years, and the prospect of being alone, even though our love had withered, was something neither of us wanted to contemplate. Perhaps we both hoped a new city would repair the fractures in our relationship and make things better.

We missed Sydney immediately. Melbourne was ugly and wet and windy, and the weather became a metaphor for our relationship. Deprived of sunlight, it began to shrivel. Within the first two months of moving, our relationship broke down. One night, Laura was in the kitchen making dinner, and I was on the sofa watching TV. I was trying to concentrate on something when Laura called out to me. I strained to hear the TV, but she kept talking.

"Shut up!" I shouted. "I'm trying to watch this!"

She walked around the kitchen counter toward me and turned off the TV. "That is the very last time; do you understand?"

I nodded. I didn't say sorry. We had reached a point where my apologies enraged her.

"The next time you speak to me like that I am leaving."

I went into the bedroom, closed the door, and slipped under the covers. I wished I could reach inside myself and tear out my rage, stomp on it until it died, or toss it into the sea and wait for it to drown. Laura needed a break from me. So did I.

I tried to think rationally. Why did I keep behaving like this? What was wrong with me? I thought about my father. My mother had tolerated his temper for the eighteen years I lived at home. Then, by the time I had moved out, his anger had left him. Disappeared. Perhaps my temper was worse than his. He was violent, but he never said hurtful things. I was rude and disrespectful. Perhaps anger was more acceptable in a man. In a woman it signaled madness. My thoughts scrambled around inside my head, and only one thing was clear to me: this was all my fault. I had slowly filed away the tether that had held us together.

Our problems were compounded by the fact that Laura had sacrificed a good life with a good job and good friends in a beautiful city for a miserable life in a city she hated. I wasn't worth the sacrifice, and she told me as much. "But you could have stayed in Sydney! You chose to come!" I reminded her.

"Biggest mistake of my short fucking life," she said.

I urged her to do something she had always wanted to do: draw, restore furniture, or go to yoga every day. My salary paid our rent and our bills, so she could do anything she liked. She wasn't interested. She needed time to decide how to fix her career. How to fix her life. She was tired of me, tired of my depression, and tired of my rage. I was the most negative person she had ever encountered. We had less and less to talk about, so we stopped even trying, and I found myself back inside my old familiar tunnel of gloom.

Jessica didn't like Melbourne much either. She resented being woken up in the dark and dragged out to a sodden park when there was frost on the ground.

Then one Wednesday night, when we had been in Melbourne around three months, Laura didn't come home. I waited up for her until three a.m. Her phone went straight to voice mail. Eventually the door unlocked and she appeared in the doorway.

"Where have you been? I was worried. Your phone was off!"

"It's over."

"What's over?"

"Us. I'm moving out on Saturday. I don't love you anymore."

I sat on the sofa staring into the black TV screen until it hit me. She took a shower and went to bed. I tried to talk to her, but she refused to speak. She didn't say another word to me until a month after she had moved out, when she told me she had fallen in love with her boss and had left me for her.

Three days' notice to end a seven-year relationship seemed a little on the short side. But I couldn't blame her for leaving. She had stuck by me for years, hoping I would change, hoping I would evolve into a reasonable person, someone who could control their emotions. The better part of a decade of her life had been wasted on me. It was time for her to start again. Time for me to learn to be alone.

Jessica and I spent Christmas together on a dog-friendly beach near home until Jen, a friend from work, invited us around to her house in the afternoon. I didn't hear a word from my mother. When we did eventually speak, all she said was, "What did you expect? You're unbearable, Sarah. I'm not surprised."

~

A few weeks later I came home from work to discover Jessica was sick. There was a coldness to her that scared me, and she could barely lift her head from her bed. I picked her up, carried her to the car, and took her straight to an emergency vet hospital.

"She's dying," the vet said after she had examined Jessica.

"Yesterday she was fine! She ran around the park chasing birds. How can she be dying?" I asked.

"It's hard to say," the vet said. "Cancer, probably. The kindest thing would be to put her down now. She won't last another few days."

I began to sob. I hugged Jessica and nodded to the vet. She shaved a patch on Jessica's leg and inserted the needle.

Can you do me next? I wanted to ask. I kissed Jessica's head and told her I loved her. She looked up at me weakly and licked my hand. The last of them was gone.

At forty-one I had managed to lose everyone I had ever loved.

10

You Can Run, but You Can't Hide

With Laura and Jessica gone, there was nothing to keep me in Melbourne, a city that had brought me little but grief in the nine months I had lived there. Luckily, the bank was bolstering its Asian operations, and when an opportunity arose for a regional head of human resources to cover Asia and the Pacific, I was the first person to put up my hand. I moved to Singapore in December 2004. I wanted to start a new life in a place where no one knew me. Laura's relationship with her boss hadn't worked out, and she had left Melbourne too, for a job in New York City.

Singapore is a country with no freedom of speech, where hangings and canings occur in a prison near the airport on Friday mornings, where it is against the law to walk around your apartment with no clothes on "while being exposed to public view," where homosexuality is illegal, where HIV-positive travelers were forbidden from entering the country[16], where a children's book about two male penguins raising a baby chick was pulped because it was believed to contradict the nation's "family values." It is also a country with one of the highest disparities between rich and poor. Pop into any Burger King or McDonald's and you will be confronted by women in their seventies and older cleaning tables. Go to the airport and you will see hunched elderly men retrieving luggage trolleys. Since the Maintenance of Parents Act was introduced in 1995, any parent over the age of sixty who is not able to provide for him- or herself may sue their children for financial support. That, of course, assumes the child has the means to provide it.

My new home was a country that had been governed by the same party since 1959, a government that had conducted a series of bizarre social engineering experiments in the 1970s, during which they paid uneducated women to stop having children and paid female graduates to encourage pregnancies. It was a government that had used public campaigns as a way of changing citizens' behavior—to make them more courteous and gracious to others, to stop them from urinating in lifts, to ban the use of chewing gum, to keep Singapore clean. For the first offense, litterers are fined. Repeat offenders are made to dress in fluorescent-orange vests that identify them as litterers while they sweep the streets. Personally, I think that last one is a pretty good idea.

The threat of punishment looms large in the psyche of Singaporeans. No one wants to be caned or hung. Only men are subject to canings, but both men and women are hung. Hangings, though rare, were known to take place at Changi Prison early on Friday mornings. Canings were more regular occurrences. The cane used is four feet long and half an inch thick, making it twice as thick and probably twice as long as the canes that had been used in Australian schools to punish unruly children while I was growing up. The maximum number of strokes is twenty-four. Before its use, the Singaporean cane is soaked in water to make it more pliable. A person is stripped naked before being caned and strapped into a trestle, which holds him in place. He is then caned across the buttocks. Each stroke of the cane opens the skin. When the caning is finished, a doctor applies a special caning cream to the wounds to stop infection. Vandalism and overstaying one's visa are canable offenses.

Singapore is a utopia and a dystopia at the same time, and you don't find that every day. The government's intrusion into the lives of its citizens has helped make the nation-state an economic powerhouse. Singapore has no natural resources, and yet its economy booms. It was true that I would have taken a job anywhere to get out of Melbourne, but I was happy to move to Singapore. Politically I found it fascinating. And there was a lot the government had done well. It was an easy place to live with excellent public transport, hospitals, schools, and roads. Asia 101, as seasoned expats liked to call it.

I had stayed in Singapore on two separate, brief occasions. During the trip that I remember, before my accident, I had lived in a cramped room on the National University of Singapore campus. The room had bathroom tiles covering the bedroom floor, fluorescent strip lighting, and no air-conditioning. At that time in my life, I mistakenly believed I was heterosexual. By the time I moved back there in 2004, in a desperate attempt to flee Melbourne and the havoc it had wrought, I had the means to live in a comfortable apartment. And I was openly gay.

Lily, the relocation agency expert who found apartments for expats, said she would take me on as a client even though my housing budget was "a fraction" of what she was used to. I was earning more money than I had ever dreamed of, and the bank covered my housing on top of that. Lily's clients were mostly investment bankers. "Very good people," she said. "Very kind." *Really?* I wanted to say but decided to keep quiet. My experience at the bank had been the opposite.

She told me she would make an exception for me as we drove around Singapore in her brand-new golden Mercedes-Benz with four-wheel drive, because she hoped that I, as head of HR, would send my better-paid colleagues her way in the future. "I look after you. You too, lah," she said.

Lily took me to see ten apartments in one day. Nine of them were what she described as respectable homes.

"You're not going to get better than this with your budget!" she reminded me. I wanted an apartment close to a train station or a bus route. In an effort to reduce the number of cars on its roads, the government had introduced a variety of taxes and levies, which made Singapore one of the most expensive places on earth to own a car. To provide an indication, in 2017 a Toyota Corolla cost $76,500. Lily had calculated that I wouldn't be able to afford a car.

We had only seen a few houses when Lily put her hand on my knee, patted it twice, and told me how sorry she was about my inability to bear children.

Thinking I had misheard her, I waited for her to go on, but she looked at me expectantly, waiting for a response.

"Um, well, thanks," I said.

"And no husband either!" she said. "Very bad luck."

I fumbled through my bag and hoped she would change the subject.

"Maybe you a bit too fussy, lah," she said, shooting me a stern look.

"He's dead," I said, with a certainty that surprised me.

She patted my leg again. "So sorry, so sorry." After a short pause she asked, "That's why no children?"

I toyed with saying they were dead too, but decided that would be too much, so I stared at the ground.

"So sorry, lah," she repeated. I thanked her again and glanced out the car window at a man tugging on the lead of a Pomeranian dog, which seemed to be either lying down on the footpath in protest or dying from heat exhaustion.

Lily was the first person I had ever lied to about my sexual orientation. The truth was I hadn't given much thought to speaking about my sexuality in a country that viewed homosexuality as a crime. It turns out, in a strange twist of logic, that homosexuality between women is not a crime, but I was yet to understand the finer points of Singaporean law. In Melbourne I had been out at work, and there was sufficient communication between the head office and the regional office to ensure word of my sexuality had reached my Singaporean colleagues. There was no point trying to conceal it. I also believed that, as a senior HR person who happened to be gay, I had a responsibility to be out at work. In doing so, I hoped I might make life easier for other gay employees.

Lying to Lily unsettled me. I had never had any qualms at all about people knowing I was gay, and denying it felt like an unnecessary betrayal. I had never felt even a shred of shame about my sexuality, and my view had always been that if anyone took issue with it, it would be their problem, not mine. My reaction to my head injury had been the polar opposite. I had fiercely guarded the truth about my accident because the shame had been crippling. Almost no one in my life at work, at university, or among my circle of friends knew anything about it. I hadn't told more than five people.

My caution over exposing my head injury was only partly paranoia. Studies have shown that society holds certain (unflattering) beliefs about people with head injuries. Many consider us to be intellectually challenged, violent, unpredictable, embarrassing, and untrustworthy. That was certainly my mother's view. As one study concluded:

> When people with brain injury become aware of how some members of society may perceive them it is possible they could withdraw from many social situations. They may fear disclosure of their injury because of the way people are likely to view them. This could lead to certain members of this vulnerable group feeling isolated and perhaps impede their seeking support.[17]

I may have been wrong, but I believed that I would not be being driven around Singapore in a gold Mercedes, looking to rent a nice apartment, as regional head of human resources for a bank, if I had been honest about my head injury.

The nine apartments Lily chose for me were decorated in what she described as local décor, which meant pink marble floors, gold chandeliers, and elaborate light fittings that resembled huge lilies sprouting from the ceiling. There was a lot of built-in furniture made from cherry-stained veneer. Some of the apartments we saw had so much built-in furniture that there was no room left for any furniture of my own.

"Very convenient. Save a lot on furniture!" she said encouragingly in one apartment that boasted a huge built-in shoe rack that accosted us as soon as we stepped inside, a floor-to-ceiling wall unit with missing shelves that took up two living room walls, a built-in bar, built-in beds, and built-in desks and wardrobes in the bedrooms. All the built-ins were covered with a light pink gloss that had been chipped over the passing years. Local décor also embraced strangely shaped rooms: there was a triangular bedroom next to a bathroom with five walls. I was learning that local décor wasn't really my style.

"Do you have anything more, um, *modern*?" I asked, after we had spent six hours traipsing through apartments.

"Ah, you prefer *Western* style?" She looked at me as if I wasn't just a barren widow, but a barren widow with very poor taste.

"I think so," I said meekly. We pulled over by the side of the road so she could make a few phone calls.

"Yes, we have, but only one that fits your budget." The last apartment was perfect. It was large, with floor-to-ceiling windows, and the only built-ins were the wardrobes in each of the three bedrooms. Best of all, the long marble-floored corridor made the perfect runway to test out the skateboard I had bought myself after my breakup with Laura. "I'll take it," I told Lily, releasing her from my barren, tasteless wasteland and back into the arms of the kindly investment banking folk.

I was the only woman on the bank's Asia Pacific leadership team. My peers were all white men who were married with children. They spent their weekends at country clubs or hosting barbecues, where they mixed exclusively with people exactly like them. Best of all, these men could pay someone less than a thousand bucks a month to provide twenty-four-hour childcare, seven days a week.

I attended only one barbecue. The women lounged around inside the host's apartment talking excitedly about the hairdresser they found after months of searching for someone who knew how to cut Western hair and had a way with peroxide. There was a lively discussion about a handbag one woman had just bought and how hard it was to find decent milk and bread in Singapore. The women also took time to complain about their domestic helpers who lived in quarters the size of broom closets while two rooms of the apartment sat empty in case guests came to stay. Their obnoxious kids tore around the house until someone literally snapped their fingers and a helper appeared to cart them off to their bedrooms.

I spent most of the time staring out the window, watching the men, who were huddled around a barbecue outside discussing their investments and the Malaysian guy who delivered illegal pornographic movies wrapped up in brown paper to their homes.

I had managed to mask my injury at work without anyone catching on ever since I had taken the policy job in aged care. Masking it in my private life had proved considerably more difficult. After the accident, I had changed in certain fundamental ways. If I let my guard down in social situations, I was seen, almost instantly, to be lacking in social graces. I had learned to keep myself from uttering the things I was thinking. But that was exhausting. I was incapable of making small talk, which was a problem given my role in HR. If I found myself drawn into idle chitchat, I would nod, smile as best I could, and hold my tongue for a few minutes before politely excusing myself.

To add to my challenges, most of my local Singaporean coworkers had never met a gay person, or someone who had admitted to it. They told me this and giggled. In my first couple of weeks in the job, there was a steady parade of people walking past my office, peering inside, eager to see what a gay person looked like. My new secretary, a woman in her early fifties, studied me with a curled lip from behind her desk. I held out my hand for her to shake, and she held her own up limply in response. *It's catching!* I wanted to tell her, but my eyes were drawn to a small wooden frog sitting on a log beside her keyboard inscribed with the words *The kingdom of God is within you, Luke 17:21.*

I had no friends in Singapore. I often went entire weekends without having a single conversation with anyone but myself. My first few weekends after I arrived were spent book shopping and reading beside the infinity pool on the roof of my apartment block. Books were cheap, thanks to a government subsidy to encourage reading. I felt like I was on a budget all-inclusive holiday in Bali. The only thing missing was the drinks waiter freshening up my fluffy duck. Occasionally, between chapters, I looked up at the sky and pinched my arm to remind myself I was alive.

I was lonely from time to time, but in many ways it was a relief to be without Laura, to be without a partner. Being alone worked wonders on my ability to regulate my emotions, and my rage vanished. Nothing made me snap. If work gnawed away at me in some way, I would stop by the gym on my way home and spend forty minutes on the treadmill. What I did miss was having a dog.

The only benefit of being dog-free was that I could travel as much as I wanted. My new job covered twenty countries and required me to travel for at least two weeks, and often three weeks, of every month. When I visited a city, I always made sure to stay on for a weekend, so I could take the time to look around. Only when I visited the head office in Melbourne did I make arrangements to take the first flight out. I was entranced by Asia, and travel was the thing I loved most about my job.

Jen, my friend from Melbourne whom I'd visited on Christmas Day after Laura had left me, came to visit me in Singapore and suggested we go out to a lesbian bar. She was a colleague of mine at the bank and one of the very few out gay people I knew in Melbourne. My track record with lesbian bars had not been stellar, and I would have rather done almost anything else, but I humored her as best I could. She sat down on the sofa with my computer on her lap and was genuinely surprised to find that there wasn't an impressive range of lesbian establishments to choose from.

"You do know homosexuality is a crime here?" I asked.

"But not for women, you said!"

"Oral sex is also a crime."[18]

"You're kidding! What's left?"

I shrugged. "There's a thriving club scene here for gay men. We could try one of those. They're usually a lot more fun." I had visited a gay club with a male friend who had visited fleetingly, and I was astonished to find it packed full of handsome young Asian men. We talked to a group of them who told us the police raided the clubs from time to time but rarely made any arrests.

"No! Come on. Here's one for women. Let's try it. Please!"

"Fine!" I'd had precious few visitors since I left Australia and would have even fewer if I was an ungracious hostess. It was nine o'clock in the evening—too early for any real action—but neither of us was looking for that. We simply wanted to satisfy an anthropological curiosity. So we found a taxi and set off in the direction of a lonely lesbian bar.

After sharing a fish-head curry and banana-leaf-wrapped prawns at a local Indian restaurant, we walked about a block before we came to a small sign that read "Alternative Bar."

"Clever name," Jen giggled as we walked up a narrow flight of stairs that led us inside a bar with bright-orange walls, just big enough for a few stools and a pool table. A handful of Filipinas stood around the pool table, chatting. They smiled and invited us to play. As the world's worst pool player, I politely declined. I have never had any talent for lesbian games. Jen, on the other hand, was pretty good. I saw the night unfold: me in a corner of the bar drinking myself into a stupor while Jen impressed her new friends with tricky pool shots.

Seated at the bar were two young Singaporean women sucking up noodles from Styrofoam containers. They looked to be in their early twenties and, like most lesbians in Singapore, they conformed to the femme/butch stereotype. One wore makeup, had long hair, and was dressed in a short skirt and stilettos. Her girlfriend wore men's trousers and a polo shirt, and her hair was cropped close on the back and sides.

"What would you like to drink?" I asked Jen.

"Do you think they have champagne?"

They didn't have champagne—or wine, or anything other than gin, rum, whiskey, and vodka—so I bought us each a screwdriver. As I reached into my wallet to pay, the butch woman lifted her head up from her noodles.

"You're too old to be here. You should try Crocs."

"Crocs?" I asked, not quite following.

"Crocs. It's a bar for *old* lesbians."

Jen, nine years younger than I am, started to laugh.

I looked at her. "Is that funny?"

"Yes," she said. "Very."

"Does she think I'm trying to pick someone up? Or does the presence of an older person offend her?"

"I'm not sure," Jen said, making no attempt to stifle her laughter.

I was forty-one and convinced, until that night, that I looked much younger. In my mind, I could pass easily for thirty-one. On a good day, twenty-eight. But living in Singapore as a middle-aged Caucasian woman had taught me to never create the opportunity for a local to guess my age. Given the chance, they would happily stack on an extra ten or twenty years, and that could be hurtful. If I managed to avoid the geriatric classification, there would always be a sting in the tail. "You look younger. It's because you're plump." But at the Alternative Bar, the damage was done. I was humiliated and ready to leave.

"I can't win!" I said, as we made our way down the stairs. "I used to get turned away from lesbian bars because I looked straight. Now I get turned away because I'm too old!"

"Crocs!" Jen said, her laughter morphing into hysteria.

"I know a place," I said, dragging her by the arm. "It's a nice bar up the road with a rooftop terrace that looks over the city, and I've never been asked to leave on account of my age. And it serves champagne."

~

I had been in Singapore for about six months when my mother emailed me saying she was planning a trip to New York to visit Laura. My mother and I had hardly spoken since Laura and I had broken up. She planned to spend ten days in a New York hotel, taking Laura out to dinner, the opera, and the theater. On the way home she would break the journey with an overnight stay in Singapore. I hoped she would stay in my spare room, but she had already booked a hotel.

I took a taxi to the airport to collect my mother, and she spent the next couple of hours telling me how wonderful Laura was, how well she was looking after our breakup, and how much fun they'd had together. Singapore was a letdown after New York, she said, and the heat was oppressive. During dinner she did not ask anything about my job or my life. The entire conversation was devoted to Laura, and as soon as we had finished eating, she asked me to take her back to her hotel. She had jet lag and needed to go to sleep. Early the next morning, I took a taxi to her hotel and then to the airport. We'd spent about two and a half hours together. It was the only time she visited me in the more than eleven years I ended up living abroad.

Alone in my apartment one afternoon, I sorted through a box of unpacked papers that I'd left in my study. About halfway through, I discovered a copy of the score to Beethoven's Spring Sonata—one of my favorite pieces of music, and the last piece I had learned to play when I was studying at the Conservatorium High School. Buried at the bottom of the box was a funeral march for piano by Mozart and Mozart's Violin Concerto in G. I used to play them all. I opened the score to the Spring Sonata and studied the notes, but nothing registered. I could identify the treble clef but that was all. Alarmed, I went into my bedroom and retrieved my violin from its spot inside the wardrobe. My violin had made every move with me since I had left Sydney. Even though one of the strings had snapped, I took it out of its case, held it under my chin, placed my left hand on the fingerboard, and examined the score to the Spring Sonata.

My fingers stuck to the fingerboard. They were slow and rigid and incapable of doing much at all. That seemed normal enough. It had been more than twenty years since I had last played. I looked at the strings, hoping my brain would tell my fingers what to do. G was the note of the open first string. *Then what?* I glanced at the score and couldn't find a G. I had no recollection of what a G looked like in musical notation. Sweat trickled down the sides of my face from my hairline: the first physical sign of panic. I had no idea at all what any of the notes signified or how they might sound. Music, I suddenly realized, made about as much sense to me as Cyrillic.

The damage to my brain from my accident had left me with a condition known as musical alexia. I had lost the ability to read or play music. People say that reading music is like riding a bicycle, and that once you know how to do it, you will never forget. But I felt like I was a young child seeing a score for the very first time. I sat for a few moments, nursing my violin in my hands, trying to understand what had happened to me. It was yet another loss, and somehow that made me feel more alone than ever. Years after my accident, I was discovering problems I never knew I had. Brain damage was the gift that kept on giving.

When I had grown comfortable being alone and given up all hope of ever sharing my life with another human being, I met Giulia. We had both signed up to a gay Asian website, looking for friends. Our profiles made it clear that neither of us wanted a partner. Singapore can be a lonely place if you are a single expat, and never more so than if you happen to be a gay woman.

We met one Saturday afternoon at three o'clock, at a bar along the river not far from my office. We said goodnight at one a.m., once we'd finished drinks after dinner at a restaurant on the opposite side of the river.

It was the longest I had spent with anyone since Laura had moved out.

Giulia was Italian, attractive, humorous, smart, and fifteen years my junior. She had modeled her way through university before finding work in fashion, first in Milan, then Paris, and then Singapore. There was an instant connection between us, and we soon started seeing each other a few times a week for drinks or dinners.

I refused to touch her for the first six weeks we knew each other. The age gap made me feel creepy and predatory.

One day, tired of waiting for me, she made the first move.

"I like older women," she said. "All of my past girlfriends have been older."

I looked at her and raised my eyebrows.

"True," she said, moving in to kiss me. From that moment on, things happened quickly.

Giulia was the feistiest woman I had ever known. She was not afraid to challenge me or to stand up to me—and not just on a small number of things, but on virtually everything. She would take no shit. And that could only be a good thing.

The first time Giulia visited my apartment, she insisted on going through my wardrobe. I watched her toss my clothes over her shoulder, forming a large pile on my king-size bed. By the time she had finished, the pile was the size of a small elephant.

"Those must go," she said.

I laughed.

"And we will go shopping. I will choose all your clothes from now on. Yes?"

"Yes," I said, relieved. Finally, at the age of forty-two, when I had money to spend on clothes, someone with good taste had come into my life to take charge of my wardrobe.

A month after our first kiss, Giulia told me that she loved me, and I told her about my accident.

"But you are fine!" she said. "Look at you! You're clever! You have a big job! Whatever problems you had have passed."

I shrugged.

There was both good and bad in having an injury, the effects of which weren't discernible to anyone else. I had done such a thorough job of disguising the signs of my brain damage, I had managed to fool the world. That disguise had given me a fellowship, a career, a few friends, and a relationship. The downside was that those closest to me often refused to acknowledge there was anything wrong. My head injury solicited zero sympathy, because no one could see the ways I struggled, the ways I'd changed. It was my word versus their observations.

I warned Giulia about the depression and the anger. I wanted to make sure I didn't repeat the same mistakes I had made with Laura. I knew there would be times when I would snap and brain-damaged Sarah would appear. I couldn't hide that side of me forever, and it was best that Giulia had some warning.

"I love you," she said. "I don't care about those things. We will manage."

Happily for me, Giulia was no stranger to anger. In fact, her temper—without any form of brain damage that she admitted to—was almost as bad as mine. My relationship with Laura had helped cement a long-standing theory I had about anger and relationships: if a person was prone to fits of rage, he or she needed a partner who was (a) also prone to fits of rage or (b) comfortable around people who were prone to fits of rage. Only a person with a terrible temper could truly understand and forgive a person with a terrible temper.

~

Giulia and I had been together three months when I invited her cat, Filippo, to move in with me. I felt bad that he was spending so much time alone. When I needed to travel, Giulia took him back to her place. My love affair with Filippo began almost immediately. He was a deeply affectionate and generous cat. He scratched me badly, but only once, and that was a mistake. It was a deep gash directly across the veins in my wrist and drew a rush of blood.

It soon became evident that I had a remarkable way with cats. Filippo adored me. *And why would he not?* He followed me from room to room, sat on my lap when I read or watched TV, watched me attentively as I worked on my laptop, and shared slices of my sashimi at dinnertime. Inside my apartment, we were never apart. He was a lot like a dog, really, without all the effort a dog required. I wasn't forced outside in the blazing heat to walk him, nor did I need to worry about his social development. Alone during the day while I was at work, he never once desecrated my kitchen. Filippo's needs were minimal, and during the six and a half minutes of each day when he wasn't sleeping, I satisfied them amply.

My relationship with Filippo was going so well that I decided to invite Giulia to join us. We had known each other for seven months and were spending every night together. I asked Giulia to move in, provided she accepted that Filippo and I had a very special relationship that she wouldn't be permitted to intrude upon. On the day she moved in, Filippo left a poo for us in our bathtub, signaling, I thought, his unhappiness with the new living arrangements. My anxiety manifested itself in more conventional ways.

The longer we spent in Singapore, the more we struggled to entertain ourselves. It is a tiny country, only 270 square miles, and there was a limit to what Giulia and I could do there. We dreamed of living in a real city like Hong Kong—a place that would allow us to do wild and crazy things like jaywalk, chew gum, tuck a durian under our arm and board a bus, engage in oral sex as an end in itself, and walk down the street holding hands. When we occasionally threw caution to the wind and held hands on the street in Singapore, elderly, stooped Chinese men would stop us and tell me how lucky I was to have such a beautiful daughter.

After three long years in Singapore, a headhunter called me about an HR job in Hong Kong, working for a tobacco company. I laughed and declined. I had left my job at the bank and taken a position at a consulting firm—and hated every second of it.

Consultants need excellent interpersonal skills to stroke the egos of their clients, and more than once my boss had kicked me under the table at a client meeting after I had said something to the effect of, "What on earth made you think *that* was a good idea?" When consultants aren't groveling to clients, they are whipping up dazzling PowerPoint presentations. Unfortunately, I have the computer skills of a preschooler. The job was a disaster, yet the global financial crisis loomed and companies had stopped hiring. If I left my job I would lose my employment visa and I'd have to leave Singapore. And Giulia. And Filippo.

The headhunter called again a week later. And a week after that. I assumed that nobody else had been interested. She nearly begged me to agree to an interview, so I ran the idea by Giulia, whose main concern was whether or not I would get free cigarettes. That would be a bonus, as she loved to smoke. She also liked the fact that the job would give us a chance to leave Singapore.

I spent a few days thinking about what it would be like to work for big tobacco. Could it really be worse than working for a bank that turned its customers out into the streets when they defaulted on their mortgages? The bank had started doing that in the months before I left. Every large corporation seemed to engage in unethical behavior—like a mining company that sends young men down mines, cutting their lives in half; or a company that makes detergents that pollute the environment; or a technology company that builds products that never disintegrate and will poison the earth forever; or KFC, which tortures the world's chickens.

I couldn't help thinking of my grandmother, who died from lung cancer without ever having smoked. Then I thought about one of my friend's fathers, who was eighty-five, in good health, and had smoked a pack of cigarettes every day of his life since he was fifteen. If you search long enough, you will find a justification for anything.

I moved to Hong Kong to begin my new job with the tobacco company in July 2008. Giulia would join me as soon as she found a job that would give her a work visa. Filippo would move as soon as I found an apartment.

My love for Hong Kong was instant. The noise and activity made me giddy. There was always something happening, something to observe. The locals were far friendlier and more approachable than the locals I had met in Singapore. Within weeks of arriving in Hong Kong, I knew it would be my home. My new employer paid for me to spend six weeks in a luxurious serviced apartment while I found somewhere to live. I eventually settled on a three-bedroom apartment in Mid-Levels that looked out onto the lush greenery of the Peak. As soon as I moved into the apartment, we made arrangements for Filippo and a second cat named Giorgio—that Giulia had acquired from a pet shop against all my urging—to join me.

It took the better part of a year before the tobacco company offered Giulia an entry-level job in marketing. I had not asked them to help, and it was a generous offer on their part. My boss at the time worried that I might leave because Giulia and I were unable to live in the same country. For nine months Giulia visited me in Hong Kong every weekend, but the four-hour flight each way was exhausting.

By the end of my first year in Hong Kong, I shared my apartment with Giulia, Filippo, and Giorgio. A friend in Melbourne had introduced me to two friends of hers who became friends of ours, and we befriended a former colleague from Melbourne and her partner who were living in Hong Kong. Life was good. All that was missing was a dog. We managed to plug that hole quite quickly with a middle-aged dog someone had found near a cargo pier. We named her Sofia.

I enrolled in a master of fine arts in creative writing. My job had given me the security to dip my toes into writing without making any real sacrifices. Other than my pride. At the urging of a professor, I started to write about my life. In a workshop, a group of eight people who barely knew me learned about my accident and my head injury from an essay I had written. The amount of people who knew about my injury doubled. It felt uncomfortable laying my life bare for strangers to poke through, but writing programs seem to attract more than their share of people with problems, and I was not the only one with a past I had kept hidden from the world.

Through writing I met two women who soon became my closest friends: a Taiwanese lawyer who had grown up in Montreal named Helena and a French woman named Isabelle. In Hong Kong, I was learning how to balance a normal life again, with friends, study, and a relationship.

There was only one problem with living in Hong Kong: the pollution had left me with a serious case of asthma. My respiratory physician there told me mine was the worst case he had seen in over a year. That was quite a feat. The only effective treatments were inhaled steroids or a pill called prednisone. Steroids and prednisone wreak havoc on damaged brains, so I would sit at home for a day or two, hooked up to a nebulizer and battling to breathe, and spend the days that followed battling to think.

I chalked my asthma up to karma for taking a job in big tobacco. But karma wasn't done with me just yet.

11

THE UNRAVELING

I went to London for a one-day meeting in April 2010 at the global headquarters of the tobacco company that employed me as a senior human resources person in Hong Kong. London is a damp, cold inhospitable place, and one night and one day there was more than enough. After dumping my suitcase in a corner of my hotel room and taking a shower under a trickle of lukewarm water, I climbed into bed.

Since the accident my fitful sleep was something I had continued to dread, like seeing my mother or getting a pap smear. But I was so tired after my flight I couldn't fight it off. It had been two years since I'd slept more than four hours on any night. Some nights I didn't sleep at all; others I was lucky to snatch two hours. When I closed my eyes, I saw hundreds of thousands of little orange lights spotted across a black canvas, like an aerial view of Delhi by night. Jet lag made it worse, and I traveled a lot, not just around Asia, but also back and forth to London. I had seen three doctors about my sleep problems, but no one had been able to help. "A residual effect of your accident," they said, offering no solution other than sleeping pills.

At nine thirty in the evening I turned off the light, closed my eyes, and drifted into sleep.

When I awoke, the electronic clock beside my bed read ten thirty p.m., or five thirty in the morning back in Hong Kong. I turned on the bedside lamp and picked up the day's newspaper. I toyed with eating the chocolates that were left on my pillow as part of the turndown service, but they'd acquired a calcified look. I wondered how many turndowns those chocolates had seen and decided instead to take a Mars bar from the minibar. Propping myself up with pillows, I opened the wrapper and bit into the chocolate.

In the six months leading up to this London visit, my memory problems had escalated to a point where I noticed problems almost daily. At first I thought my problems might have been caused by the steroids I was taking for my asthma, but I had stopped taking prednisone, which seemed to have the worst effect upon my memory. Even when I went weeks without any kind of breathing difficulties, the troubles with my memory persisted. I might struggle to remember something I agreed to do at work or forget my own telephone number. Lack of sleep made matters worse. On a bad day it felt like I'd been scalped and then wet cement had been poured inside my head. Something was wrong. I just didn't know what.

Finishing my Mars bar, my eyes rested on a banner in the top-right side of the paper that invited me to "Test Your IQ!" I groped around for a pen, sat upright in bed, and summoned all my powers of concentration. It was the first time I'd taken any kind of IQ test since meeting Toby at the brain center following my accident. The questions were tougher than I had expected, and it took me a while to answer them. I finished the test and struggled to tabulate my score. Ninety. My IQ was ninety—just ten points higher than it was days after my accident. Thirteen relatively normal years after three bad ones had led me to believe I was out of the woods. Perhaps I wasn't.

Distressed, I switched on the TV. The first channel showed a man in his sixties, his head in his hands, weeping. The TV guide told me it was a program about the writer Terry Pratchett and his diagnosis of

Alzheimer's. I watched this man wrestle with a puzzle while a woman I presumed to be a psychologist watched. He started to cry again. My body trembled. I decided to watch a show about a woman with tattooed eyebrows and her pole-dancing studio in industrial London, but nothing could erase the image of Terry Pratchett inside my head.

~

Back in Hong Kong, I talked to Giulia.

"You do not have Alzheimer's!" she shouted. She insisted that she hadn't seen any signs of diminishing cognitive functioning or memory problems in the five years we had been together.

"But you don't know the effort it takes me to remember things, to recall, to think clearly!" I said. "It gets harder and harder."

"Sorry," she said, shrugging, "but I don't see it."

We continued to have this same conversation on almost a daily basis for the next six months, until she threatened to leave unless I saw a doctor.

An internet search revealed that I needed blood tests to rule out some of the more obvious things that caused memory loss and impaired cognitive functioning in middle-aged women. The big ones were thyroid disease, vitamin B12 deficiency, perimenopause, and menopause. The doctor who called with my lab results told me that I'd tested negative to everything. The results added a new dimension to my panic.

Another internet search produced an article in the *Journal of Head Trauma Rehabilitation* that warned moderate to severe traumatic brain injury was associated with "later seizures, cognitive deficits, depression, aggression, unemployment, or social isolation." That part wasn't a surprise. The article went on to say that brain injury was also associated with "premature death, progressive dementia, Parkinson's disease, and endocrine dysfunction, particularly hypopituitarism."[19]

I felt like I had been dropped into an ice bath. The prospect of a progressive form of dementia terrified me.

In the years since my accident, I had grown accustomed to my anger and depression. They had cost me dearly, killing my relationships with family and lovers. They had *become* my family. The type of family that visited, overstayed their welcome, left their crap everywhere, and refused to budge from the sofa. I hadn't chosen them, but I knew them intimately and had learned to live with them. But a progressive form of dementia caused by my head injury was something I had never even considered.

Back on the internet again, I learned about the term "miserable minority." The term had been coined in the mid-1990s but was still in popular usage and refers to victims of mild traumatic brain injury whose symptoms had lasted beyond twelve months. The neuropsychologists who coined the term believed that most mild traumatic brain injuries resolved themselves within a period of one to three months. The miserable minority were individuals (mainly women according to the case studies provided) who typically suffered from "emotional risk factors," coexisting medical problems, or were motivated by financial gain through litigation. Their problems, the authors contended, were not necessarily "brain-based."[20] It is an offensive and unhelpful designation, leading one researcher to remark:

> When we unwittingly communicate the message that "this is all in your head" (pun intended) we may unintentionally foreclose scientific inquiry, drive persistently symptomatic patients away from the resources meant to proffer support (to them and their families), reinforce ugly gender stereotypes, and risk coming up on the wrong side of history (again).[21]

I had never suffered any emotional or psychological problems prior to my accident, besides the grief around my father's death. Nor had I been motivated in any way by the fruits of litigation after my accident. There was no litigation. Nor compensation. I found work as soon as I was able, and I had been employed ever since, apart from my year as a Harkness fellow and the year I spent as a full-time student and in recovery from hepatitis. The problems I'd experienced after my accident—including depression, anger, short- and long-term memory loss, and challenges with word finding and coordination—may not have been visible to the outside world, but they were part of my life, part of me. They were not in my head.

Years after the research into the so-called miserable minority, we know, through MRI technology, that the brain does *not* return to normal after a traumatic brain injury.[22] That explains why subsequent blows to the head can be so dangerous. We also know that a small proportion of sufferers of mild TBI experience the effects of their injury for many years afterward. We do not yet know why.

Recently, attention has been drawn to the fact that the very notion of recovery among brain-injured people is fraught with difficulty. Most clinicians consider an individual to have recovered if they are able to show some improvement in functioning independently. As one article published last year in the journal *Neural Plasticity* notes:

> It is important to point out that sometimes even when an individual appears to have "recovered" [from a brain injury] and is able to function independently, they may continue to show "silent" cognitive and motor deficits in areas such as emotion, attention, or fine motor control.[23]

I summoned all my courage and called my neurologist in Sydney to explain my problems. He asked me to make an appointment so he could talk to me in person, scan my brain, and test my brain waves. I had no choice but to return home to see him.

It was October 2010 by the time I visited my neurologist in Sydney. By that time, I had decided that my problem was chronic traumatic encephalopathy (CTE), a progressive degenerative disease of the brain I had read about in the *New York Times*. Its garden-variety name is *dementia pugilistica*, and it had recently been discovered that boxers and football players who have taken multiple blows to the head were particularly affected. Its symptoms take around seventeen years to manifest, and it had been sixteen years since my accident. Of course, I had suffered only one blow to the head, but who was to say it was impossible to develop CTE after a single traumatic brain injury? What was known about traumatic brain injuries was tiny compared to what *wasn't* known. My anxiety was compounded by the media. There was a stretch of about three months before my appointment when I swear the *New York Times* ran something about another NFL player with CTE a couple of times a week. Most of those men ended up with a gun in their mouths.

A taxi dropped Giulia and me off in the entranceway to the hospital, and we walked inside to the reception desk. Giulia tried to catch my hand, but I didn't want my hand held. Nothing she could do could allay my terror. We took an elevator to the seventh floor and walked around in a loop before finding the right office. I had never known more fear than in those moments, circling the hospital floor.

The waiting room was empty, and the doctor invited us in almost immediately. I had only seen him once before, when I started noticing problems with my memory after I stopped working at the newspaper, but there was something about this man I liked from the moment I met him. He was respectful and kind, and he listened without passing judgment.

"So what's going on?" he asked.

"I'm losing the ability to think. Some days it feels like I need jumper leads to get my brain working before I can process even the simplest things."

He looked at me and nodded. Giulia looked at him and rolled her eyes.

"You don't see it?" he asked her.

"I see no problem at all. Nothing."

He looked at us both in turn and gave a slight smile.

"English is her second language," I said, only half joking.

Giulia rolled her eyes a second time.

"The worst thing at the moment is my problem with words. I can't spell anymore. A couple of weeks ago I tried to spell 'friend.' It took me an age, going back and forth. In the end I had to pick up a dictionary.

"I used to be an excellent speller. And it's not just spelling. The meaning of words I once used conversationally are no longer clear to me. Words that are not complicated. Like 'adjudicate.' Or the wrong word hijacks my sentences, changing the meaning. When I mean 'book,' the word 'chair' pops out of my mouth. Or I use words that sound vaguely similar to the word I am trying to say, like 'beyond the *course* of duty' instead of 'beyond the *call* of duty.' It happened a lot after my accident, and it's started to happen again.

"When I write, my sentences are clunky and awkward, and I can't use punctuation anymore. I've forgotten how. I used to write well, but now writing feels like torture. I'm doing a master's of fine arts in creative writing, and every time I submit something, a professor red pens the whole thing and asks, 'What is up with your grammar?' My grammar was excellent before the accident."

"They sound like problems caused by your accident."

"Do you think it could be CTE?"

He looked at me and creased his forehead. "That would be highly unlikely, unless you have had other blows to the head."

"Just the one, as far as I know. But you can't rule it out without an autopsy.[24] Is it *impossible* to get CTE after one hit to the head?"

"Not impossible, I suppose. But I would be extremely surprised. Let's organize an MRI and some brain-wave tests," he said. "Then we will have a better idea. I'll get my assistant to book those now, and you can come back and see me at two o'clock."

The last time I had a brain MRI, when I was forty, I felt like my head had been stuck inside the propeller of a helicopter, so I was doubtful about my ability to endure it. Thankfully, technology had come a long way since then, and the MRI passed quickly and without incident.

An elderly woman in a spotted dress administered the brain-wave test. She told me she was seventy. She looked even older and smelled like a room that needed airing. After coating my head with a thick, sticky paste, she attached a lot of tiny electrodes to my scalp. Each electrode was linked by a wire to a machine. The test lasted forty minutes, during which time she asked me to alternate deep breathing and shallow breathing. During the course of the test she turned the lights on and off several times. As I watched the white-haired woman shuffle around me, performing the electroencephalogram, I couldn't help thinking it should have been her sitting in the chair, with me doing the testing.

When the tests were finished, I returned to the doctor's waiting room sick with fear. I would gladly have taken any disease, any illness, had my body paralyzed—anything—as long as my brain still worked. The next twenty years of my life flashed before me. I saw myself sitting in a nursing home—an environment I knew quite well—surrounded by people forty years older, eating nursing home food, sticking my hand up the skirt of every pretty nurse that passed. I had already decided the only sensible thing would be to kill myself as soon as I learned I had a form of dementia.

To be prepared, I had spent a few hours searching assisted dying online and had learned that if I could fork out around eight thousand dollars, the best place to go would be Switzerland. The budget version consisted of making a trip to Mexico and getting myself a couple of bottles of Nembutal. Mexico seemed an awfully long way to go when all I wanted was to sleep.

Giulia sat beside me, oblivious to my inner monologue. She had heard it all before.

The last time I'd brought up my plans, she had said to go right ahead, just as long as she didn't have to listen to me anymore. I watched her in the waiting room as she calmly flicked through a pile of old issues of *Newsweek* and *Woman's Weekly*. In the interest of medical science and preventing some other poor sucker from ending up in the unhappy situation I found myself in, I planned to donate my brain for research. My body, I'd decided, would be sent to the Chronic Traumatic Encephalopathy Center at Boston University, which led the world in research into damaged brains.

"Can we go to Hawaii this year?" Giulia asked as she thumbed through a soiled, dog-eared copy of the *Woman's Weekly* that she had laughingly pointed out was from June 2004. She put her hand on my leg, which was bobbing up and down violently.

"What?"

"Hawaii! Can we go this year?"

"Okay," I said without really registering her question. Then it occurred to me that in Hawaii I might be able to hurl myself inside a smoldering volcano and be done with it.

I wanted to take Giulia on a tour through my brain—to show her what had been going on behind my skull for the five years we'd spent together. I imagined it would look like a house that had been destroyed by fire. Nothing would be left but the frame and foundations. I'd take her through the belly of the badly charred living room and point out the remains of furniture and personal belongings, things I barely recognized. Everything would be covered in a thick blanket of ash. I would lead her by the hand from room to room and she would see it for herself, so that when I told her my brain no longer worked, she would understand what I was saying.

My mind churned until the neurologist finally opened his office door and invited us inside.

"Look, there is definitely something wrong here," he said, staring at his computer screen at pictures that showed my brain from multiple angles. "But it's not Alzheimer's."

"No signs of amyloid?" I asked, in a barely veiled attempt to show him I knew what I was talking about. I had read enough in the *Lancet Neurology* to know that amyloid is an indicator of Alzheimer's disease.

"None," he said.

"What is it then?"

"I don't know."

"Is it progressive?" That word was harder for me to say than any word I had ever spoken. I couldn't bring myself to utter the word "dementia." My mouth refused.

"I don't think so."

I was so anxious about being there and having my brain tested, and so relieved to hear the words "I don't think so," that I forgot all the questions I had meant to ask him.

Giulia leaned across and hugged me. "What did I tell you?"

He handed me the radiologist's report. My eyes skipped down the page to the paragraph headed "Conclusion" and came to rest on the phrase "significant atrophy." I read the section carefully.

> There is significant atrophy of the central sulcal motor cortex and post motor cortex and some atrophy of the posterior parietal region as well as parieto-occipital cortex parasagittally. There is mild ventricular prominence.

I felt like I was reading a different language. The only words that meant anything were "significant atrophy." The doctor interrupted my reading. He told me the atrophy accounted for the problems I had been having—poor concentration, short- and long-term memory issues, the time it took messages to leave my brain, problems with spatial aware-ness, diminished vocabulary, and difficulty spelling. I completely forgot about the report from the electroencephalogram, and he didn't offer to share it with me.

"What happens next?" I asked.

"Watch and see."

"What can I do?"

"Cut back on alcohol. No spirits, no cocktails. One glass of red wine a day, no more than five times a week. The more expensive, the better."

I could live with that if I had to. Giulia was not a big drinker, and I drank considerably less with her than I had done when I was with Laura. The problem was weekends, when we went out with friends. Alcohol made everything so much more fun.

"What else?"

"Exercise at least four times a week. Read, write, keep working. Take up a foreign language. Chinese or something with different char-acters," he said.

"I don't want to learn Chinese. I'm too old; I don't see the point. Languages aren't my thing. These days I struggle to string a sentence together in English."

He looked at me and nodded. "Well, writing is great, so keep that up.

"There's just one more thing," the neurologist said. "Try to keep a positive outlook. That can make a big difference." I looked at him, and the expression on my face must have signaled that a positive outlook was about the last thing I was capable of keeping. "Well, try anyway," he offered.

When we left the hospital, Giulia wanted to celebrate—to go shopping and have a nice dinner. Her optimism made me feel emptier than ever.

"You don't have Alzheimer's!" she said jubilantly.

I hadn't even thought I had Alzheimer's! Well, maybe I had for a while, but that was before I'd discovered CTE.

"Are you *never* happy?" she asked as we hailed a taxi outside the hospital.

I reflected for a moment before answering, "Lately, no," and hanging my head.

She clicked her tongue. "Jesus! You are such a drama queen! It's great news! Be happy!"

I smiled and ignored her. I wasn't in the mood for a fight. What I really wanted to do was curl up under a tree for a few hours and sleep the whole trip off. I thought back and remembered another *New York Times* article, in which a number of neurologists said they often didn't tell patients with progressive dementias their diagnoses because the knowledge sent people into a downward spiral. It was easier to keep living with a sliver of hope. I didn't really want to know about another hopeless prognosis, but I couldn't help wondering what significant atrophy meant. And what was left after significant? Total? Comprehensive? Extreme? Absolute? Whatever it was, it wasn't good.

I called my mother right after the appointment to tell her I was in town and to ask if Giulia and I could pop around and say hello. We had emailed each other on a few occasions since her lightning visit to Singapore, and I had contacted her when I had been in Sydney for work visits, but she had never been free to meet me. This time I caught her off guard.

"Oh," she said, and began to fumble for an excuse. "Well, I suppose if you're quick. I'm going out soon."

"We will be quick," I promised.

After my mother disposed of my father's rare book collection, she sold the family home and moved into the apartment she had inherited from my grandfather. We turned up at her apartment, which wasn't far from the hospital, and I introduced her to Giulia. I could tell instantly that my mother didn't like Giulia. I wasn't sure whether it was the fact that Giulia was fifteen years my junior, or if it was just my mother's long-standing prejudice against pretty blonde women. She did her best to be polite and invited us in.

I told her I was in town to visit the neurologist and that I'd just had an MRI. That I was concerned about a deterioration in my memory.

"Don't be ridiculous! Why would you have dementia? What a silly thing to think!" she said, looking to Giulia for support. Giulia nodded at her in agreement. I resisted the impulse to scream.

While we drank a cup of tea, my mother told me that all her friends were sick or dying. She discussed each in turn. Then she glanced at her watch. "I need to get ready now. I'm going to the opera."

As we rode the elevator to the ground floor, Giulia looked at me, shook her head, and leaned in to hug me. "Your mother is horrible!" she said.

There was still a small part of me that was wounded every time I had contact with my mother. I couldn't help wishing things were different. I couldn't help hoping she would change.

~

Back home in Hong Kong, I visited the Wanchai Computer Center. A colleague who had just had her first baby and struggled with "baby brain" mentioned that Nicole Kidman had endorsed a Nintendo DS game with brain exercises. I love Nicole Kidman and considered her a credible spokeswoman for neuroplasticity, so I decided to get one for myself.

I stumbled inside a shop selling computer toys and attempted to haggle with an old man who had a thick clump of lucky hair sprouting from his chin. I failed and paid full price for a Nintendo device and the brain games disc. All my hopes hung on a game that had Nicole Kidman's stamp of approval.

I took my Nintendo home, turned it on, and inserted a disc the size of a postage stamp marked *Brain Age*. A cartoon likeness of a Hawaiian man who claimed to be a famous neurologist popped up on the screen and invited me to test my brain age. I did as I was told. To my horror, all the questions involved numbers. Seconds later a message flashed up on the screen: *Sorry, your brain age is 87!* Hands trembling, I picked the Nintendo DS up and shoved it inside a drawer of my desk. That little device had seen in a matter of seconds what Giulia and Laura and my mother had failed to see. Days later I gave the Nintendo to a friend's son.

~

Eight months after my visit to the neurologist, Filippo died from kidney failure. Giulia and I stroked his belly, and I kissed his head as the vet slipped a needle into his leg. His death and the decline that led to it left me devastated.

The day after Filippo died, I lost my job at the tobacco company. My old boss, whom I liked, had moved to London and been replaced by a new boss I didn't like. He came into my office, closed the door behind him, and said, "Look, your performance is excellent, but you don't fit in here." It was hard to argue with that.

Giulia had spent two years with the tobacco company. She was a perfect fit, so in a rather awkward twist, she stayed and I left.

Days after I packed up my office, Giulia told me she had fallen out of love with me. She had just been promoted and loved her new job. I was heartbroken. I had known for more than six months she was drifting away from me, but there was nothing I could do. There wasn't anyone else. She had just grown tired of me, and my depression, and my mood swings, and my anxiety. It had stopped being fun. *I* had stopped being fun.

My life felt like a plane falling out of the sky. In my relationship with Giulia, I had tried so hard to avoid repeating the same mistakes I had made with Laura, and yet here I was again. The problem was me.

Things got worse. I subscribed to a brain-training website called Brain HQ, which was developed by a neurologist who was an exponent of brain plasticity. I did the most basic exercises under the following categories: Attention, Brain Speed, Memory, and People Skills (facial and voice recognition), and I was horrified to learn I scored in the bottom quarter on each dimension. My brain was in worse shape than I had thought it was.

I called my neurologist and explained my frustrations. I was noticing problems with my brain almost every day, but the people I'd worked with, my best friends, and the person I'd lived with for six years had noticed nothing. Giulia left me because she had tired of hearing me complain about something she could not see, or so she said.

"Well, if she didn't want to stick around, she wasn't worth the effort," my doctor said over the phone. "You haven't invented anything. You have a problem. The scans show that. We just don't know what kind of problem yet. I have a patient with Alzheimer's who is a professor of architecture. He's cut his teaching load, but he still works."

I fell silent.

"You do not have Alzheimer's! I'm just trying to make the point that no one has noticed his problems. That's how it is for many smart people with brain conditions. They may notice a decline, but it is not necessarily evident to others. It might not be for some time."

I exhaled.

"Any decline with you is happening very slowly, if at all," he added. "Keep writing."

I thanked him and hung up the phone, thinking that losing one's memory and cognitive abilities was a lot like draining a dam using a bucket. It could take a while.

~

I found a job working four days a week in HR for a construction company, and Giulia and I both decided to move across town to the greener, cheaper side of Hong Kong. We took leases on two apartments in the same block. Our goal was to continue to coparent our dogs and cats. Between us, we now had four rescue dogs; Giorgio, the cat Giulia had bought in Singapore; and two cats I had rescued. We wanted them to be able to move between our apartments with ease. We split the costs of a domestic helper who could care for our pets when we were at work. I made Giulia promise she would care for them forever should anything happen to me, and she gave me her word. I told her if she ever changed her mind that I would come back from the dead and make every day of her life hell.

"That's okay," she said, suppressing a smile. "I lived with you long enough. I know what hell feels like."

I spoke to my two closest friends, Helena and Isabelle, and told them about my significant atrophy. Both of them were adamant that they couldn't detect any problems with my brain but promised that, if they did, they would tell me. Isabelle offered to take me to Zurich if things got really bad. "I'll hold your hand," she said. "I promise." That meant a lot.

I began to retreat from life. When I wasn't at work, I spent my time at home with our dogs and cats. Sofia, a black-and-white dog who looked eerily like Bess, would not leave my side. We had rescued her within a week of Giulia moving to Hong Kong, after someone had found her starving, without fur, and doing her best to raise seven tiny puppies. Her puppies found homes quickly, but she had shifted around in foster care for more than a year before we saw a sign in a vet surgery saying she needed a home urgently. Sofia and I had formed the kind of bond I had shared with Bess. She was an incredibly loving and empathetic dog who sat at my feet when I was at my desk or beside me on the sofa when I watched TV. At night she took Giulia's place in my bed, stretching out alongside me, under the covers whenever it was cold, making sure that part of her was in contact with part of me. On the few occasions I cried, she licked my hand and would not stop until I did.

Things continued to get worse in my head. In early 2013 I emailed my neurologist and explained that I had entered what seemed like the next wave of deterioration. What felt like a bad day less than a year ago was now the best of days. I could no longer trust my memory. It didn't matter if I was talking to friends about a movie we had seen or trying to remember something about a place I once visited. I was almost invariably wrong. For someone who had spent most of her life reminding everyone around her she was right, this required some adjustment. My dining room table was smothered with Post-it notes—things I had forgotten and finally remembered, and things I needed to remember in the future. I felt like I was stepping down a ladder into the sea, with every couple of months bringing new, unwelcome challenges.

I told my doctor I had found a new job that allowed me to work a four-day week because I needed the money and a visa to allow me to continue living in Hong Kong. The problems with my brain were not impacting my work, as long as I went everywhere with a notebook and wrote everything down. My coworkers had only commented on my memory once. Two of them had giggled when I offered to buy them coffee and wrote their orders down inside my notebook. "Three coffees and one of them is yours," one laughed. "Can't you remember?" I shrugged and smiled. It had become exhausting. I promised myself that I would stop work as soon as I turned fifty and use what time I had left to write.

I told the doctor that my brain felt exhausted—one part was always trying to pick up the slack from another part that had perished. I worried that soon the parts of my brain capable of compensating would shrink and I'd have nothing left at all.

He wrote back: "I share your concern about your impaired cognitive function. It is difficult to know without studying you closely whether the condition is progressing or whether you had a monophasic insult that has left its damage, and now, over time, your reserve of memory and capacity for multitasking has started to reduce." Come back and let's repeat the tests, he suggested, and do some psychometric tests.

The last time I had submitted to psychometric tests, I had learned my IQ was around eighty. That news had devastated me. The IQ test I had taken in the newspaper the night I found myself unable to sleep in London had increased that score to ninety. It was still a very low number. I would never submit to the stress of another series of psychometric tests.

Without much in the way of an alternative, I decided to stay in Hong Kong, sharing my dogs and cats with a woman who no longer loved me and spending the hours I wasn't working writing in an attempt to preserve whatever memories I had left.

I longed for the day when I could finally give up.

12

MELANCHOLIA

I stopped working in December 2013, three months after my fiftieth birthday. My days in HR were finally over. I would never fire another person, hire another person, discipline someone for absenteeism, or tell another chief executive that "cunt" was not an acceptable term to use in the workplace.

I had reconciled myself to arranging my own death, rather than lose my mind to the dementia I was convinced awaited me. I prepared a will and started giving my favorite possessions away to my friends. I stopped buying things that I wouldn't use immediately. The last thing I wanted to leave was a legacy of clutter. In fact, I wanted to leave no trace at all. I sold my car. I sold my house in Sydney. I promised my cousin I would buy her a house in return for taking care of my dogs, should anything happen. She lived on Queensland's Sunshine Coast and worked only part-time. The pups would be happy enough there, where they could gambol along the sands of Coolum Beach.

I planned to be dead by the following Christmas.

I downloaded paperwork from Dignitas, an organization based outside Zurich that assists terminally ill people to die. I wasn't terminally ill, of course, but that seemed, to me, a minor stumbling block. It had taken me months to summon the courage to even open the link on their website. Once I had, everything became much simpler. I was taking matters into my own hands and choosing to die a peaceful, dignified death, before dementia ravaged what was left of my brain. I started thinking about my last supper, a fondue and chocolate dinner with my closest friends at a fancy restaurant in Zurich, followed by all the champagne I could drink. I toyed briefly with the idea of paying for a high-end call girl. Sadly, perhaps, that was something I would not be able to follow through on. Assisted suicide I believed I could manage. Hiring a call girl I could not.

~

In April 2014 I traveled to Sydney to see my neurologist. I planned to ask him to sign the paperwork saying I was a suitable candidate for assisted suicide. We talked for a couple of minutes before he sent me off to imaging for a brain MRI and a new scan I had never had before, a spectroscopy. Brain spectroscopies are performed on the same machine as an MRI, but they measure changes in brain chemistry.

An attractive woman with perfect teeth and short dark hair invited me into a small, stark, white room and helped me lie down on the bed.

"The tests are going to take forty minutes," she said, and I looked at her with horror.

"I don't think I can lie in there for forty minutes. That's a very long time." I had struggled in the past to lie still even for twenty minutes.

"This is a brand-new machine," she said gently. "It's much quieter than the older ones, and it has a rearview mirror. You can watch the street if you like. It helps the time pass. There's music too. Buddha-Bar."

Normally I would rather stick a pitchfork through my foot than listen to world lounge music, but what choice did I have? She placed a set of headphones over my ears, clamped a plastic frame tightly over my head, and asked if I was comfortable.

"No," I said, and she laughed.

"In an emergency, just press the red button and I'll come in right away. And no swallowing or twitching during the tests or we'll need to repeat them. Keep perfectly still," she said, and winked.

I couldn't help wondering if she was gay. She was doing a good imitation of flirting, but perhaps it was just a ploy to keep me docile. I waved goodbye with one hand, and she pressed a button that sent me deep inside the large plastic cone.

Her voice came through a microphone, calm and crisp. "Hi, Sarah. Are you okay?"

"No!" I wanted to say, but I croaked, "Yes," trying to be brave.

The tests began. First the drilling, then the whirring, then the jack-hammering, and then a noise that sounded like someone was trying to crack open the shell of my machine with an ax and steal my brain. My mind darted across the Pacific to China, where people woke up in ice baths to discover slits down their fronts and sides and organs missing. I strained to hear the dreary sameness of Buddha-Bar through the clatter.

Saliva leaked down my throat. My chest heaved. I needed to swallow or I was going to cough—one of those coughing fits that come on in a theater or a concert hall and won't let go. *I will choke,* I thought, *and drown in my own spittle.* I closed my eyes and pretended I was dead.

After what felt like ages, I glanced up at the rearview mirror and looked at the street: an intersection with a café on one corner, a flame tree on the other. A woman trailed behind her dog, and a gaggle of people walked to work. I drifted off and imagined I was the sole witness to a robbery, a knifing, a kidnapping. Like Jimmy Stewart in *Rear Window.* What would happen then? For a moment or two I forgot my damaged brain.

Finally the nurse pressed a button that slid me out from inside the machine and entered the room.

She took my hand, squeezed it, and looked at me with a mixture of sadness and pity. *Your skull is empty. It's like a giant cicada shell. We can't find anything inside it,* was what I expected her to say.

Instead she said, "Sarah, I'm so sorry. We're going to have to repeat the tests. I've never done a spectroscopy before, and it seems I've made an error."

I was convinced my brain had shown something so shocking that it needed to be viewed from new and different angles. People needed to be assembled to witness the void inside my head and that would take time.

She must have detected my terror because she said quickly, "The problem isn't you. It's me."

Her boss, an unambiguously heterosexual older woman, walked in to explain. "It's a new machine, and not everyone knows how to use it. It's just not as simple as it seems. We're very sorry."

"This will only take twenty minutes," the pretty nurse said, squeezing my leg. "You're going to be fine."

I tried to smile. I had come a long way for these tests, and I needed them if I was going to be allowed to fly to Switzerland to die.

When the second test ended, I wandered off to another part of the hospital where a middle-aged woman with a rash across her face attached electrodes to my head and conducted an electroencephalogram.

I returned to my neurologist's office after he had taken the time to examine the results of my MRI, spectroscopy, and electroencephalogram. It wasn't until that point that I told him about the documentation I needed for Dignitas.

"I can't sign that!" he said, shaking his head.

"Why not?"

"It's way too soon."

I told him about my cousin and the house I had promised to buy her.

"Well, you're going to need somewhere to live too, so tell your cousin to cool her heels."

"I've sold my house here! Sold my car!"

He eased himself back into his chair.

"What exactly are we talking about?" I asked. "Another couple of years?"

"I can't give you a time frame."

"Two years?"

Nothing.

"Three?"

Nothing.

"Five?"

"You're a very unusual case. I can't possibly give you a time frame. I honestly don't know."

"I want to die. I'm ready for it."

"You are not ready to die. Not even close. You need to talk to someone about that. I have a colleague who is excellent. I'll write you a referral. You can see him next time you're in Sydney."

I exhaled slowly.

"I've looked at the scans and compared them to the last ones, and I don't think it's progressive. The changes we see on your MRI scans are happening very slowly, and they are in the parts of the brain that took the impact from your accident. There's another important factor here: your sense of taste and smell is fine. That's not the case with most progressive dementias."

"Oh," I said, unable to mask my surprise.

"I will say, though, that I think your head injury was severe rather than mild. It's unusual to see the kinds of changes that show up on your scans with a mild traumatic brain injury. You had a very bad knock to the head."

"But wouldn't a severe head injury mean my speech and movement would be affected?" That was what I had learned from reading about the Glasgow Coma Scale, which was used to help distinguish between mild, moderate, and severe types of head trauma.

"Not necessarily. I'd like us to repeat the tests in four years from now to determine any changes. That will give you time to get on top of your anxiety. How does that sound?"

"So I'm not going to Switzerland?" I asked, with a mix of shock and disappointment.

"No, you are not. How long do you plan on staying in Hong Kong?"

"I don't know. I planned to die."

"Perhaps you should think about moving home."

"Sydney?"

He nodded. "And remember to exercise, limit your drinking to one glass of red wine per day, eat healthily, and make an appointment to see Peter. He's the best psychiatrist I know, and I have a feeling you two will get along well. Remember, depression and anxiety make everything worse."

"I wish it were so easy."

"I know. Peter will be able to help. And keep writing!"

"Okay," I said, realizing I may have been too hasty with some of the decisions I had made.

"Here are the MRI pictures," he said, handing me a large envelope. "There is no report this time, because I asked them to send me the scans urgently, given you're only in town for a couple of days. I'll email you a summary letter. You can email me anytime with questions."

I got up, thanked him for all his help, hugged him, and walked outside into a bright Sydney day.

Once you convince yourself you'll be dead by Christmas, the idea of another few years of life can take some getting used to. I had been given a reprieve, and that made me sad. To complicate matters, I had made a lot of life decisions I could not undo.

Back in Hong Kong, I took to my sofa and spent my days slumped in front of the TV, watching shows about overfed, precocious children; about Long Island mediums; about creepy American men who married mail-order brides in ninety days and then were shocked to discover that their chosen one didn't want to have sex with them; about the Kardashians and the Amish; about the parents who sexualized their five-year-old girls and sent them out to compete in beauty pageants; and about the guy who looked like a plainer version of Jon Bon Jovi who went into people's homes to remove their rattlesnakes.

I mused about my own idea for a reality TV show, *The Aspiring Writer*. It would be filmed with hidden cameras and show the lead character, a melancholy white woman of around fifty, transfixed in front of her own TV, or scrubbing her air-conditioning machines with a wire brush, or sorting through her collection of chopsticks and organizing them according to hue, or picking through the contents of her desk and discovering things she never knew she owned: photos of old boyfriends and girlfriends, a small plastic box full of erasers shaped like dinosaurs. I would watch a show like that.

I took Giulia to dinner at Nobu in Tsim Sha Tsui to celebrate her birthday. Living next door to one another had done nothing but prolong the agony of my heartbreak. We still saw each other almost every day, and I was no closer to falling out of love with her than I had been when she broke up with me. Isabelle and Helena both told me I was crazy for living next door to Giulia, but I couldn't break free. I was pathetic—I knew that—but I still hoped there was a sliver of a chance she might turn around and tell me she wanted me back. "She doesn't love you," Helena said to me each time I saw her. "You have to move on!"

In the taxi on the way to the restaurant with Giulia, I made the mistake of remarking on the fact that this was the first occasion for which I had left my apartment in over a fortnight, for any purpose other than to walk the dogs. Longer, in fact. I had glanced in the mirror as I was getting ready to leave the house and had been surprised to find my face was the color of a button mushroom.

As soon as we were seated, Giulia told me I was wallowing. Depressed. And lazy. Not that any of those states was a surprise to her.

"What the hell do you do all day?" she asked.

"Watch TV, eat popcorn, stare out the window."

"Jesus, Sarah! You gave up a good job for that?" she asked, waving her hands in the air.

"I hated it."

"You've hated every job you've ever had!" she said.

"True."

"You're meant to be writing. That's your life's dream, remember?"

I sighed and tapped my fingers on the table, waiting for her to stop.

"You need to exercise! Leave the house! Go outside. Do something! Find another job and write on weekends."

I stared at the table and felt a rush of hatred toward her.

My dream was to write. But it was more complicated than that. Writing had saved my brain after the accident. Had I not returned to my research and retaught myself how to read and write, I don't believe that my brain would have repaired itself. What Giulia didn't understand, because I hadn't told her, was that I still harbored the dim hope that writing might be able to save my brain a second time. That was why I had clung to it so fiercely. But depression fuels lassitude like petrol fuels fire, and until I found a way out of this last stretch of gloom, writing, like every single other activity apart from watching bad TV, seemed impossible.

The waiter brought us two glasses of champagne, and as I took my first sip I decided Giulia was right. I wallowed. I was depressed. And I was lazy. I needed boundaries. With work, I never had enough time to write. Now I had too *much* time. Freedom creates a prison all its own.

I lay in bed the next morning, awaiting the moment I'd finally manage to stir myself from this torpor. Eventually I heaved myself off my mattress, threw on some clothes I found in a heap on my bathroom floor, and went for a walk. I needed to think about my future, a future in which I would write and walk and try not to wallow.

I needed to change my life.

I walked down my street, along the edge of the Shing Mun Country Park, before coming upon three of the sickliest-looking puppies I had ever seen. They were nestled underneath a few bushes by the side of the road where men were digging trenches for sewage works. Two were black and one was brown. They looked to be around five weeks old. The puppies had made their home on a concrete ledge at the top of an embankment, less than twenty feet away from one of Hong Kong's busiest roads. They were wild dogs whose mother had probably ventured out from the country park behind the embankment in search of food. Hong Kong's country parks were full of wild dogs—dogs whose ancestors were dumped by their owners, dogs who struggled to fend for themselves.

I raced home, grabbed a bag of kibble, ran down the hill, crawled up the embankment, and deposited three large piles of food. The puppies scampered out from their hiding place and gobbled down the food.

The next morning I woke early, eager to feed the puppies. I scrambled up the embankment to deposit the mounds of kibble, and one of the black puppies came out to greet me. I placed a handful of dry food in my palm and offered it to her. She ate from my hand. I had been feeding packs of wild dogs in the Shing Mun Country Park for more than eighteen months, but I had never had a dog or puppy come close enough to allow me to touch it. The puppy glanced up at me with a worried look and wagged her tail, and I was so entranced by this scrawny black puppy, and its mixed message of anxiety and relief, that I forgot to remove my hand. Eager for more food, the puppy gnawed a small hole in one of my fingers. I pulled my bleeding hand away.

My neighborhood in Hong Kong was eight train stops away from China, and China happens to have the second-largest rabies problem of any country in the world. A wire fence separated Hong Kong from China, and although Hong Kong was supposedly rabies-free, between 2007 and 2010, twenty-five people had died from rabies after dog bites in Shenzhen, a city that borders Hong Kong. I called the local hospital. "Come here right away," the nurse on reception told me.

The nurse cleaned the wound on my finger with disinfectant, jabbed my arm with a needle full of Verorab, and told me to return for four more shots over the course of a month. Rabies shots are like tetanus shots: they hurt. It wasn't the first time I had been treated for possible rabies exposure. On holiday in Langkawi once, at Giulia's insistence, I fed a stray kitten a small piece of fish. Ravenous, the kitten bit through my flesh, puncturing the skin in two places. I was talking to a friend at work three days later back home in Singapore, when, alarmed by my story, my friend told me two things I didn't know: there was rabies in Langkawi, and a person needed to start treatment for a rabies infection within seventy-two hours. It had been over seventy hours since the bite, but not quite seventy-one, so I raced out of the office and took a taxi to the local hospital, where I had a needle in my arm with one hour to spare.

As I stood in line waiting to pay the cashier in the hospital in Hong Kong, it occurred to me that repeating the same mistakes was an incontrovertible sign of my own idiocy. But that didn't change my compulsion. Nothing jolted me out of my depression more than an animal in need of care.

Anxious about the state of the puppies, I woke at six the next morning and headed down the hill, a large bag of dog food tucked under my arm. I felt useful, invigorated. I reached the top of the embankment, and one of the black puppies rushed toward me. It may have been the same one that bit me, but I couldn't be certain. Emboldened by the Verorab coursing through my veins, I held out my arm, and she stepped inside the palm of my hand. I clutched her to my chest and climbed back down to the road. This tiny wild puppy, who weighed no more than a mango, was happy to be held. She looked at me, her brow furrowed and her head cocked, but she made no attempt to struggle. She seemed to be asking *Where are we going?* rather than *Why are you holding me?* And both of these would have been good questions. Why *had* I picked up this sickly-looking dog and what were my plans for it? I had no clue. A tick crawled up my arm, and I flicked it off with my wounded finger.

I carried the puppy under my arm for three blocks to the nearest vet, where together the vet and his nurse used tweezers to remove sixty ticks from her tiny body. The vet wormed her and injected her with fluids.

"She would have died out there," he said. "In a matter of days. She's very malnourished."

Back home I bathed her with a medicated tick shampoo and jumped in the shower to rid myself of the fleas and ticks that had migrated from her body to mine. I fed her and put her to bed on my sofa next to Ambrose, my other wild dog. He glanced at her and pretended she wasn't there. Sofia, my oldest dog, stared at her before shooting me a look that said, *Tell me this is temporary.*

The puppy curled up on top of a stuffed reindeer and fell asleep almost instantly. I looked at her body, alarmingly thin and missing large patches of fur. Something had bitten her on the snout, leaving an open wound. I soaked a cotton ball in saline solution and cleaned the gash. She looked at me with a steady gaze before dropping back into a deep slumber, her chest rising and falling as she breathed. I studied her, marveling at the size of her enormous, donkey-like ears. Her eyes were set too close together. She was odd looking, with a face that reminded me of Vladimir Putin.

What am I doing? I asked myself. I was the coparent of four dogs already. Two of the dogs I had rescued with Giulia spent their days with me and their nights with her. Sofia and Ambrose, who lived with me, were middle-aged dogs whose needs were met with two meals a day, four short walks, a spot on my sofa, and as many cuddles as they could stand. Luca and Toby, the two street cats I had adopted after our breakup, did as they pleased. A puppy was a different commitment altogether.

I called Giulia at work and told her the news. "I left the house," I said.

"Finally!"

"And I found a puppy."

"What?"

"Well, I found three puppies, but I only managed to catch one."

"Are you fucking crazy?"

"Not yet," I said.

"Jesus, Sarah! The last thing we need is another puppy!"

"There is no 'we' anymore."

"Jesus Christ."

"It was going to die!" I said. "What should I have done? Leave it there?"

"Well, as long as you find it a home," she said, and I pictured her nostrils flaring on the other end of the telephone.

"That's the plan."

"Did you look for a job yet?"

"No," I said, and hung up the phone.

After lunch I walked down my street with more food in search of the other two puppies. I scaled the embankment and called for them, but they had disappeared. I left the food and went home to tend to my new puppy. Her name, I decided, would be Scout.

I checked again on the puppies early the next morning, but the work-men digging trenches had laid live electrical cables through a clearing in the bushes. A piece of plastic tied to the cable warned "Live Wires." I could no longer crawl up to the concrete ledge without risk of electrocution. From the road, I searched for any sign of the two puppies, but they had vanished. The food I had left the day before had not been touched. That evening I ran into a neighbor who said she had just seen a black puppy lying dead in the gutter at the bottom of our street.

I raced inside to Scout, picked her up, kissed her, and told her how lucky she was. I decided not to tell her about her siblings. She curled up in my lap and started to snore.

By the time I had finished with my third rabies shot, Scout had fallen ill. She lay on her bed, unable to lift her head. She tried to wag her tail but even that was a struggle. Perhaps the gash on her snout was a bite from an animal that had slipped across the border from China.

I decided to educate myself about the rabies virus. Googling something other than "head trauma" and "dementia" invigorated me. I learned that the incubation period for rabies usually lasted between one and three months but could vary anywhere from one week to one year. That wasn't terribly helpful, so I moved on to symptoms. The first symptom in animals and people seemed to be fever, followed by a burning sensation at the wound site and then by pica, or the desire to eat things that don't have nutritional value (a word I would never have known the meaning of had I not watched a TV show about a pregnant woman in America who ate chalk). Like most puppies, Scout enjoyed chewing shoes and books—she'd devoured the spine of David Foster Wallace's *A Supposedly Fun Thing I'll Never Do Again* and the corner of a ceramic Chairman Mao statue I had in my living room. Other, more advanced symptoms included seizures and an inability to swallow.

The more I read, the more absorbed I became. Rabies was probably the oldest infectious disease in the world. Pliny the Elder (23–79 AD), my first point of contact when it came to medical matters, believed that dogs could become rabid by tasting the menstrual blood of a woman and that dogs were most susceptible to rabies while the Dog Star was shining. Pliny's recommendation for protecting a dog against rabies was feeding it chicken droppings. People were counseled to ward off rabies by carrying the worm of a dead dog or the menstrual blood—again!—from a female dog, or by placing the tongue of a dog in one's shoe underneath the big toe, or by carrying a weasel's tail—provided the weasel has survived and been returned to the wild.[25] Elsewhere, I learned that life expectancy at the time was thirty-five.

Rabies was a horrible way to die, but it happened quickly. A few days of frothing at the mouth, biting people, madness, and life was over. Dementia took years or, at worst, decades. It was the descent into craziness, the disorientation that seized its victim between moments of lucidity, the knowing, and the complete and utter powerlessness. I was terrified of seeing out my days in a stupor in a nursing home's communal area, oblivious to the smell of terrible food and incontinence, clapping my hands while a nurse with a guitar sang the theme song to *Skippy the Bush Kangaroo*.

I decided Scout didn't have rabies. Her illness came on suddenly, so it was more likely something she had eaten. Her tendency to chew books, statues, furniture legs, blankets, the ears of one of my cats, and toothpaste tubes, and her ability to pry open a remote control, pop out its batteries, and chew on them had me worried. I turned off my computer, called a taxi, and took Scout over to Hong Kong Island to the best vet in town.

The vet took one look at Scout and decided to take a blood sample for tick fever. I sat in the waiting room, Scout asleep in my arms. Half an hour later, the vet appeared to tell me Scout had tick fever and ringworm. Her platelets were dangerously low, and she needed to begin treatment immediately. "It's very expensive, I'm afraid."

"Of course it is!" I laughed.

"It's the same treatment they use for malaria in humans," he said. "But it's her only chance of pulling through."

I watched him prepare the medication she needed for the next two weeks.

"Could she die?" I asked as he handed over a large plastic bag full of pills and a small bottle of fluorescent-yellow liquid.

"Let's see how she responds to the medication. Hopefully we have got to it in time. But it's babesiosis, and that can be fatal. Bring her back in two days' time and we'll repeat the blood tests."

I paid the enormous bill and carried my floppy puppy home. "Don't die, don't die, don't die, little one. I really need you to live," I whispered as the taxi took us home. Scout rested her head on my shoulder, and I stroked the top of her head.

Two days later the blood tests showed that Scout was improving.

"She's doing really well!" the vet said. "Have you decided what you're going to do with her?"

"I'll try to find her a home. When she's better." I have no idea where those words came from. I had zero intention of ever letting this puppy out of my sight.

Scout had made a full recovery by the time I trundled off to the hospital for my final rabies shot.

"If you feel unwell, come back right away," the nurse said as she flicked at the needle and jammed it into the muscle in my shoulder.

I started feeling dreadful by the time I found my car in the hospital parking lot, but I remembered from the course of shots I had had in Singapore, the last one was the worst. Verorab is very potent. I drove home and put myself to bed. I ached all over, and my body throbbed. Scout, now big enough to hop onto the bed unassisted, walked up and down me like a Thai massage therapist, spreading the vaccine through every last inch of my body. Once done, she curled herself up inside my arm and fell asleep.

I leaned over and kissed her head. "It's a big question for a tiny pup, but will you fill the hole in my heart?" She turned her head to face mine and held my gaze with her dark-brown eyes.

It took a few days before I started to feel better. I was no longer at risk of dying from rabies.

In a matter of weeks, Scout had changed my life. I had discovered the joy of waking each morning to a wriggling puppy whose tail refused to stop wagging, who licked my face, whimpered excitedly, and left me in no doubt that I was her favorite person in the world. Giulia had never once done any of those things. For the first time in three years, I stopped worrying about dementia. I was thinking about Scout, Sofia, Ambrose, Luca, and Toby, and about what our future might hold.

I knew that part of the reason I had made the decision to keep Scout was because she was a puppy—a puppy who would likely live for at least ten or eleven years. Which meant that I, as her person, would need to also live for ten or eleven years. Scout had not only given me a reason to get out of bed in the morning but, perhaps more important, also robbed me of a reason for dying.

I entered my study for the first time in months and inspected my father's 1527 edition of the *Decameron*, marveling at the ornateness of the print, the robustness of the hand-carved leather spine, the intricacy of the gold lettering. This book had endured nearly five hundred years. I thought about my father and what he would have made of Scout and the life that had unraveled before me. He would pop open his mouth, shake his head, and say, "Not another bloody dog!" He would also, I hoped, be proud of my grit. My mother was fond of saying, "Well, what you lack in talent, Sarah, you certainly make up for in determination." Perhaps she was right. I returned the original Boccaccio to its shelf and picked up the Penguin Classics version I kept on a shelf below. Boccaccio believed that to be noble, a man had to embrace life as it was, to face adversity without bitterness, and to accept the consequences of his actions. It wasn't as easy as it sounded.

The time had come for me to regain control over my life. I had no choice but to move back to Australia. To leave Giulia. It was the only way I would ever get over her. I loved Hong Kong and my closest friends were there, but it was time to leave. It was also time for me to make one last attempt to reconcile with my mother. She had suffered a number of small strokes during the past two years and was experiencing problems with her memory. Whatever her future held, I wanted us to try to make peace while we were both still able.

Giulia agreed with my suggestion that I should take Sofia, Ambrose, Scout, Luca, and Toby. She would keep our two elderly dogs who were not fit to fly and one cat. I consulted the vet about the process required to move pets from Hong Kong to Sydney and discovered that it would take at least six and a half months, maybe longer. They could live normally in my apartment for that time, but they weren't allowed to fly until six months had passed from the date they tested negative to the rabies virus. Upon arriving in Australia, they would spend ten days in quarantine. Then we would be reunited. The whole rigmarole would cost about the same as a small German car, but there was no alternative. We were a family, and no one was going to be left behind.

13

NEXT OF KIN

Pearl Beach is a pristine strip of coast nestled beside thick bushland a ninety-minute drive north of Sydney. There is nothing there but a café, a general store, an upmarket restaurant with limited hours, and a community hall that offers seniors yoga, stretching, and Pilates, depending on the day. The neighboring beach towns offer little in the way of attractions, but each has a shop selling motorized scooters. Then there are the funeral parlors, each with slight variations on the same shop front display: a vase of white flowers standing on a wooden coffin, set behind a wispy white curtain. I didn't go to Pearl Beach to die, but being there certainly encouraged me to spend a lot of time thinking about it.

Like most introverts, I have few social needs, and if I cannot enjoy the company of the small handful of people I love, I would rather be alone. One of my many contradictions is that I don't like people much, but I find comfort in having them around. I prefer sprawling, crowded cities like Bangkok, Manila, or Mexico City, where I can wander the streets without anyone noticing me. Not so in Pearl Beach, where the sight of a stranger aroused alarm. "What is *she* doing here?" I heard an elderly woman ask her companion as we passed each other in the street days after I arrived. It was a good question.

Twelve years earlier I had bought a house in Pearl Beach over the internet. I rented it out while I was away and had paid down the mortgage. It was the only place where I could live rent-free.

No one came to meet me at the airport when I landed in Sydney. I had told my mother and brother my arrival date, but I didn't expect to see them. Three weeks earlier, I had received an email from my brother telling me my mother had just been diagnosed with vascular dementia. The news was devastating.

Walking out into the arrivals hall into the jaws of a city that was no longer my home made me want to spin around, march back inside the airport, and buy a ticket for the next flight out.

Instead I caught a taxi to a serviced apartment in Zetland, a dingy suburb on the outskirts of the airport, and checked myself in for the night. Dinner was a squashed piece of almond cake I had wrapped in a napkin on the plane and a bottle of water bought from a hallway vending machine outside my room. I called my mother, and she was understandably distressed. She was about to live out my own nightmare, and I promised I would do anything I could to help her. It was a strange homecoming. The next morning I picked up a car and drove to Pearl Beach.

I had visited Pearl Beach three times in my life before deciding to buy a house on a street one block back from the beach. It had not been much of an investment.

"I'd be lucky to get my money back, wouldn't I?" I asked the real estate agent when I went to collect the keys.

"It's been a bit flat here," he said.

I didn't recognize my house. I had only been inside it once and had no memory of the layout or its size. I thought the garden was bigger, the house smaller. It was a ridiculous size for one person, or one person with three big dogs, one large cat, and one normal-sized one.

There were four bedrooms. Too much space. I had spent years purging myself of belongings so I could live in Hong Kong, where space was at a premium. Now I needed clutter to fill the void.

I had started renovations from Hong Kong, and by the time I arrived, builders had installed half a new kitchen and a third of a new bathroom. The pink carpet that had smothered the house had been pulled up to reveal pristine pine floorboards that needed nothing more than a sand and a polish. The house was dirty and covered in sawdust. It was uninhabitable, so I bought a mattress, some sheets, a pillow, and a towel, and I took up residency in the cabin at the back of the garden.

In the absence of a better use of my time, I decided to wake each morning at six and paint the inside of my house. It would be another six weeks before the first batch of pets arrived from Hong Kong, and at least another eight weeks before my furniture would be delivered. I had nothing else to do.

Every morning at eight o'clock when the café opened, I wandered across the road dressed in the same pair of paint-splattered jeans and the same soiled T-shirt, and I ordered muesli and two caffe lattes. For lunch I had ice cream and chocolate. Each evening I visited an Indian restaurant in a nearby suburb and ordered takeaway. I ate vegetable curry from a plastic box with a plastic fork, propped up on my bed inside the cabin, under the glare of a long strip of fluorescent lighting. I felt like a squatter, not someone who had just moved home after years abroad.

The house hadn't been painted in decades. The walls soaked up four coats of paint, and the woodwork was scabby so I had to scale, sand, patch, sand again, add a coat of primer, and apply three coats of paint. My task seemed endless. Then one day, after almost finishing the living room ceiling, I decided to put my mental health first and stop. Could I live in a house that was almost painted? Of course I could. Painting taught me two important things: First, I was lazy by nature, and despite a fondness for grandiose plans, I wasn't a great "finisher." I knew this already. Second, it's always a good idea to use drop sheets to cover your freshly polished floorboards.

A couple of weeks after my arrival, I visited the local pharmacy to buy an oral contraceptive. Not because I had been entertaining prospects of sex, although I wasn't without options. One gentleman in his late seventies had already asked me if I wanted to go for a bushwalk with him, as he winked and squeezed my forearm, and another older gentleman I met in the vegetable section at Woolworths had invited me home with him to help make tomato sauce. As tempting as those offers were, I was looking for the pill because I had reached an age where I needed a dose of hormones each day to keep me balanced, and without them, my moods swung with a ferocity that frightened even me.

The pharmacist looked at me like I had fallen from another planet and said, "You need a prescription for that."

"Not in Hong Kong, you don't," I said, and he stared at me without speaking.

Luckily the building next door had a sign outside that read "Surgery."

The receptionist, who looked to be in her sixties, snapped at me and told me I needed an appointment. I was happy to wait, I told her. All I needed was a prescription.

"It doesn't matter what you *need*," she hissed. "You still have to see a doctor."

She glowered at me and asked how I liked to be addressed. Ms.? Mrs.?

"Doctor, thank you," I said. I couldn't recall the last time I had used the doctor honorific, or even the last time I had told anyone I had a PhD. But at that moment, I wanted that woman to call me doctor. As soon as the word left my mouth, I realized my pettiness, but her tone changed instantly.

"I'm terribly sorry," she said.

And still I wanted to lean across the counter and hiss, "You should be, you rude bitch," because it had been five days since I had run out of my hormone pills and I was at risk of doing something rash.

"Doctor," she said, smiling, "can I ask for your next of kin?"

I looked at her as my mouth fell open. Could I tell her Sofia was my next of kin? Or Scout? I told her I would get back to her, and she passed my new file to a doctor who saw me almost instantly and gave me a script for my hormone pills.

I left the surgery in a daze. The fact was, I had no human next of kin, or at least none with whom I had any kind of relationship. My brother and I didn't speak, and I'd seen my mother only five times in the last twelve years. I had never thought of her as my next of kin. I had driven down to Sydney a few times to meet her. I would pick her up from her apartment and take her to lunch, but our meetings were always strained and uncomfortable, my mother tight-lipped and me doing my best to avoid saying anything that might inflame her.

I had no kin at all except my cousin, who lived an eleven-hour drive away on the Sunshine Coast. We had seen each other once in twenty years. At the age of fifty-one, I had three dogs, two cats, and an ex-girlfriend in Hong Kong I still loved who didn't love me back. In Australia I was completely alone.

Moving three dogs and two cats from Hong Kong to Australia proved more stressful than I had hoped. Scout failed her rabies antibody test twice, and it looked like she would never leave Hong Kong. The next challenge, which the vet handling our relocation had neglected to mention, was Australia's requirement that dogs test negative to ehrlichiosis, a type of tick fever, within twenty-one days of travel. A dog that failed that test is forbidden from ever entering Australia. Scout had tested positive to babesiosis, a different type of tick fever, but it wouldn't be a stretch to think that one of those sixty ticks may have exposed her to ehrlichiosis. If Scout was refused entry to Australia, I would have no choice but to move back to Hong Kong and rethink my plans. Fortunately, after an agonizing wait I got the news that she'd passed, and everyone was cleared for travel.

Scout and Sofia arrived first, and Ambrose and the two cats followed a fortnight later. For dogs who had never known the sensation of grass underfoot, much less had their own backyard, their new home was a paradise. On their first visit to the beach, they stepped gingerly through the sand, sniffing it and looking at one another with surprise. *What* is *it?* they seemed to ask. Moments later they were charging up and down the shoreline, dodging the waves, and chasing after each other in huge loops. I had never seen them so happy. The cats were delighted with their new home. It was vast and offered two large balconies from which they could observe, but not touch, the native birds. And for the next two months, their joy became my joy. Until one evening I assembled all five pets around me on the sofa and took up a pen and a piece of paper.

"I need to show you something," I said. I drew a large *X* and pointed to the line that ascended sharply. "That's your happiness here," I said as they shuffled around me, yawning and trying to get comfortable. "And that," I said, pointing to the line that descended sharply, "is mine."

They looked dumbfounded.

I went ten days without having a single conversation with a human other than Brian, the checkout boy at Woolworth's with the unusually small head.

"How are you doing? Alright?" he asked as he scanned my tins of cat food and placed them into plastic bags.

"Good, thanks," I said. "And you?"

"I'm good," he answered.

Can people die from being alone? I wondered as I drove back to the house with my car full of pet food.

At night, unable to sleep, I wondered what would happen if I dropped dead in my home or fell down the stairs and broke my neck. How long would it take before anyone found me? No one knew I was there, except for my friends overseas, and they weren't going to be much help. In my darker moments, I thought about which of my dogs would lie beside me and die of heartbreak and which would eat me. In the end it was Luca, the street cat I had rescued as a kitten in Sai Ying Pun, who had the shrewdest instincts for survival. He would make a meal of me until someone discovered us and opened up a couple of tins of cat food.

I found a good friend, Sue, who had grown up with James, my gay friend from Parliament House. Sue happened to live one beach away and worked in Sydney. The travel time back and forth took three hours a day, so her weekdays were long. But a couple of months after I moved to Pearl Beach, we started meeting for dinner each Saturday night at a tiny Japanese restaurant not far from her place. Sue suffered from depression, and for the first time in a long time, I felt I could finally talk about mine. My friendship with Sue stopped me from losing my mind.

In July 2015 my mother was admitted to the hospital with heart problems. She knew the warning signs of a stroke—the nausea, the dizziness, the headache—and had the number of an ambulance on speed dial.

I drove down to Sydney, and found her propped up in bed in a public ward. A frizzy-haired stranger in her seventies, dressed in a white hospital gown, was standing at the foot of my mother's bed.

"Oh, it's you," my mother said softly when she saw me. She looked at the frizzy-haired woman who, it turned out, was the patient occupying the bed opposite hers. "I'm sorry. I've forgotten your name."

The woman glanced up at the ceiling. "Me too," she said. "I think it's Heather."

"Heather, this is my daughter, Sarah." I shook Heather's hand, and she made herself comfortable on the end of my mother's bed. I was grateful, because as long as she sat there, it was unlikely my mother would say something unpleasant. The three of us talked about the news and the loathsome American dentist who had killed Cecil the lion.

"I never wanted children," Heather said. "I always preferred animals."

I agreed.

"Not me!" my mother said, and we turned to her with interest. "Of course, I wanted children," she said. "I just never wanted girls."

"Well, you only had one," I said.

"One was enough!" She grinned at Heather.

A nurse came to take Heather's blood pressure, and my mother and I were left alone. We talked about the hospital food, which my mother said was delicious, and the bird that peered into her window from the ledge outside.

"What do you call that bird?" she asked.

"That's a magpie," I said.

"Yes! Magpie."

I, too, forgot words and names. The last time I was in Sydney, I had met a friend for coffee. He'd told me he planned to travel to Muscat, the capital of Oman, which I had visited three years earlier.

"It's beautiful," I said. "You must go out into the desert. What do you call those things in the desert with water?" I asked, unable to remember the word. I felt my heart stop. Every missing word seemed an indication of some fresh damage.

"Oases."

"Yes!" I said, doing my best to compose myself. "You must see an oasis."

My mother was trying to solve the daily anagram in the newspaper. We studied the letters, and she wrote down words that started with *P*. Suddenly overcome with concern that she would be better at it than I was, I blurted out, "Parlatory."

"That's not a word," my mother said immediately.

She was likely right. Since my accident, she usually was when it came to language. I took out my cell phone and typed in "parlatory."

"It is a word. It means the parlor of a convent or a monastery."

Unconvinced, my mother demanded to see the evidence.

I noticed that the newspaper she was working on was from the day before. The current day's paper sat on her bedside table, so I picked it up and flicked to the page with the solutions. "Portrayal," the paper said. I felt my hands tremble.

My mother seemed unsurprised that I was wrong.

I drove to Sydney from Pearl Beach each day for the week my mother was in the hospital. Perhaps my fear was that she might die without us having a chance to reconcile. On the day she was discharged, she thanked me for coming. "It's a long drive you've made each day," she said.

~

I turned fifty-two alone but for the dogs and cats. My friends phoned from Hong Kong, and I got text messages and emails wishing me happy birthday, but it didn't feel like a celebration. Giulia had forgotten. I had not drunk anything other than the occasional light beer since moving back to Australia, but that afternoon, I found a bottle of beer in the fridge and took the dogs down to the beach. I sat on the sand under a huge pine tree, with Sofia and Ambrose on each side of me, and looked out to sea. Scout had learned how to dig, and her new trick was to position herself in front of me and cover me in sand before leaping on top of me and licking my face.

I survived six months in Pearl Beach before the transition from Hong Kong to a sleepy beachside village proved to be too much. I missed living in a city—in a place with energy, where things happened. Thinking I was going to die, I had sold my house in Sydney before the market boomed, and eighteen months later prices had become so inflated I couldn't afford to buy anything like my old place. I settled on a small house in Sydney's Inner West, a short walk from a large off-leash dog park.

~

Now that I had moved back to Sydney, I felt a responsibility to see more of my mother, to do what I could to salvage the remains of our relationship before the opportunity was lost forever. I wanted us to create even one happy memory to temper all the unhappy ones.

My mother's illness compounded my anxiety about my own memory problems, and that anxiety bled into a depression. There was nothing I could do to stop the progression of my mother's illness. I felt I was about to watch her lose her mind in a loud and lurid dress rehearsal, before I lost my own.

Once she had recovered from her stroke, I offered to take my mother to lunch. I picked her up as planned, and she asked me to take her to the bank.

We drove to an ATM, and I helped her out of the car and stood behind her as she removed the leather watch band from her wrist and examined the four-digit code she had written on its back.

"Don't look!" she shrieked. "I don't want you knowing my password!"

On the way to the café, a man dashed out in front of my car, and my mother shrieked, "You drive like a lunatic! You could have killed him!"

At twelve miles an hour, it was unlikely I could have killed anyone and I told her as much. When she screamed at me again, I stomped on the brake, did a U-turn, drove her straight back to her apartment, and stopped outside her front door.

"Let's never see each other again," I said as I removed her walker from the trunk.

"Fine by me," she replied.

By the time I left, tears were streaming down my face. What kind of person fought with their demented mother and then suggested they never see one another again? I sank into the same well of gloom and failure I seemed always to inhabit after seeing her.

As soon as I got home, I rang my mother and apologized.

"Thank you for apologizing," she said, and hung up.

In desperation I started seeing the psychiatrist my neurologist had recommended once each month. Toby, one of the two street cats I had adopted in Hong Kong, had developed kidney failure, and his health had deteriorated quickly. I took him to four different vets, and after the various treatment options failed, I decided the best thing for Toby would be to have him put to sleep. With Toby's death, my depression grew worse, and I realized if I was to keep going, I needed help.

Peter was a gentle man with kind gray eyes and a fondness for perfectly pressed shirts. I liked him from the moment I met him. We talked about Beethoven's string quartets, Philip Roth, contemporary art, and famous psychiatrists in history. He told me that he believed the role of a psychiatrist was to provide a patient with hope. I told him that hope was something I looked forward to experiencing, although I had my doubts that it was possible.

Peter had studied my brain scans and talked to my neurologist. He told me he couldn't detect any sign of cognitive decline from our conversations and promised he would let me know as soon as he did. He agreed that losing one's memory was one of the most horrific things that could happen to anyone. He also told me he had patients who were judges and surgeons and scientists and that in his opinion, I could hold my own among any of them.

"You have a wonderful mind," he said.

I raised my eyebrows and told him I couldn't remember what I did yesterday. "I've spent more than twenty years learning how to disguise my cognitive shortcomings," I said. "I'm pretty good at fooling people."

"You've fooled me," he said without hesitation.

"Last time I saw my neurologist, he told me he considered my injury to be severe. So much for mild."

"I think he's right," he said. "You suffered a serious blow to your head. But you've made the best cognitive recovery of any person with a TBI that I've ever seen."

We talked about my mother and her dementia diagnosis.

He wanted to know more. "Mothers are important, you know," he said, giving me a half smile.

I explained that in the eleven-plus years I lived in Asia, my mother and I had barely spoken. I told him about showing her my short story when I was twelve, and her telling me I wouldn't make much of a writer. And how, when I told her at age fifteen I wanted to be a journalist, she had said, "But you need to be clever to be a journalist. You'd better think of something else."

"Why is she like that?" he asked.

"I honestly don't know. My mother loves conflict. She hasn't spoken to her only sibling for nearly three decades. My mother adores my brother and has always enjoyed pitting him and me against one another."

Peter raised his eyebrows and waited for me to continue.

"I come from a long line of difficult people," I said. "We're all difficult. But my mother, she is divisive."

I told Peter everything I could remember. My mother and I had gone four years without seeing each other. During that time, she was either "busy" when I traveled home or didn't "feel up to" seeing me. She sent me an email most years on my birthday, always with the same message: *Happy Birthday. Cheers, Hilary.*

I sent her an email for her birthday, telling her about the places I had visited, hoping she was interested, hoping she was doing well. I always signed mine, *Love, Sarah.* I'm not sure why. For a long time, I wished I could feel nothing for her at all.

"She's an unusual woman," Peter said. "An unusual *mother.*"

I saw Peter a fortnight before Christmas. We talked more about my mother. I would be her only company on Christmas Day; my brother and his wife had planned an overseas trip. Fourteen days separated me from alone time with her, and I was starting to panic.

"If it gets to be too much, just leave," Peter said.

I told him how upsetting it was to watch my mother's decline, to watch her live my imminent future. I wanted to make damned sure I was able to end my own life as soon as I started exhibiting obvious signs of dementia. When the time came, Peter said, he would write me a script for a box of fifty tricyclic antidepressants that I could keep at home and take when I was ready.

Euthanasia is illegal in Australia, and I had worried about how hard it would be to find a doctor who was prepared to help.

I asked him if I could get drunk before I took the pills, thinking it might make the experience easier. And more enjoyable.

"No. You might vomit, and then they will have no effect."

"I never throw up from alcohol."

"Well, you might if you wash down fifty of these tablets with alcohol."

I sighed. "There's no pleasure, even in death."

He gave me a wry smile.

"If it were me," he said, "I'd just wait till evening, go to bed, take them all, and fall asleep."

As relieved as I felt that Peter was willing to help, I wasn't charmed by the idea of swallowing fifty pills in a single sitting and dying alone shortly thereafter. What if something went wrong? The idea of going to Switzerland and being handed a green juice by an attractive Swiss nurse was much more appealing.

My mother took a taxi to church on Christmas morning. After my father died, she had begun attending weekly services at an Anglican church in the city. My father was an atheist, and I had always assumed my mother was too. I had been brought up to believe God was like Father Christmas. A couple of years after my father died, I asked my mother if she believed in God.

"Well, that is a private matter, but yes," she said. As shocked as I was, I felt glad she had something to believe in. "I'm happy for you," I said, and I was.

I took Sofia, the least neurotic, best-behaved of my three dogs, to my mother's place on Christmas Day. Sofia, I hoped, would be our Switzerland, the neutral territory between my mother and me. She would distract us from each other. Sofia was boundlessly amiable—which made one of us.

I left the elevator on the fourteenth floor of my mother's apartment building with Sofia by my side, my shopping bags stuffed with groceries. My mother was outside her front door, leaning on her walker. She looked older and frailer than when I last saw her.

"What's his name?" she asked, beckoning my dog.

"Sofia."

"What a pretty name."

As soon as we were inside, my mother asked Sofia's name again. She eased herself onto the sofa, and I coaxed Sofia up beside her. My mother reached into her pocket for a treat called a Schmacko, snapped it in half, and offered a piece to Sofia. She put the other half to her own mouth.

"No, Mum! That's dog food!"

"Oh," she said, surprised.

Sofia sat at my mother's feet, waiting for the next treat.

"What a lovely dog," my mother said, stroking Sofia's ears.

She inspected the name on the tag hanging from Sofia's collar. "Sofia," she said, before digging into her pocket for another Schmacko.

Sofia swallowed the second Schmacko and started to pant. I told my mother Sofia needed a drink, and my mother pointed to a water bowl in the kitchen set out for a neighbor's dog who occasionally came to visit. "She's not stupid; she'll find it," she added.

"Don't bet on it," I said, and I led Sofia to the water bowl.

"Did you say she's stupid?" my mother asked.

"I did not. But she is not the smartest of my dogs."

Sofia drank from the bowl, and my mother produced another Schmacko from a packet stuffed into a crevice in the sofa. She motioned to Sofia and whispered just loud enough for me to hear, "That's why she has you. So she can feel clever!" She gave my dog a smug smile and glanced up to make sure I heard her.

Watching my frail, elderly mother trying to conspire with my dog overwhelmed me with a bewildering flood of pity, dismay, and helplessness. I went inside the kitchen and hid.

The walls and doors of my mother's apartment were festooned with yellow sticky notes full of commands:

Turn off the coffee machine!

Don't forget to put coffee inside the machine! You have broken it TWICE already!

Don't leave the house without your keys!

Don't forget to take your medicine! It's next to the kitchen sink.

The more important notes—the ones that prevented her from locking herself out or leaving the stove on and burning down the apartment block—had been fastened to the wall with tape.

A whiteboard on an easel stood in the middle of her living room. Written across the top in black marker were the names and phone numbers of people my mother might need to contact in an emergency: my brother, my aunt, my sister-in-law, the fire department. I noticed my name was not among them. At the bottom were the times when Vicky and Tracey would visit. Vicky and Tracey were the nurses my brother had employed to check on my mother each morning and afternoon while he and his wife were abroad.

Vicky and Tracey didn't work on Christmas Day.

Between feeding treats to my dog, my mother told me that she planned to kill herself. When I asked how, she simply said, "I know people."

This felt like dangerous territory. I understood exactly how she must be feeling, burying herself in sticky notes, reminding herself how to function. What lay ahead of her was an inevitable and devastating decline. But I couldn't help thinking of my father, begging me to help him die, and my mother's reaction. Telling our doctor and an aunt on the phone I wanted to kill him. It had almost felt to me as though she wanted to drag out the last weeks of his life, no matter how painful or horrific. And yet here she was, talking about ending her own life. I felt stuck. I could not help her because euthanasia was against the law, but it angered me that she was not able to make that decision herself. That my father had not been able to make that decision himself. In the end, I reminded her that it was illegal and mentioned that, if she wanted help, she'd better make arrangements while she was still able.

"I can do it myself," she said.

"It's not as easy as it seems," I replied.

A decade before that Christmas, when I was in my early forties, I had written to my mother apologizing for my part in our relationship. I hadn't been an easy child, I admitted, nor had she been an easy mother. I hoped we could put the past behind us and start anew. She never responded to my letter.

I waited a month before sending her an email to make sure the letter had reached her.

"Yes," she replied.

"Did you plan to answer?"

"I didn't think I needed to," she wrote back. "Of course we are friends."

I didn't respond. I had friends already. What I needed was a mother.

In preparation for our Christmas feast, my sister-in-law had emailed me my mother's detailed dietary restrictions, beginning with *NO LEAFY GREENS!* As a fish-eating vegetarian, I wondered what I could prepare for the two of us. It would also be fair to say my culinary skills are somewhat underdeveloped.

Alcohol is a wonderful salve at Christmastime, but neither my mother nor I was allowed to drink. Between my neurologist's advice that I cut back to one glass of red wine a day and Peter, my psychiatrist, suggesting I stop drinking altogether, I was moved to action. Eager to conserve what few healthy brain cells I had left, I stopped drinking almost entirely. By that Christmas, half a glass of light beer made me giddy.

My mother nudged at the food I had prepared for her; without the leafy greens or the myriad other ingredients she was forbidden, it was a pretty Spartan meal. A large piece of Tasmanian salmon sat atop her noodles. She liked salmon, or so she had said before I put it in front of her.

"Is there anything wrong?" I asked. "Mine is nice!"

"No," she said, but I could tell she was lying. I glanced out the window at the Opera House, and when she thought I wasn't looking, she broke the salmon in half and fed part of it to Sofia.

"Dessert will be better," I said. "I brought some goat cheese to eat with poppy-seed crackers and two mangoes."

"What's a mango?" she asked.

I wondered if she was joking. Growing up, mangoes were a luxury we couldn't always afford, but when the price was right, my mother would buy three or four at a time, and we would share them after dinner.

She placed her knife and fork together on top of her plate. I took it to the kitchen, tossed the food (minus the remains of the salmon), and returned with a mango.

"What's that?"

I looked at her, incredulous.

"A mango. Smell it."

She held it up to her nose and shook her head. Nothing. I wondered if, like many people with dementia, she had lost her sense of smell. She examined the mango closely. "I have never seen anything like it!"

I went back to the kitchen and returned with a cutting board, a knife, and two plates. I placed the mango on the board and sliced it down either side of its pit. Then I took the two sides, crisscrossed the flesh with the knife, and turned the skin inside out, the way she taught me when I was a child.

My mother looked on in wonder.

I passed her a half and waited for her to try it.

She held the mango half up to her mouth, juice streaming down one arm. I offered to cut the flesh away from the skin, but she refused.

"I can feed myself," she said, returning the mango to the plate and using a fork.

She took a mouthful and closed her eyes.

"Oh, my. This is the most delicious thing I have ever tasted!"

I passed her the rest.

Somehow, we survived our lunch. Afterward my mother said she felt tired, and I emitted an audible sigh of relief and suggested that she should nap while I washed up and let myself out.

"No!" she said. "I like washing up."

I yielded to her wishes and retrieved my belongings from the kitchen.

"Thank you," she said. "It was a lovely lunch."

I smiled, gave her a quick hug, summoned my dog, and left.

As soon as I stepped into the elevator, I knelt down and hugged Sofia.

"That was all your doing," I said. "You are the best dog in the world."

Sofia leaned against my leg and looked up at me lovingly. *Your mother is hard work,* she seemed to say.

"Tell me about it," I said to no one in particular.

That evening the phone rang. It was my mother.

"I can't find your phone number!" she said in a panic.

"Don't worry. You've found it!" I answered.

"What?"

"You're ringing me now."

"Oh." She laughed. "I suppose I am. I wanted to thank you for lunch."

"My pleasure," I said.

"And to say that I enjoyed meeting your dog . . ."

"Sofia."

"Yes, Sofia!"

"Thank you," I said. "Well, call me if you need anything. You have my number."

It was the most cordial conversation I could recall us having in recent decades.

I put down the phone and squeezed onto the sofa between Scout and Ambrose. Sofia curled up on her dog bed to sleep off her Christmas lunch.

I had a fleeting hope that my relationship with my mother would improve as her dementia progressed. And I wondered how long I had left before I forgot what a mango was. Before my home was festooned with sticky notes. Before all my mother's deficiencies became mine. Seized by panic, I got up, went to the fridge, and opened my emergency stash of beer. I poured two-thirds of a bottle into a glass and the rest down the sink. Then I turned on the TV and watched a blonde woman in a long dress sing "Have Yourself a Merry Little Christmas."

14

SYNCHRONICITY

During my appointment with Peter the following February, I told him that 2015 was the loneliest year of my life—that since moving back to Australia, I often went weeks without talking to anyone other than my friends who lived overseas. Peter and I talked about my mother, whose health was slowly fading, and I told him that after each visit to her apartment, I longed to be dead.

He smiled and told me I could not keep living that way, that leading the life of a hermit was not helping my atrophied brain, and that it was time for me to start looking for a new partner.

"But I don't want a partner! I'm fine on my own."

"You're not really fine," he said. "The dogs are something, but they aren't enough. You need someone in Sydney who loves you and you can love back. When your mother dies, you are going to need support."

"I've lost every person I ever loved. They either died or left me."

He waited for me to finish, a sad smile passing across his face.

"I've been alone so long, I don't think I could adjust to life inside a relationship. I'd drive her crazy. She would drive me crazy too. I can tolerate human company for about forty minutes; then I need to be alone. To recover. I find people exhausting."

"I honestly do believe there is someone out there for you," he said.

"Truly, there isn't."

"But you have so much to offer! I have patients who frankly deserve to be alone. People who are not particularly nice or kind or attractive; people who don't have a lot going for them. And *they* have someone who loves them. You *deserve* to have someone and you don't. You shouldn't be alone."

I wasn't convinced. Beyond my obvious challenges with rage and social propriety, I didn't think I was capable of falling in love with another human again. I am fussy, intolerant, and judgmental, and I feared that no one would ever measure up. My list of requirements in a partner was long, with subsections and subclauses. If I did find someone who satisfied my exacting list of criteria, the chances of them liking me, I suspected, would be infinitesimal.

Let's imagine that lesbians make up around 5 percent of the population, and introverts around one-third of the population.[26] My ideal mate—the only one I was interested in pursuing—was an introverted lesbian who loved animals and was kind, clever, interesting, feisty, and serious and lighthearted in equal measure. And that list didn't even take into account any of my deal breakers, like having bad table manners or being a noisy eater. My pool of possible partners was a puddle.

Slowly, over our monthly meetings, Peter wore me down, and I signed up for the hamster wheel of online dating for middle-aged lesbians.

It was worse than I imagined. I met a woman for coffee who bore no resemblance whatsoever to the photo she sent me. I had just sat down when she told me she never had sex with anyone until she knew them well. I assured her that sex was the last thing on my mind. Next she told me how wealthy she was, and how she needed to be careful because women only liked her for her money. I drank my coffee as quickly as I could, scalding my esophagus in the process, thanked her for her time, and left.

Another woman I met for coffee was a petite platinum blonde with a mouth that looked like it had been drawn on with a ballpoint pen. Despite clearly labeling her profile "gay," she announced that she had never slept with a woman before and then added, "I don't find you attractive at all."

"Oh, well that's, um, fine," I said, feeling my face redden. I'm not sure she noticed. She immediately launched into details about her husband, who was at home dying from bowel cancer. Their house was in his name, so she couldn't exactly kick him out, she said, but she'd decided it was time to put herself first. She was training to be a psychologist, she told me. I excused myself as soon as she drew breath.

At each appointment I regaled Peter with my latest horror story. "There is evil out there. That's why I don't like leaving the house." He laughed and asked me if I would ever consider pursuing a relationship with a man.

"A man who satisfies an exacting set of criteria, I suppose."

"It might be easier."

I registered a new online dating profile—woman seeks man—but my heart wasn't in it. I was surprised by the number of messages I received from interested men, but something about the whole endeavor smacked of desperation. I wanted someone who could love me but was also comfortable being alone. Someone who would be comfortable leaving me alone when I needed it. I removed both profiles days later.

In August a friend invited me to a drinks party for single women that her friends had arranged at a pub close to my home. Ever since the accident, the way I approached social gatherings with strangers was by either drinking a lot, which I had decided not to do any longer, or setting a clear time at which I'd allow myself to leave. I decided on the drive to the pub that I would stay one hour. When I arrived I bought a mineral water for myself and a beer for my friend, and proceeded to panic as soon as she left my side.

Scanning the room, I recognized some women from my single years in Sydney around twenty years earlier. We were older now, with slightly thicker waists and worry lines etched into our faces, and still trying to find partners from the same group of eligible women. I scoped out the exits; climbing out a window onto the street and disappearing started to feel like the best option. Or pretending to go to the bathroom like a normal person and never returning. A kind woman noticed my distress and introduced herself, and while we were in mid-conversation, someone I had never met before took me by the arm and deposited me in front of a beautiful woman with high cheekbones and a perfect mouth. She wore glasses and appeared slightly awkward.

Her name was Louise, and she told me right away that she dreaded these gatherings because they made her feel even more of a misfit. Two of her friends had dragged her along.

"I never fit in anywhere!" I laughed.

She told me that she had planned her departure before she arrived. She would give it one hour.

I asked her if she liked animals. "Absolutely! More than I like people," she said enthusiastically before pausing for a moment. "I probably shouldn't say that. I'm a doctor. I *do* love old people."

"Old people are fine," I said, realizing that her preference could work to my advantage since she appeared to be at least a decade younger than I was, "and babies. I love babies."

Louise and I talked for more than an hour. I told her about the dogs and cats I had brought home from Hong Kong, and she told me about her own dog, her "soul wolf" that she had stolen from a neighbor's balcony. The malamute had been locked out on the balcony all day and all night for months. Louise told me that one day, she'd knocked on the apartment door and begged the owners to let her take the dog for a walk. They agreed, and she took the dog out and never returned. A vet friend had changed the dog's microchip. "You have no idea how sickly she was when I got her. They had locked her outside with no bed, no shelter from the sun or rain." She dipped inside her handbag and pulled out her phone to show me a photo. "Isn't she gorgeous? I had to have her put down three months ago. Cancer." Her eyes welled up.

I touched her elbow. "Are you real?"

At ten the next morning I was wandering around a Cate Blanchett installation at the Art Gallery of New South Wales when my phone rang. It was Louise, asking me to dinner the following Saturday. She explained that her time was limited since she was traveling to Mexico in two weeks' time to participate in the world triathlon championships, so she needed to spend all her spare time training. All her friends complained that they never saw her. It was one of the joys of being a doctor, she added.

"What kind of doctor are you?"

"A psycho-geriatrician."

"A what?"

"I specialize in dementia. I split my time between a hospital and my own practice."

"Dementia?"

"Yep."

"Wow."

I got off the phone and folded myself down on the steps outside the art gallery. My memory leapt back to the serendipitous meeting I had more than twenty years earlier with the woman in the park who told me about neuroplasticity. She was the reason I had picked myself up and applied for a job. And now in another baffling sleight of chance, I had met a woman I knew I could fall in love with, a woman who happened to specialize in dementia. I shook my head and laughed at the improbability of it all. Strange things happened when I left the house.

Louise and I had dinner at a Turkish restaurant that I'd suggested after reading the lackluster reviews of the restaurant she had suggested. Doctors, in my experience, will eat anything. As soon as our food arrived, she mentioned that her best friends hated the place I had chosen.

"They sound like philistines," I said.

"One is Dutch and one is British," she responded.

"Two nations well known for their fine food," I said, and she laughed.

Louise took charge of the conversation, and I responded with gibberish. The food arrived. "It's delicious!" she said.

I had never been so nervous on a date in my life. There was something about Louise I had never found in anyone before, and I wanted her to like me as much as I liked her.

"You have an anxiety disorder," she said with a smile.

"That's the very least of my problems."

She laughed and told me she was nervous too.

To help matters I blurted out, "I've been single for more than five years! I haven't even been on a date!"

I stopped just short of telling her I hadn't had sex in six years, although I'm sure she worked that out for herself. She struck me as someone with a flair for numbers.

Assuming Louise might come home with me after dinner, I had spent the day cleaning my house, washing my dogs, and changing the sheets. But when dinner ended, I kissed her on the cheek and watched her drive away.

The next week she flew to Mexico. She had been training for the race for more than a year. She would be gone for three weeks.

On the day she left, I sent her a text message letting her know that I would judge her interest in me by the quality and quantity of her text messages.

Good! she answered. *I like a challenge.*

~

I saw Peter the second week she was gone and told him my news.

"You aren't going to believe it," I said. "It's early days and it's likely to be a disaster, but I met someone! Someone I really like! It's almost as if she was conjured up from my imagination after our last meeting. She is the composite of my perfect person."

Peter looked astonished. "Wonderful!"

"And you'll love this. She's a psycho-geriatrician! Who trained in neurosurgery!"

"How extraordinary! Are you sure she's gay?"

"Seems so!"

He asked her name and for the hospital where she worked, and I was relieved to know he had never heard of her.

"How do you think she'll feel when I tell her about you?" I asked. "Is there a protocol for telling the psychiatrist you want to date that you are seeing a psychiatrist?"

"I don't think so, but it shouldn't be a problem. Lots of people see psychiatrists."

"Do they?"

He laughed. "Yes!"

"Then there's the head injury, and all the fun things that come along with that."

"She'll be lucky to have you."

"Let's see."

To avoid Louise discovering any nasty surprises about me in the future, I sent her a text message about my accident, my atrophying brain, my depression, my temper, and my problems with impulse control. It was a long text message. She read it but didn't answer, and I spent the night feeling incredibly foolish.

I waited until it was morning in Mexico, then called her to explain. The silence on the other end of the line was excruciating. When we hung up, I was sure I had scared her away.

I phoned Helena in Hong Kong, whose judgment is impeccable and whose counsel I sought often.

"Are you insane? You're trying to sabotage this before it's even started! She is the only woman you have liked since Giulia. What is wrong with you?"

"I just thought she needed to know."

"Why didn't you tell her about the good things? Call her back and tell her you are kind and generous and funny and smart!"

"It's too late!"

I lightened things up with my next text messages. I sent photos of my dogs and cats and a picture of a T-shirt I bought online that said, *Sorry I'm late, I didn't want to come.*

Then, as if to leave her in no doubt at all that I was neurotic, I asked her the one question that bothered me most: *Are you worried about my brain?*

No. Your brain seems fine, she answered almost instantly. Relieved, I bombarded her with more dog photos. The next day she messaged me saying she wished I was there, and that if she had met me a few months earlier she would have bought me a ticket to Mexico.

We exchanged more than six hundred text messages during the three weeks Louise was gone, and despite a mutual dislike for telephones, we spoke on the phone every other day. The similarities between us were astonishing. Impossible as it seemed, at the age of fifty-three I had found the first person who seemed to see the world through the same lens as me.

The day before she flew home, I sent her a message. *I have no impulse control, I know, but I am falling in love with you.*

For the hour it took until my phone pinged, I paced around my house like someone possessed. Finally my phone lit up. *I think I am too.* Moments later it pinged again. *Have you ever felt so much for anyone so quickly?*

Never, I answered.

Louise flew back to Sydney via San Francisco and arrived on a Sunday morning. We agreed that she would sleep for a few hours before I visited her.

On the drive to her place, I stopped and bought flowers. My hands trembled as I rang the doorbell. She opened her screen door, and I couldn't bring myself to look at her. She was even more beautiful than I remembered. She laughed, kissed me for the first time, and told me she had never met anyone who was shier than she was. I followed her into the kitchen and watched as she took a bottle of champagne from the fridge. She filled two glasses and led me by the hand to her sofa. I drained my glass almost instantly and she refilled it.

"I shouldn't drink. It's bad for my brain."

"A couple of glasses isn't going to hurt. It's not like you do it all the time."

"I'm not good at stopping. That's the problem."

"I'll make sure that you stop."

After my third and final glass, we began to relax.

"You don't just like me because I'm a doctor, do you?" she asked.

"What do you mean?"

"Some women like going out with doctors."

"Do they? I like you in spite of that. I'm not a huge fan of the medical profession. If you were a vet, it would be different."

She laughed.

"You don't just like me because I'm an aspiring writer who hasn't written much yet, do you?"

"That's a big part of it, yes." She smiled, took my hand, and led me upstairs to her bedroom. An elderly cat with gray curly fur used a set of cat stairs to join us on the bed. "Sarah, meet Smokey. Smokey, be nice." I tickled Smokey in that spot beneath the chin that cats seem to love, and she started to purr.

"I can't believe I told you I was falling in love with you before we had even kissed!" I said.

"Have you changed your mind?" she asked.

"I've never been more certain of anything."

"Me either," she said.

The next night, I went to Louise's place to cook her dinner. I had never cooked dinner for anyone I wasn't living with, but I wanted to impress her. I had one recipe that was foolproof: salmon noodles. Or at least I had thought it was foolproof until I tried it out on my mother on Christmas Day and watched her feed most of it to my dog. Anyway, it was all I had. As soon as we finished eating, she told me that she wanted to spend the night at my place, to meet my dogs and cat. I warned her that Scout could be protective and snappy. That she had never met a person other than me she had really warmed to, and that Louise shouldn't take it personally.

We arrived at my place, and the dogs started barking as soon as they heard my car door close. I opened the front door and walked in first in an attempt to calm them. Scout looked up at Louise and fell silent. Louise extended her hand for Scout to sniff, and Scout's ears reclined and she started wagging her tail. We walked through the hallway, Scout trailing behind Louise and sniffing at her legs, and we sat on the sofa so I could make the proper introductions: first Sofia, who was already licking Louise's hand; then Ambrose, who was sniffing at her knees; then Scout, who had climbed up beside us on the sofa and was licking my face. Finally Luca appeared from the bedroom, hopped up onto the back of the sofa, and sniffed Louise's hair.

"That's incredible," I said. "It's the first time Scout has ever welcomed anyone into the house. I didn't want to alarm you, but two friends refuse to come inside unless I lock her in the bedroom. She can seem ferocious when she wants to."

"She knows you like me. And she knows I love dogs."

"She knows you are wonderful."

We stretched out on the sofa and drank red wine, and Louise told me she had moved to Sydney from Johannesburg with her ex-girlfriend seven years earlier. That as soon as they had arrived here their relationship began to disintegrate. That she had dated two women since and, on the basis of those experiences, decided she would never have another relationship.

I told her that since I had moved back to Australia, life had been joyless, and that after nearly six years alone, I was convinced I would never have another relationship. That had it not been for Peter, it would never have even occurred to me to try to meet someone new. And then I told her something I had never told anyone but Peter: Three months earlier, I had been so worried I was going to kill myself, I had locked all the kitchen knives inside the back shed and thrown the key into my garden so I wouldn't be able to find it. That day I had taken something called 5-HTP, an alternative drug that was meant to help depression. A depressed friend in Hong Kong swore by it. I couldn't buy it in Australia, so I had ordered it from New Zealand. I had taken one tablet and two hours later found myself curled up on the floor, thinking I had to kill myself. The experience was terrifying. After locking up the knives, I managed to drag myself to bed with Sofia and Scout on either side of me, and I lay there trembling for hours. Scout lay on her back beside me with her head on my shoulder, and Sofia rested her head on my pillow. I waited until the morning and searched the garden for the key. I found it and brought the knives back inside.

"That makes me so sad," Louise said. "I was living only a couple of suburbs away and didn't even know you existed. You'll never go through that again. I promise."

"Even though I only just met you, I'm happy. And happiness is something I thought I would never feel again. It's quite a lot to get my head around."

~

A fortnight later Louise moved in with her two cats. I had never started a relationship with complete and utter certainty that the person I had chosen was the one with whom I would spend the rest of my life.

"You are the only person I have ever met who makes me feel normal," she said one night before we fell asleep, a week after she moved in. "I have never felt this way about anyone."

"You are the only person I've ever met who doesn't make me feel lonely," I said. "I can't believe I've found you."

A month or so after she moved in, Louise asked to see my brain scans.

"You do not have dementia," she said, before I put the envelopes in front of her. "You have to trust me on that."

She worked back chronologically, looking at the three batches of scans, holding up each slide to the light that came in through our kitchen window.

"I look at brain scans of people with dementia all day. These scans show a brain that has suffered a traumatic brain injury. They show the area where you landed. Your memory problems are caused by your accident. If you did have dementia, it would be happening a lot more quickly. These changes are happening slowly. You're doing all the right things: you eat well, you drink in moderation. You write, or at least you claim to. I have never actually seen you write, but I trust you. You could certainly do more exercise, but I can help with that," she said, nudging me with her elbow.

"Do you notice problems with my memory?"

"Your serial memory isn't great. Chronology and so on. A couple of times you've said things that didn't add up in terms of timing. And you definitely have problems with word finding, but that's because of the area you damaged. You can't multitask, and your executive functioning isn't great. You struggle to focus, and you have visuospatial problems because of your injury. You know, bumping into things, tripping over stuff. So yes, of course I notice problems. But remember that's what I do all day. All the problems you are experiencing have been caused by your accident."

"It's not just my short- and long-term memory, or my serial memory. I lose track of things while I'm talking. And it's weird stuff too. I went to a music school. I played the violin and the piano for eight years. Now I can't read music, and I have lost the ability to play."

"That's the temporo-parietal region again." She spoke as if it was all so obvious. That I had hit my head badly in a particular spot, and that dead brain tissue accounted for all the problems I had experienced. She was not in the least bit alarmed.

"I've felt like I've been banging my head against a wall for years. Which is probably not a good analogy, but no one except my neurologist and my psychiatrist have believed there was anything wrong. My mother, Laura, Giulia—none of the people closest to me even believed I had a problem. My mother thought I was manic-depressive!"

"Head injuries like yours are invisible. You look fine, so no one is going to think otherwise. If you'd had cancer everyone would have understood what you were going through."

"We brain-injured folk get a really raw deal. Doctors blame us for our accidents—as if we wanted a brain injury. Neuropsychologists think we invent our symptoms because we are emotionally unstable or trying to cheat the legal system. Society thinks we are violent and unpredictable. Families and partners tire of our mood swings. And I'm one of the lucky ones. There are scores of brain-damaged people who can't speak for themselves.

"Why do we know so little about head injuries?" I asked Louise.

"Because the brain is complicated."

"So is space travel! Lots of things are complicated. When I had my accident, I was told I'd suffered a mild traumatic brain injury. But *mild* meant I lost my job, was put on a disability pension, and told I would never be able to work again or finish my PhD. Now my neurologist thinks my injury was *severe*. I guess most people would shrug their shoulders and say, *Well, there's nothing I can do about it, so I'll wait and see.* I wish I could think like that. But the uncertainty of it all, the *not knowing*, is distressing."

"I think your neurologist is right. The longer-term effects you've experienced are more consistent with a severe head injury."

"But why can't anyone give me a prognosis?"

"Because no one knows. Every TBI is different. Every brain is different. It really is impossible to tell."

"Listen to this." I rustled through a notebook and found a quote from the only source on medical matters I happened to trust, Pliny the Elder.

Nothing whatever, in man, is of so frail a nature as the memory; for it is affected by disease, by injuries, and even by fright; being sometimes partially lost, and at other times entirely so. A man, who received a blow from a stone, forgot the names of the letters only; while, on the other hand, another person, who fell from a very high roof, could not so much as recollect his mother, or his relations and neighbors. Another person, in consequence of some disease, forgot his own servants even; and Messala Corvinus, the orator, lost all recollection of his own name. And so it is, that very often the memory appears to attempt, as it were, to make its escape from us, even while the body is at rest and in perfect health.[27]

"That was Pliny the Elder back in AD 77. In a single paragraph he covered traumatic brain injury and a disease that sounds a lot like Alzheimer's," I said.

"Wow," Louise said, taking the notebook from my hands and reading the quote herself.

"My memory has attempted to make its escape from me," I said.

"But you managed to catch it in time."

"That remains to be seen. I'm due for another brain MRI two years from now."

Louise put the notebook down and looked up at me. "It's up to you, but I really don't see much point," she said.

"What do you mean?"

"If the scans show more atrophy, what are you going to do?"

"I expect that they will show more atrophy. I don't see how they can't."

"Maybe so. But more atrophy doesn't necessarily mean you are developing dementia. And I can imagine how you'll react if the scans look worse than they did last time."

I looked at her and said nothing.

"Listen," she said, taking hold of my hands. "You've wasted the last seven years of your life worrying about something that hasn't happened. Do you want to waste the next seven years?"

That night, unable to sleep, I crept out of the bedroom with Scout and Sofia, and we curled up together on the sofa. I stared at the moon suspended above the magnolia tree in our backyard and realized that Louise was right. I had lost seven years of my life to depression and anxiety, worrying about dementia. And it hadn't happened yet. It was time to think about the possibilities that lay ahead of me, of us, and to do something with my life.

∿

I introduced Louise to my mother.

Her doctor now believed my mother was suffering from Parkinson's disease. My mother had been robbed of her mobility and her mind, and the person Louise met bore little resemblance to the woman who caused me so much grief.

"It's lovely to meet you," my mother said when Louise leaned over to shake her hand. I told my mother we planned to travel to New York to marry, and my mother asked, "Can you marry there?"

"You can marry everywhere in the Western world but Australia," I said.

"That's wonderful," my mother said, and looked like she meant it.

An hour later my mother forgot my name. She remembered I was her daughter, and when I reminded her I was Sarah, she said, "Sarah! That's right."

Louise told me she could live two years or more, unable to move on her own, unable to think. I wished nothing more for my mother than a swift and easy death.

On another visit my mother snapped at me and demanded we leave. "That's the mother I remember," I said to Louise as we made for the door.

We moved my mother into a nursing home when it was no longer possible for her to have in-home care. It took a while for her to settle in, but her mind deteriorated quickly and it wasn't long before she forgot where she was.

Each time I visited, she thanked me for being there. "You didn't need to come, given everything that has happened. But you did, and I appreciate that so much. You really are lovely." When Louise was there, she chimed in and told my mother how lucky she was to have me. "I know," my mother said, "I know."

Sometimes she pleaded with me to stay. "I just like having you here. You're such good company." And I pulled up a chair beside her and stayed until she fell asleep.

"Why is she so nice to me now?" I asked Louise one day after my mother told me I was beautiful, kind, and delightful. "She's like a different person!"

Louise told me that she had seen a number of patients who were prickly before their dementia diagnosis lose their sharp edges as the disease took hold. That prickly people often have a facade that vanishes when their frontal lobes begin to deteriorate.

"Someone like your mother may lose her ability to manipulate. Underneath the veneer, your mother is probably quite a nice person."

One of Louise's patients, a woman around my mother's age, had been charming to everyone all her life. Her daughter couldn't recognize the monster she had become since she developed dementia. "This woman is horrible!" Louise said. "Rude, nasty, a real piece of work. Yet she and her daughter were incredibly close. Perhaps her charm ran out. Perhaps she was hiding some of her self. And now, with her veneer gone, that side of her has appeared for the first time."

"Strange."

Louise agreed.

"Do you think Mum means the things she says now?"

"Yes. She's still the same person. Dementia takes things away from us. It doesn't add things that weren't there before."

"It's terrible to say, but I like my mother a lot more now. We've lost the need to control each other, the need to compete. It's not just her who has changed; it's me too. We've both softened. We're kinder to one another. It's like we've been on a parallel journey that has brought us together, her with her brain, me with mine."

One Saturday morning Louise and I drove across town to visit my mother, stopping on the way for a box of Italian pastries. I opened the box and my mother stared at me and started to cry.

"I was a terrible mother to you," she said. "And yet you are always here for me." There was a sadness, an earnestness in her eyes I had never seen before. I hugged her and told her to stop crying. The sight of my mother crying caused me physical pain. I told her that we were both to blame. That what mattered now was that we had finally found peace.

"I'm so sorry," she said when she finally stopped crying.

The more I visited my mother, the more I looked forward to seeing her. Before her mind had started to fail her, I couldn't recall a single occasion when I had appeared at her door with anything other than a sense of dread. I always expected the worst, and usually I wasn't disappointed. Now I arrived and her face lit up. She was genuinely happy to see me. I pulled up a chair beside her and took her hand, and she looked at me and smiled.

"I love you, Mum," I said, and I meant it.

"I love you too," she said. It was the first time I had ever heard her say it.

"Why couldn't we have been like this years ago?" I asked.

"I'm sorry," she said. "It's not too late."

One night, lying in bed waiting to fall asleep, I told Louise how devastating it was to see my mother stuck in a wheelchair unable to move, to watch her life ebb away and her mind deteriorate. "She would be horrified to think her life had come to this."

Louise looked at me and squeezed my hand.

"I reminded her about my accident not long after I moved back home from Hong Kong. Her memory was better then, but she didn't remember anything about it. I tried to prompt her. The farm. A horse. I landed on my head. She didn't seem to register. I have never been able to understand why she didn't try to help me back then, why she disappeared and left me alone, and now I never will. I shouted at her in the hospital parking lot the day I had my brain scanned, and she never mentioned my accident again. Not once."

Louise shrugged. "Some things don't have answers."

In April 2017 Louise and I married in a small room in the New York City Marriage Bureau. Our honeymoon started in New York and ended in Paris.

Home in Sydney, we lead a simple life. Louise leaves each morning to tend to her patients, and I walk the dogs. I try to write. Writing is suffering, and Louise tells me that being spat on and punched in the face by elderly patients isn't a walk in the park either. My social life has shrunk since moving back to Australia, but Louise and I are happiest at home, alone with our dogs and cats, sharing a meal she has prepared and a glass of red wine.

Love cannot fix everything. I still have a temper, and while I do everything within my power to contain it, occasionally I erupt. Depression is like a tattoo across my shoulders I can never seem to remove. Over the past two years, Louise encouraged me to try five new types of antidepressants (taking my lifetime total to thirteen) before admitting my depression was treatment resistant. Exercise will save my life, she says, or at least prolong my quality of life, and the available research suggests she is right. We are now one of those strange couples who visit the gym together. A couple of weeks ago, she came home excitedly, telling me she had bought me a present. I was hoping for chocolate or a book, but she handed me a small plastic bag with a running bra inside. The saddest present ever.

Pinned to the wall of my study is a Post-it note with a warning I want to confront every day. It's a quote by Norman Cousins:

The tragedy of life is not death but what we let die inside us while we live.

At Louise's urging, I decided to skip my next brain scan. I chose not to know. I have managed, somehow, to build a new life in place of my old one, and my goal now is to live. Learning to live from day to day is not as easy as it sounds. Neither, I've realized, is it impossible.

"Do you remember who I am?" I asked my mother during a recent visit.

"Are you my sister?"

"No. You don't have a sister."

"Are you my mother?"

"I'm Sarah," I said, and squeezed her hand.

She laughed and shook her head. "You're certainly not Sarah."

Perhaps she was right.

ACKNOWLEDGMENTS

I would never have started this book without the encouragement and support of Xu Xi, the founder and director of the MFA program at City University in Hong Kong, a program, sadly, that no longer exists. Sincerest of thanks are due to Robin Hemley, Suzanne Paola, Ravi Shankar, and Justin Hill, and to my fellow students in the program, most particularly Sophie Monatte (my closest writing buddy), Mags Webster, Jacinta Sweeting Read, Adnan Mahmutovic, Andrea Brittan, and Rebekah Chan. Two of my favorite writers, Shannon Cain and Rawi Hage, provided me with invaluable advice on earlier drafts of this manuscript, and I am grateful to them both. Thanks are also due to friends who have read all or part of this book at some point: Kira Legaan, Michelle Leung, Nick Avery, Warren Cahill, Brooke Green, Vedna Jivan, Justin Hocking, Phil Glist, and Amy Shea. Big thanks to the support provided by the team at Little A: Emma Reh and Merideth Mulroney, as well as Michael Townley, Chad Sievers, and Zoe Norvell.

A number of literary journals published essays of mine that appear in this book in slightly different forms. They include the *Gettysburg Review*, the *Sun*, *Two Thirds North*, the *Pinch*, *Post Road*, *Bellingham Review*, and the *Asia Literary Review*. My thanks to them all.

Special thanks and love to Helena Hu, a gem of a friend, who read multiple versions of this book, and to my beloved wife, who patiently read every iteration and draft. Without you, this memoir would have ended bleakly. Thanks also to my previous two long-term partners, "Laura" and "Giulia," for putting up with me for as long as you did. I would also like to thank my psychiatrist and my neurologist, without whom I probably wouldn't be here. I hoped Sofia, my much-loved dog, who sat patiently at my feet while I wrote this book, would live to see its publication, but sadly she did not.

Finally, this book would not exist without the wisdom, kindness, and patience of my agent, Sarah Levitt, and my editor, Laura Van der Veer. I cannot thank them enough.

ENDNOTES

1   In the US, between 2001 and 2005, there were five activities in which traumatic brain injury accounted for greater than 7.5% of Emergency Department visits for that activity. The five include horseback riding (11.7%), ice-skating (10.4%), riding all-terrain vehicles (8.4%), tobogganing/sledding (8.3%), and bicycling (7.7%). American football accounted for 5.7%. J. Gilchrist, K. Thomas, M. Wald, and J. Langlois, "Nonfatal Traumatic Brain Injuries from Sports and Recreation Activities—United States, 2001–2005," *Morbidity and Mortality Weekly Report* 56, no. 29 (July 2007): 733–37.

2   BBC, Leeds Press Office, "Inside Out Reviews Dangers of Riding" (March 23, 2007), http://www.bbc.co.uk/pressoffice/pressreleases/stories/2007/03_march/23/riding.shtml.

3   Years later, someone will tell me I suffered a coup-contrecoup injury. That happens when a moving object (one's brain) smashes inside one's skull when it collides with a stationary object (in my case, a rock). This ricocheting within the skull is what causes brain damage. The coup part occurs at the initial site of impact, and the contrecoup on the opposite side of the brain to where the initial impact occurred.

4   My mother was lucky. In the US, from 2003 to 2012, equestrian sports accounted for the majority (45.2%) of all sports-related traumatic brain injuries. E. A. Winkler et al., "Adult Sports-Related Traumatic Brain Injury in United States Trauma Centers," *Neurosurgical Focus* 40, no. 4 (April 2016): E4.

5   See for example, C. Prince and M. E. Bruhns, "Evaluation and Treatment of Mild Traumatic Brain Injury: The Role of Neuropsychology," *Brain Sciences* 7 (8), August 2017. The authors also describe the differences in diagnostic criteria of mild traumatic brain injury, as determined first by the American Congress of Rehabilitation Medicine and later the World Health Organization.

6   In 2001, eight years after my father died, a book launch was held for *Nature's Investigator: The Diary of Robert Brown in Australia, 1801–1805*. Two of my father's colleagues in Britain who shared his interest in Robert Brown had finished the book. See *Nature's Investigator: The Diary of Robert Brown in Australia, 1801–1805*, compiled by T. G. Vallance, D. T. Moore, and E. W. Groves (CSIRO Publishing, 2001).

7   Institute of Medicine, *Cognitive Rehabilitation Therapy for Traumatic Brain Injury: Evaluating the Evidence* (Washington, DC: National Academies Press, 2011).

8   Y. S. Su, A. Veeravagu, and G. Grant, "Neuroplasticity after Traumatic Brain Injury," in *Translational Research in Traumatic Brain Injury*, eds. D. Laskowitz and G. Grant (Boca Raton, FL: CRC Press/Taylor and Francis Group, 2016).

9   S. J. Redpath et al., "Healthcare professionals' attitudes towards traumatic brain injury (TBI): The influence of profession, experience, aetiology and blame on prejudice towards survivors of brain injury," *Brain Injury* 24, no. 6 (May 2010): 802–11.

10   "TBI: Get the Facts," Centers for Disease Control and Prevention, last modified April 27, 2017, https://www.cdc.gov/traumaticbraininjury/get_the_facts.html.

11   M. I. Medved and W. Hirst, "Islands of Memory: Autobiographical Remembering in Amnestics," *Memory* 14, no. 3 (April 2006): 276–88.

12   J. Strizzi et al., "Sexual Functioning, Desire, and Satisfaction in Women with TBI and Healthy Controls," *Behavioural Neurology* 2015, Article ID 247479 (2015), http://dx.doi.org/10.1155/2015/247479.

13   M. Nagasawa et al., "Oxytocin-Gaze Positive Loop and the Coevolution of Human-Dog Bonds," *Science* 348, no. 6232 (April 17, 2015): 333–36.

14   V. Rao et al., "Aggression After Traumatic Brain Injury: Prevalence and Correlates," *Journal of Neuropsychiatry and Clinical Neurosciences* 21, no. 4 (October 2009): 420–29.

15   D. Goleman, "When Rage Explodes, Brain Damage May Be the Cause," *New York Times*, August 7, 1990.

16   The law was relaxed in 2015 to allow short-term visits. The ban on long-term visits for HIV-positive people entering Singapore remains.

17 M. A. Linden and I. R. Crothers, "Violent, Caring, Unpredictable: Public Views on Survivors of Brain Injury," *Archives of Clinical Neuropsychology* 21, no. 8 (December 2006): 763–70.

18 The law was changed in 2007 to permit oral and anal sex between consenting heterosexuals.

19 G. W. Rutherford and J. D. Corrigan, "Long-Term Consequences of Traumatic Brain Injury," *Journal of Head Trauma Rehabilitation* 24, no. 6 (November–December 2009): 421–23.

20 R. Ruff, L. Camenzuli, and J. Mueller, "Miserable Minority: Emotional Risk Factors That Influence the Outcome of a Mild Traumatic Brain Injury," *Brain Injury* 10, no. 8 (1996): 551–65.

21 K. A. Gorgens, "Women and Mild TBI," *Spotlight on Disability Newsletter*, December 2014, https://www.apa.org/pi/disability/resources/publications/newsletter/2014/12/women-brain-injury.aspx.

22 Z. Kou and A. Iraji, "Imaging Brain Plasticity After Trauma," *Neural Regeneration Research* 9, no. 7 (May 2014): 693–700.

23 M. J. Hylin, A. L. Kerr, and R. Holden, "Understanding the Mechanisms of Recovery and/or Compensation Following Injury," *Neural Plasticity* 2017, Article 7125057, https://doi.org/10.1155/2017/7125057.

24 Since I wrote this book, a test to identify CTE has been developed by researchers at UCLA and is available for trial, although it has not yet acquired FDA approval.

25 A. A. King et al., eds., *Historical Perspectives of Rabies in Europe and the Mediterranean Basin* (Paris: World Organization for Animal Health, 2004).

26 These are rough guesses. It is very difficult to be precise about the percentage of lesbians in any particular place as (a) people are not always honest about their sexuality; (b) there is a blurry line for many people between homosexuality and bisexuality, which may skew survey results; and (c) the surveys that have been done often use questionable methodologies. In terms of introverts, it has been suggested that between one-third and one-half of all Americans are introverts. That seems a little on the high side to me.

27 Pliny the Elder, *The Natural History of Pliny*, trans. J. Bostock and H. T. Riley (London: Henry G. Bohn, 1855), vol. 2, 165.

ABOUT THE AUTHOR

Photo © 2018 Nicole Cooper

Sarah Vallance was born in Sydney. She graduated from City University of Hong Kong in 2013 with an MFA in creative writing. Her essays have earned her a Pushcart Prize. She has been published in the *Gettysburg Review*, the *Sun*, the *Pinch*, *Asia Literary Review*, *Post Road*, and *Bellingham Review*, among other places. Sarah was a Harkness Fellow at Harvard and holds a doctorate in government and public administration. She lives in Sydney with her wife and their three dogs and three cats. *Prognosis* is her first book.